The Silent Garden

Praise for *The Silent Garden*

I don't often come across a resource that thoughtfully looks at the decisions families must make and the complexities of raising a child who is Deaf/Hard of Hearing. I would recommend this book to all families who are beginning their journey.

—Janet DesGeorges,
Executive Director, Hands & Voices

I will share this insightful book with new parents knowing that this is a publication that speaks to their hearts and souls in a powerful and truthful manner.

—Gerard Buckley, President,
National Technical Institute for the Deaf

Ogden and Smith empower readers, parents and professionals alike, with a treasure trove of ready-to-use tools and copious amounts of information to support the decision-making process.

—Jennifer Blohm, Early Intervention Deaf
and Hard-of-Hearing Specialist

This invaluable book cuts through emotional issues, identifies subconscious struggles, and demonstrates successful pathways for living with deafness.

—Glenda Lane, Parent

As a Deaf individual raising a Deaf daughter, this book affirmed for me the importance of following the child's lead in what is best for his/her cognitive, social, and language development.

—Michelle L. Bronson,
Parent and Executive Director,
Deaf and Hard of Hearing Service Center, Inc.

The Silent Garden was a valuable resource for my Deaf/Hard of Hearing students and their parents. This wonderful, informative book gives unbiased information and guidance to newly identified Deaf children and their families. Parents often shared that the book spoke to them like a good friend.

—Rosie Ruelas-Wasser, Educator

The *Silent Garden*

A Parent's Guide to Raising a Deaf Child

Paul W. Ogden
David H. Smith

Gallaudet University Press / *Washington, DC*

Gallaudet University Press
Washington, DC 20002
http://gupress.gallaudet.edu

Printed in the United States of America

Library of Congress Cataloging-in-Publication Data
Names: Ogden, Paul W., author.
Title: The silent garden : a parent's guide to raising a deaf child / Paul W. Ogden,
    David H. Smith ; foreword by Marlee Matlin.
Description: Third Edition. | Washington, DC : Gallaudet University Press, 2016.
    | Revised edition of The silent garden, 1996.
Identifiers: LCCN 2016026123| ISBN 9781563686764 (paperback) |
    ISBN 9781563686771 (ebook)
Subjects: LCSH: Deaf children—Family relationships. | Deaf children—
    Education. | BISAC: FAMILY & RELATIONSHIPS / Parenting / General.
Classification: LCC HV2392.2 .O34 2016 | DDC 649/.1512—dc23
LC record available at https://lccn.loc.gov/2016026123

∞This paper meets the requirements of ANSI/NISO Z39.48-1992
(Permanence of Paper).

Digital painting of the *Silent Garden* by Tracey Salaway, 2016.

This book is dedicated to Harry and Jean Smith, David's parents. They expected nothing less than great achievements from their son in response to naysayers and skeptics.

Dedication from the second edition:

This book is dedicated to Dunbar H. Ogden and Annegret S. Ogden, my brother, sister-in- law, and close friends. They refused to be my ears. Instead they taught me to read the world.

Dedication from the first edition:

This book is dedicated to Dorothy C. Ogden, Paul's very special mother, who cherishes the following poem:

Heaven's Very Special Child

> A meeting was held quite far from earth!
> "It's time for another birth."
> Said the angels to the LORD above,
> "This Special Child will need much love."
>
> His progress may be very slow,
> Accomplishments it may not show,
> And it'll require extra care
> From the folks it meets down there.
>
> So let's be careful where it's sent;
> We want its life to be content;
> Please LORD, find the parents and teachers who
> Will do a special job for you,
>
> They will not realize right away
> The leading role they're asked to play,
> But with this child sent from above
> Comes stronger faith and richer love.
>
> And soon they'll know the privilege given
> In caring for this gift from Heaven;
> Their precious charge, so meek and mild,
> Is Heaven's Very Special Child.
>
> by Edna Massionilla

Contents

Foreword

Marlee Matlin

WHEN I SEE and meet deaf children and their families, I often observe how they interact together, and I especially note how, or even if, communication is happening. Does it seem to be happening naturally and spontaneously? Is there a bit of a struggle, but the parents are making a good effort to help their child understand? Or is there very little communication happening at all? The first two situations are always good to see; however, when little or no communication is taking place, I see a tragedy happening before my eyes, because a deaf child is being deprived of the chance to learn language. I doubt it is because the parents don't care. Most parents love their children. Perhaps it may be because the parents have no idea how or what to do. If you are a parent who wishes to know the "how" and "what" and wants the best for their deaf child, you have come to the right place: the Silent Garden. It is actually a very vibrant and colorful place, with much going on to see and enjoy. This is the kind of place where all deaf children and their families will thrive and grow together.

It is rare to find an academic who is committed to writing for everyday folks rather than exclusively for scholars and professionals. It is even more rare to find deaf academics, but thanks to improvements in communication access over the years, their ranks are growing. Two of them who you will meet here, authors Paul Ogden and Dave Smith, have stated that their philosophy is to get information to the people who need it the most—the parents of deaf and hard of hearing children. Four characteristics make this book a radical departure from other works in the field of deaf education. The authors both are deaf, whereas most literature on parenting is written by hearing professionals; they use their personal experiences and understanding of being deaf as their reference point in discussing the special needs and problems of deaf children from birth to age twenty one; they include findings from interviews with more than 350 parents of deaf children as well as discussions with at least 500 deaf adults as an additional reservoir of experience from which to draw; and the book's overall purpose is to channel the knowledge and expertise available to academics and professionals to nonacademic audiences and primarily parents. This information may often be lost along the way due to the technical language in which it is often presented, in addition to the stress of the moment that parents are experiencing. What is needed is straightforward guidance in resolving the inevitable issues that come up and in making the necessary decisions. The authors have provided it here.

Dr. Ogden and Dr. Smith proceed with the understanding that a deaf child is not merely "a deaf person," but a complete and complex human being who happens to be deaf. The distinction is subtle but important. Historically, deaf children have been treated as having deficiencies merely because they cannot hear or speak well. Often, they have poor literacy outcomes as part of a self-fulfilling prophecy with low expectations for achievement. But the authors make it clear that children who are deaf, when provided full access to communication and taught to partake of the full range of human experience, have the potential to lead productive and ultimately independent lives. The authors themselves are a living testimony to the kind of potential that deaf individuals can reach, given good parenting and a good education. Dr. Ogden, although retired from California State University, Fresno, with the honored title of professor emeritus, is still active in promoting effective practices in raising and educating deaf children. He still travels to meet with parents and their children throughout the United States, a rare venture for an academic. Dr. Smith is the director of the Center on Deafness at the University of Tennessee in Knoxville. Dr. Ogden and Dr. Smith's work strikes an ideal balance of achievement, between teaching students and writing for and working with parents and professionals in the language each is comfortable using.

It is my hope that you find this book a useful companion on your own personal journey with your deaf child and family through the real silent garden that you cultivate in your home and in the Deaf community. Yours will be one more successful deaf child and family that I can delight in and not worry and wonder about. Who knows, your child could even be the next deaf Academy Award or even Nobel Prize winner. Nothing is impossible with good communication and literacy skills. But the bottom line is that just knowing there is another happy stroller in the silent garden of life would be wonderful. Get ready for an interesting adventure and great outcomes!

Preface to the Third Edition

IF YOU'VE picked this book up, there is a chance you are a parent or an interested individual looking for information about being deaf. Welcome to the Silent Garden! You've come to a good place, where we will show you that you are not alone; that there is a thriving Deaf community that revels in sharing information. In fact, information-sharing is the cornerstone, or in keeping with our gardening theme, maybe we should say the "fertilizer," of the Deaf community. This book is intended to be reader friendly, without too much of the technical or academic jargon professors like us are prone to write. As you will find, there is plenty of that sort of information available, and we have placed some references in the chapter endnotes to help you get started on the deeper topics.

Much has changed in the years between the publication of the first edition of *The Silent Garden* (1982) and this third edition. American Sign Language (ASL) has evolved from its formerly inferior status to become fully recognized as a language capable of expressing the most abstract concepts. ASL is currently the third-most-taught second language in the United States according to the Modern Language Association. Cochlear implants, once a controversial medical experiment, have improved drastically and are small enough to fit completely behind the ear. They are now becoming commonplace in children as young as twelve months old, when language development is most critical. Even hearing aids have gone digital and can do things that were previously not feasible. Visually based technology has removed many of the communication barriers that restricted deaf people from information access, which has made it much easier for them to succeed in work environments and to stay in touch with family and friends.

It is no longer surprising to see deaf people working in professions once thought impossible—as professional sports figures, actors, lawyers, doctors, dentists, scientists, engineers, politicians, stockbrokers, and college professors like us. Also, thanks to a wealth of websites, movies, videos, television programs, books, and news articles on deaf people, more people now recognize that being deaf is not about hearing, but about access to communication. Although many people in the hearing world think that all deaf people sign, we know there are plenty of deaf folks who also communicate by spoken language at various levels of ability.

Increased awareness, as well as the presence of deaf and hard of hearing people working and creating in the mainstream of life, has helped to nudge into the collective consciousness an idea once apparently incomprehensible—that being deaf is not a disability, but a state of being that is different from but no more limited, restricted, or disabling than the hearing state.

If things are so much better since the last edition of this book, why are we undertaking the considerable task of revising and expanding a book for parents of young deaf and hard of hearing children about the issues and decisions they will face? Don't parents have access to all they need to know about what to do when they discover their child is deaf? Aren't the lives of deaf people finally understood?

It is true that many writers have explored deaf lives during the past few decades; however, on a practical, day-to-day, detailed level, most parents of young deaf children lack comprehensive information about the complex challenges they face. These parents, especially if they are hearing, must learn quickly about a whole new world and probably a new language and culture. More than ever, these parents need a companion and guide. The maze of information sources, professional philosophies, educational options, and communication styles has become even more complicated, thanks to the proliferation of Internet websites. Parents today need to educate themselves quickly and thoroughly to the many conflicting points of view on what is best for their deaf children.

These conflicting viewpoints and biases about how best to raise deaf children can cause quite a bit of consternation among parents and, in turn, the deaf children themselves, as they become older and transition into adulthood. As you will see or may already know, there are two primary viewpoints, and we ourselves have experienced both sides of the debate. We both grew up learning and using only spoken language, and we learned ASL after our teen years. Although we don't regret our upbringing and think our parents did a great job, we both definitely wish we had the experience of learning ASL as young children.

The purpose of this book is to put forth various points of view as neutrally as possible; however, like everyone else, we do have some biases. We think deaf children should be taught sign language, exposed to deaf adults as role models, and yes, definitely have access to listening and learning spoken language, if possible. But we also want you to know the potential pitfalls. Let your children lead the way to communication access, because they will naturally crave and need it any way they can get it, and develop their own preferences and communication style.

One thing hasn't changed over the years, and that is parents' urgent desire to do the best they can, to make the decisions that will enable their children to grow into strong, healthy, autonomous adults and productive members of society. The sense of loving responsibility that all parents feel can weigh particularly heavily on the parents of deaf and hard of hearing children.

As deaf professionals and writers, we also feel a sense of responsibility toward the children. This reason, as well as the success of the original *Silent Garden* and the ensuing second edition, inspired us to produce a third edition, to bring information up to date with the current times. This book is intended to serve as a thorough, up-to-date reference comprising all the bits and pieces of advice, encouragement, and hard data that parents need in order to make decisions.

Over the years, Paul Ogden interviewed more than four hundred parents of prelingually deaf children; in addition, he has discussed the deaf life as it relates to childhood, learning, and communication with five hundred deaf people. The first decade of that research is reflected in the original *Silent Garden*. The second edition incorporated what was gathered from the second decade of interviews and discussions, and it reflects the broadening of his experience and perspective. Because many of the issues and life stories from the interviews gathered for the first and second editions are still relevant all these years later, we have decided to leave them mostly as-is for this edition. Some things may never change, especially on a human level, in spite of all the great advances we have seen.

If you are familiar with deaf life and the wide variety of communication and cultural issues associated with it, you may nevertheless find ideas here that will help you to be your child's greatest advocate. If you are entering this world for the first time, expect to encounter new ways of learning and communicating. What seems strange at first will slowly gain definition until it coheres into a way of being that is full of meaning and magic.

〜

Being deaf isn't about being *silent*; it isn't anything describable in a single word or phrase. Rather, it is a range, a spectrum of conditions. The term is applied to people who are profoundly deaf, with little or no hearing, to people who are only slightly hard of hearing, and to everyone in between. It is kind of ironic that many of the old publications and newsletters published by the Deaf community had the term *silent* in the title, such as *The Silent Worker*. Contrary to stubborn stereotypes, deaf people are definitely not silent. Many speak, and all laugh, cry, and rejoice aloud. In fact, you may be surprised how loud and proud they can be.

Some deaf readers of the original *Silent Garden* objected to the word *silent* in the title. They suggested that it misrepresented the life of deaf people to those who needed most crucially to understand it—the parents of young deaf children. Once again, we decided to keep the word *silent*, not because of its descriptive quality so much as its poetic and evocative meaning. We will end our beginning with a quote from Paul,

> I am profoundly deaf; I don't hear a single sound. Instead, I experience the world through vision. When I think of a silent garden,

I think of my version of paradise, which means perfect communication: no more breakdowns, misunderstandings, confusions; no more floundering for words. In my imagination, I can see the place where this smooth interaction takes place. It is located on top of a hill with breathtaking views of the ocean close by and snowcapped mountains in the distance.

I don't hear the waves crashing—I feel the spray of water on my face. I don't hear the wind—I feel the breeze in my hair. I don't hear the sunrises and sunsets—I catch the spectacular blend of orange, pink, and gray over the horizon. I don't hear the stars—I see tiny, piercing lights shining in the night sky. I don't hear the wildlife— I enjoy the places where they live. I don't hear a friend call my name—I feel his touch on my shoulder or see his wave of greeting.

Welcome to the silent garden, a world of color and movement so beautiful, so engaging, so rich in information and meaning that we are completely engrossed in the life of it all. Enjoy your journey, and don't forget to stop and linger among the various flowerbeds that make up the unique mosaic of our garden.

Acknowledgments

MANY PEOPLE along the way have encouraged, urged, and coaxed us to finish this book. Our wives, Anne and Rachel, have shared their thoughts sensitively and have willingly taken up many of our distractions to enable us to write. They have also given up many evenings and weekends, normally reserved for our time together, so that we could continue working. They have been extraordinary coaches, encouraging and loving wives.

Other family and friends have cheered us on to do this new edition of *The Silent Garden*. Dr. Nan Barker was instrumental in the shaping of one chapter to which she contributed a lot of feedback. Antonina Cardinalli read much of our work and offered many helpful comments.

The book would not be the same without these people: Jake Arcanin, Carol Brautigam, John and Marilyn Cassidy, Carolee Clayton, Suzanne L. Conway, Dr. Nancy Delich, Kathy Yoshida Doerksen, Alice Tenscher Dunbar, Linda Hammer-Brown, Jeanne Glad, Sandy Harvey, Susan Kane, Nancy Kanta, Peggy Kelly, Carl Kirchner, Barbara Lincoln, Jessica Marshall, Karen Mistry, Barbara Montan, Dunbar and Annegret Ogden, Laura and Mike Peterson, Dr. Stephen D. Roberts, Kathleen Ruccione, Debbi Silberg, Jim Vincent, Cathy Walsh, Pamela J. Warkentin, Pat Wasserman, Lenore Williams, Megan Williams, and the faculty, staff, and students at California State University in Fresno.

Our warm hugs for all the families and deaf and hard of hearing adults we have met along the way and who have contributed so generously and openly during their interviews, discussions, and social visits with us. Their personal recollections and insights have added a vivid life to *The Silent Garden.*

Finally, our deepest appreciation to Ivey Pittle Wallace and the staff at Gallaudet University Press. With their encouragement and support, we have navigated this project with much greater ease. Very special thanks go to these people for their unique proofing skills: Rachel Smith, Kim Holly, and Marilyn Weinhouse, who also found ways to add clarity and insightful comments to the book. We thank Tracey Salaway for the perfect book cover with her digital painting, THE SILENT GARDEN.

The Silent Garden

1 *First Things First*

1 Introductions

IN THE PREFACE, we said that being deaf is not about hearing, but about communication. To communicate requires full access to language. To clarify this observation, it makes sense to begin with terminology. What do we mean when we say that people are *deaf* or *hard of hearing*, and to whom, precisely, do these terms refer?

There's a good explanation for the confusion that surrounds these questions: Deaf and hard of hearing people do not constitute a homogenous group; rather, they form a group that is diverse in many ways. Yet as our peer, Dr. Thomas Holcomb, notes, they do have the four following common threads that tie them all together:

1. the desire for full access to communication and language,
2. the capability to access information about things around them,
3. the need for developing a positive self-identity, and
4. the ability to make their own decisions, or self-determination.[1]

We cover all of these topics in one way or another in this book, often in overlapping ways.

Certain terms and labels can be confusing, such as *hard of hearing* and *deaf* with a lowercase *d* or a capital *D*, depending on identity or membership in the Deaf community. Some terms, such as *hearing impaired* and *deaf-mute*, are currently considered passé and even offensive. Also, it is usually unnecessary to use "people first" language, as in "people who are deaf." Using the terms *deaf people* or *hard of hearing people* is perfectly acceptable and is the format we follow here, as you may have already noted. Finally, as with any other sort of label, the best approach is often to just ask individuals what they personally prefer. Some may proudly proclaim themselves Deaf, whereas others would rather nobody knew and declare that their hearing status does not define them at all. We have decided to use *deaf* only for the sake of brevity and not to single out or exclude any particular identities that we have in this diverse population.

Here is a partial list in alphabetical order of some the possible self-identifications that people may use to describe themselves:
• Deaf
• Deaf and cochlear implant user
• Deaf and partially sighted
• Deaf-Blind
• Deaf with cerebral palsy
• deaf
• deaf and cochlear implant user
• deaf-blind
• deaf and partially sighted
• hard of hearing
• hard of hearing and partially sighted
• hard of hearing and blind
• hearing
• late-deafened
• late-deafened with neurofibromatosis Type 2
• oral deaf

Given the wide variety of people within the deaf population, it is not surprising that outsiders are often confused about who we are. In recent years, as writers and researchers have tried to describe us with greater precision, it has become obvious that generalizations are futile without reference to agreed-upon criteria. The following questions outline the ten distinguishing features that are used to define the spectrum of possibilities within the deaf population.

1. *How much hearing ability does the person have?* Hearing people often wonder why some people benefit from wearing hearing aids or cochlear implants while others receive no benefit at all. They

wonder why some deaf people can talk on the phone while others cannot. Levels of hearing loss vary from person to person, ranging from slight loss to mild loss, moderate loss, severe loss, and profound loss. Only a handful of deaf people have what most people would call total deafness.

2. *At what age did the hearing loss occur?* Keep in mind some people were born with their current hearing status and thus never "lost" what they never had in the first place. Conversely, there are those who did lose their hearing ability after birth. We know of people who are deaf, speak very well, and can play the piano brilliantly. Many people marvel at what to them is a contradiction in terms—a deaf musician—but in one instance, we know a person who took piano lessons for twelve years before she contracted spinal meningitis and lost her hearing completely at the age of seventeen. She sometimes gives in to the temptation to mystify hearing folks by pretending she has always been deaf. It is not uncommon for deaf people to amuse themselves by taking advantage of hearing people's naiveté with regard to deafness.

3. *What type of hearing loss does the person have?* Hearing loss can be defined as any loss of sound sensitivity, partial or complete, produced by abnormality anywhere in the auditory system. For the purposes of this discussion, we will define the four following types of hearing loss.

a. *Conductive hearing loss* is caused by a disruption or blockage within the ear canal or a defect in the bones of the middle ear that inhibits sound from reaching the inner ear. People who have conductive hearing losses often benefit from corrective surgery and/or wearing hearing aids.

b. *Sensorineural hearing loss* is caused by disruption of the transmission of sound information to the brain in one or more of three possible locations: The hair cells of the cochlea in the inner ear, the nerve synapse between the inner ear and the auditory nerve, or in the auditory nerve between the cochlea and the cortex of the brain. Sensorineural hearing loss is usually incurable, and hearing aids do usually provide some benefit for most people. This type of hearing loss is specifically targeted by the use of cochlear implants, as we will discuss later.

c. *Mixed hearing loss* is a combination of conductive and sensorineural hearing loss. Mixed hearing loss is the sum of losses resulting from abnormalities in both the conductive and the sensorineural mechanisms of hearing. In such a case, the hearing loss caused by conductive problems usually is treatable, but the treatment of sensorineural loss currently available does not restore the physiological structure of the cochlea or nerves used for hearing.

d. *Auditory neuropathy* is a condition in which sound enters the inner ear normally, and the inner hair cells react normally, but the transmission of signals from the inner ear to the brain is disrupted. People with auditory neuropathy may, at times, appear to have normal hearing, or hearing loss ranging from mild to severe; but they usually have poor speech-perception abilities. They may be able to hear sounds, but they have difficulty recognizing spoken words. Although few people have it, we are learning that more and more people have this condition.

4. *What caused the hearing loss?* Although there are just four types of hearing loss, the number of possible causes, or etiology, is much greater. The known causes of hearing loss are heredity, disease, toxicity, noise exposure, and injury. Medical professionals estimate that inherited genes are the cause in half of all babies born deaf. In 25 to 40 percent of cases in children, the cause is unknown. Hearing loss may occur at any point in the life cycle—before, during, or after birth. During pregnancy, for example, the mother having rubella or cytomegalovirus (CMV), or ingests certain drugs can cause hearing loss in a fetus. During delivery, complications in the birth process, the presence of a sexually transmitted disease in the mother, or Rh incompatibility between mother and child may result in hearing loss. After birth and throughout life, a host of possibilities exists: otitis media (infection of the middle ear), spinal meningitis, bacterial or viral infections, automobile accidents, allergies, the ingestion of toxic substances, and so on.

Some causes of hearing loss, such as maternal rubella, CMV, trauma, or prematurity, are associated with other health problems or disabilities. Deafness that is genetically inherited is the least likely of all kinds of deafness to be accompanied by additional disabilities.

5. *Are the parents deaf?* According to commonly accepted estimates, about 5 to 10 percent of deaf children have deaf parents. Deaf children of deaf parents tend to score higher in cognitive, language, and academic areas than do deaf children of hearing parents.[2] Three factors have been proposed for this finding: (1) Most deaf parents have a fluent and intelligible communication system in place in the form of ASL, which they use to communicate with their infant from birth; (2) deaf parents are more likely than hearing parents to expect and identify deafness in their child; and (3) they are accepting, and surprisingly to many people, hopeful of having a deaf child.[3] You will read and learn a great deal about these factors in this book. Early diagnosis of hearing loss, access to fluent language models, and Deaf parents' response and acceptance of the diagnosis of deafness in an infant can often serve as a model for hearing parents who are unexpectedly thrust into a new and (to them) unexplored world. Deaf parents are also good models for how constant exposure to language and communication globally affects a child's overall development in positive ways. Of course there are exceptions with some not-so-great deaf parents, just as there are not-so-great parents in the general population.

6. *How much and what kind of education has the person had?* Deaf and hard of hearing children can attend a variety of school programs. Some go to schools specifically for deaf students, either private or public, which can be far from home. Most are mainstreamed in classes with hearing children, with or without support services, such as interpreters, note takers, tutors, and resource specialists. Children who have hearing aids or cochlear implants should receive appropriate support for the use of these devices in and out of the classroom.

The education levels of deaf people are as varied as those of hearing people. Some deaf students attend mainstream colleges, which are now required by the Americans with Disabilities Act (ADA) to provide support services when requested. Others take advantage of the college programs specifically targeted to deaf students that are available throughout the United States.

7. *What are the person's distinguishing personal characteristics?* With regard to personality, intelligence, genetic makeup, and the other

characteristics that contribute to each person's uniqueness, the deaf population is no different from the hearing population. Humans who are deaf do not differ from those who are not, except in their levels of hearing and modes of communication. Nevertheless, throughout history and until recent decades, educational and employment opportunities for deaf and hard of hearing people were extremely limited, and these limitations squeezed much of the deaf population out of the mainstream of society and into "special" (often specially *limited*) schools and jobs. In recent years, the Deaf community has succeeded in defining itself more clearly to the hearing community and in actively taking advantage of expanded educational opportunities. As a result, career possibilities have become unlimited. We know of doctors, veterinarians, lawyers, professional magicians, accountants, contractors, automobile mechanics, actors, and actresses, all of whom are deaf. And, by the way, we have known obnoxious deaf people, deaf slackers, deaf criminals and convicted felons, and deaf alcoholics and drug addicts. The only limits on what deaf people can be are those that make all of us human together.

8. *What are the person's parents or other family members like?* Family climate has a lot to do with the psychological, educational, and vocational opportunities afforded to young people. In the families of deaf children, the decisions affecting the child's schooling and communication opportunities are heavily influenced by the parents' personal, social, and cultural backgrounds; communication style; value and belief systems; economic status; and orientation toward education. We will explore these factors later. One thing we will emphasize here is this: Research has shown that parent involvement and parent expectations are an important factor in deaf children's success.[4]

9. *What is the person's primary mode of communication?* A large portion of this book is devoted to in-depth exploration of modes of communication, both deaf–deaf and deaf–hearing. Members of the public are often surprised to learn that deaf people use a variety of communication modes—a large and impressive variety. In fact, it is not unusual to meet hearing individuals who completely misunderstand the nature of being deaf itself, even confusing it

with blindness—a good number of us deaf folks have been handed braille menus in restaurants. Even worse is being treated as if we have an intellectual disability. Most people believe that deaf people communicate by some combination of speechreading (or "lipreading"), the ease and effectiveness of which is often overestimated, and sign language, which is routinely underestimated, because they lack experience with its power and richness. Uninformed folks who see deaf people signing usually assume that the signs are equivalent to visual shorthand in English. The truth is that there are four major categories of communication practiced in the American deaf population, as follows:

1. ASL, the native language of American deaf people,
2. Listening (with assistive devices) and Spoken Language (LSL),
3. strictly English-based signing with grammatical influence from English (generally called *Manually Coded English*, with specific approaches, such as Signing Exact English and others), and
4. a combination of speech, speechreading, audition, and signing going along an expressive continuum from signing to oral language. It has been called a variety of names such as *simultaneous communication (Sim-Com)*, *Pidgin Sign English (PSE)*, and *contact sign*.

The ultimate choice reflects the person's own preference, based on facility and comfort with the particular mode. That choice is influenced by a complex interaction of factors, which we will explore in later chapters. The important thing to remember here is that the choice is a personal one, and it is shaped and influenced by all the personal, cultural, social, and genetic factors that make individuals unique.

Just as in the hearing world, where people range from monosyllabic grunters to great orators, in the deaf world, you will find a tremendous range of communicators, including the following:

• fast-and-furious signers,
• people who "mumble" in sign,
• bilingual people who are articulate in both ASL and English (spoken or written),

- people who are articulate in ASL, but not in English,
- people who are articulate in spoken English, but not in ASL, and
- signers who enjoy and develop the natural drama and aesthetic qualities of sign.

Gone are the days of the stereotype of deaf people as depressed and dispirited stay-at-homes. Today, we have made ourselves known in all walks of life for who we are—unique individuals who happen to be, among many other things, deaf or hard of hearing.

10. *What are the person's ties to the Deaf community?* How a person who is deaf relates to the Deaf community is also a matter of personal choice. Some deaf people prefer to live and function primarily in the Deaf community, others exclusively in the hearing society, and others spend varying amounts of time in both worlds or go freely back and forth according to circumstances.

As you can see, deaf people encompass a range of communication styles and levels of community involvement. They contribute in many different ways to the diverse deaf population and to society as a whole. Although our diversity is our strength, it is also the origin of many questions and problems that need to be clarified and understood. For you as parents, facing these issues perhaps for the first time on behalf of your child, the jumble of possibilities to be sorted out no doubt seems overwhelming. Our aim is to take you step by step through this thicket, not as the proponents of a single point of view but as guides and facilitators, helping you gather the information and insights you need to make your own decisions.

In serving as your child's advocate, you will be facing a whole raft of decisions you never anticipated. We hope that this short introduction on the deaf population will help acquaint you with the reality that is the deaf experience. And more, we hope it reassures you that, although different from the hearing experience in its orientation toward communication access, the deaf life can be a rich, productive, exciting world full of promise and potential. The challenges lie in bridging the two worlds. We are writing here with the goal of helping you meet those challenges as you guide your child along the path toward autonomy.

Notes

1. Thomas K. Holcomb. *Introduction to American Deaf Culture* (New York: Oxford University, 2012).

2. Paul Miller, Tevhide Kargin, and Birkan Guldenoglu, "Deaf Native Signers Are Better Readers Than Nonnative Signers: Myth or Truth?" *Journal of Deaf Studies and Deaf Education* 20, no. 2 (2015): 147–62.

3. Thomas K. Holcomb, *Introduction to American Deaf Culture*, 220–21.

4. Stephanie W. Cawthon and Jacqueline M. Caemmerer, "Parents' Perspectives on Transition and Postsecondary Outcomes for Their Children Who Are d/Deaf or Hard of Hearing," *American Annals of the Deaf* 159, no. 1 (2014): 7–21.

2 Lifeboating: Caring for Yourself

ALL PARENTS are their children's lifeboats. Like other parents of children with characteristics that require special attention, you need to take special care of yourself because—not to stretch the metaphor too far—with the news that your child is deaf—you may find yourselves in rough waters. With your child depending on you for direction and guidance, you cannot do better than by first turning your attention to yourself. We want to emphasize here that you need not be alone in this journey. There are other parents who are or have been through this process and are willing to lend a hand.

Before we continue, we want to make note of the fact that the availability of information and the structure of families have changed dramatically since the last edition of this book was published. Janet DesGeorges, a founder of the national parent support group Hands and Voices, reinforces this fact in the box on the following page.

As a parent, you will be making many complex, interrelated decisions in the coming months and years, such as the following:
- what kinds of professional help to seek for your child and your family,
- how to begin communicating most effectively with your child,
- which modes of communication to make available to your child through education,
- what type of school to choose for your child—and where, and
- how to help your child transition from school to an independent and successful adulthood.

Families are not the same as they were ten or fifteen years ago. Today's families are busier and more complex. Access to information has also been completely transformed by the Internet and other media. Support to families across the spectrum—from professional support through telemedicine to parent-to-parent and deaf or hard of hearing adult support via blogs and listservs—has increased the opportunity for families to gain access to information and resources, including research on the topic of being deaf. This brave new world brings many advantages, but at the same time can lead to confusion for families. Inaccurate, incomplete, or misleading information is readily available. Knowledgeable professionals must provide *unbiased* (italics ours) guidance to help families meaningfully process all this information.[1]

These important decisions will affect your child all through life, socially, emotionally, and intellectually. In many ways, your decisions are more significant than are the analogous ones by parents of hearing children. To decide what actions to take—even to learn about the alternatives and think them through—you'll need to be clearheaded, emotionally stable, and physically hearty. It is no overstatement to say that you may have to extend yourself further than you ever have before. Your first need is to absorb the new knowledge that has shaken you so deeply: Your child is deaf or hard of hearing and will be for the rest of his or her life. The time that directly follows confirmation of this fact is *your* time to gather yourself together. For the child who has been deaf from birth or shortly thereafter, nothing has altered. For you, life has changed permanently but not for the worse, just differently than you expected.

The Response Cycle

Every child is unique; every parent is, too. Furthermore, as is explained in Chapter 1, types, levels, and causes of hearing loss vary from person to person. The combinations of personalities, potentials, family constellations and patterns, and social and economic variables that shape deaf people's particular situations are infinite. As with all things human, the uniqueness of each and every situation is all we can really count on. Just as varied as all these shaping influences are also the reactions of individual parents when they first learn that their child is deaf or hard of hearing. There is really no one "right way" to react to a diagnosis, but most do follow a similar pattern.

People react to life-altering events through a cycle of responses that are recognizable and describable—and, most important, *functional.* Although each person responds differently, everyone experiences the cycle in some form. The responses in the cycle, which do not occur in any predictable order, are normal and can be healthy if they are addressed and not repressed. They are the steps we humans need to take to come to terms with radical changes in our lives and, eventually, to incorporate the changes into an adjusted worldview.

The response to crisis is a lifelong process—not a neat and tidy movement from problem to solution, but rather a shifting and changing in response to new information and conditions. The purpose of this chapter is to help you understand and accept your own feelings in each part of the cycle and to see how they function in the adjustment process. The ultimate goal is to help you to be the reliable, seaworthy lifeboat you hope to be for your child.

What is a crisis? Why does it require so much of us, emotionally and intellectually, and why is it so difficult to respond to? The answer is that by its very nature, a crisis is an occurrence that permanently alters our understanding of reality; frequently, it is an event we have not anticipated or prepared for. Something happens that throws everything we know, feel, and understand about our lives and those around us into a new light. We don't have to tell you that learning that your child is deaf is this kind of experience.

As you begin to react to the many dramatic and subtle changes that this single discovery brings to your family life, you may find yourself experiencing intense and painful emotions. On the basis of our long experience with families of deaf children, we urge you not to resist, but to let yourself feel everything that comes to you. Do not be frightened or disgusted by the strength of your feelings or the forms they take. Do not deny your feelings; allow them to come and go. Above all, do not try to change them or force them away—you will never succeed. Sustained denial is like pretending that your lifeboat is not filling up with water.

Simply understanding that you are in the process of adjusting to a fundamental change in reality can be helpful. And you may find comfort in the fact that others have also experienced what you are going through in the same situation. You can be sure that, like the many parents before and after you, you will move through the more painful states into a position of strength. At that point, you will see more clearly, think more clearly, and perhaps act more effectively than ever before in your life.

The sections that follow examine each of the identifiable stages in the response process. Before we begin, though, we want to underscore a point made in passing earlier: *Responding to having a deaf child is not a one-time experience.* You will be called upon to respond time and time again as your child matures and faces new challenges. At each rite of passage, when complexities seem to loom larger for your deaf child than for other children, you are likely to go through the response cycle again. Some parents have described the process to the authors as being more like a spiral, with the cycle becoming shorter and less intense each time. Remember, everyone's response may be different. Also, rest assured that you are not a bad parent if you do not even feel a response other than typical parental pride or anxiety. Experience has shown that families of deaf children go through periods of stress particularly during developmental milestones, such as the following:

- when the hearing loss is identified,
- when the child enters school for the first time,
- when the child enters adolescence, and
- when the child transitions to early adulthood.

Although these are not the only high-stress periods you can anticipate, the very nature of these chronological events makes it reasonable to expect that you and perhaps your child will be called upon emotionally to respond anew.

If you know what to expect from yourself during high-stress transition periods, you will be less likely to be taken by surprise or overwhelmed, and you may find reassurance in the experience of others (see "Welcome to Holland" on page 16). Despite the

Welcome to Holland

Emily Perl Kingsley

I am often asked to describe the experience of raising a child with a disability—to try to help people who have not shared that unique experience to understand it, to imagine how it would feel. It is like this . . . .

When you're going to have a baby, it is like planning a fabulous vacation trip—to Italy. You buy a bunch of guidebooks and make your wonderful plans. The Coliseum. Michelangelo's *David*. The gondolas in Venice. You may learn some handy phrases in Italian. It is all very exciting.

After months of eager anticipation, the day finally arrives. You pack your bags and off you go. Several hours later, the plane lands. The stewardess comes in and says, "Welcome to Holland."

"Holland?!?" you say. "What do you mean, Holland? I signed up for Italy! I'm supposed to be in Italy. All my life I've dreamed of going to Italy."

But there's been a change in the flight plan. They've landed in Holland, and there you must stay.

emotions you may feel, eventually you will emerge with a clearer understanding of the challenges you and your child face together.

GRIEF

Time is the greatest teacher. Not only do we collect insights and information with the passage of time, but also we come to understand more about what we already know. When the first edition of this book came out in the early 1980s, the literature on grieving provided an analogy for the emotional responses parents experience upon learning they have a deaf child. Today, our understanding has deepened, and we view grief not as an analogy, but as the very phenomenon these parents undergo. But, you may ask, isn't grief the response to the death of someone close? So, let's start

The important thing is that they haven't taken you to a horrible, disgusting, filthy place, full of pestilence, famine, and disease. It is just a different place. So you must go out and buy new guidebooks. And you must learn a whole new language. And you will meet a whole new group of people you would never have met.

It is just a different place. It is slower-paced than Italy, less flashy than Italy. But after you've been there for a while and you catch your breath, you look around, and you begin to notice that Holland has tulips. Holland even has Rembrandts.

But everyone you know is busy coming and going from Italy, and they're bragging about what a wonderful time they had there. And for the rest of your life, you will say, "Yes, that's where I was supposed to go. That's what I had planned."

And the pain of that will never, ever, ever go away, because the loss of that dream is a very significant loss.

But if you spend your life mourning the fact that you didn't get to Italy, you may never be free to enjoy the very special, the very lovely, things about Holland.[2]❏

with a definition: *Grief* is the process by which we separate from someone or something significant that has been lost.

Wait a minute, you say. No one has died in our family. Yes, we have received difficult news, and we are facing a crisis. But we haven't sustained any sort of permanent loss. Consider this definition of *loss* by Kenneth L. Moses, a well-known psychologist.

Losses are . . . occurrences or events that shatter dreams that are core to a person's existence. . . . The initial diagnosis oftentimes marks the point when a cherished and significant dream has been shattered for the parent. . . . The parent oftentimes does not understand that it is a dream that he has lost, and therefore he is frequently confused by the grief process that follows.[3]

As an example, Terry, a former teaching colleague of one author, went through just such an experience. He was particularly supportive of the deaf students in his classes. One day, he discovered that his three-year-old son, Ted, who had just recovered from meningitis, had lost his hearing completely as a result of the disease. Terry went to his boss to talk about the situation and, much to his own surprise and embarrassment, broke down crying. Once he began, he couldn't stop. For days, then weeks, he found himself breaking down in tears. Why did he weep? At first, he says, it was because he was afraid that his son would grow up to resemble the deaf children in his class, none of whom could read past the first-grade level. Then it was because his marriage, which had been happy and stable, had shattered under the weight of the crisis. His wife had left him and Ted, fleeing to her parents' home on learning that her son was deaf.

Terry was surprised and bewildered by the force of his emotions, but if we recognize that he had lost two of the dreams that made up his fundamental reality—a hearing son and a happy marriage—we can see that grief was an appropriate response.

What is not as evident without some understanding of the grief process is that grief is not only an appropriate response but also a productive and helpful one. Although there was a time when mental health professionals were as likely as well-meaning friends and relatives to *discourage* grieving, today we understand that grieving is an essential part of the normal healing process that enables us to come to terms with change.

Grieving in the face of the initial diagnosis of having a deaf child is an unlearned, spontaneous response that is necessary to successful lifeboating. Each stage in the grieving process plays a specific role in enabling you to let go of old, shattered dreams and acquire new, attainable ones.

In different ways and at different times, everyone experiences the following stages in the grief process: shock and denial, anger, guilt, depression, and anxiety. Healthy parents who mourn the lost child of their dreams eventually learn to deal with the feelings as they come and go over time, and turn their attention to the real, living child. Soon they find that, yes, the child is different from their original idea of him or her—but only with respect to being deaf. The child's personality, the identity that has been unfolding from birth, is still the same. Once the parents' initial grief period has passed, they find that they have moved away from their "loss" and closer to their child. Better yet, they gain the realization that their child can still lead a successful life, just not the way they had originally envisioned. Keep in mind that parents also may find themselves recycling through the grief process during life's milestones; but with a good support system, they can learn it is okay and normal to have these feelings and not let them control their behavior.[4]

Shock and Denial

The first reaction to life-altering news is *shock*. This response, which lasts from a few hours to a few days at most, is a stunned calm in which you try to absorb the mere truth of the situation apart from its implications. Typically, parents say something like, "The audiologist told me my child was deaf, but it didn't really sink in." Shock is a protective device that enables you simply to sit with bad news without being immediately overwhelmed by emotion.

You may wonder, or even worry, about your detachment upon first hearing the news. You may be surprised to find that you remember the design on the audiologist's dress or the pattern of the shadows on the wall. For those of you who have been aware that something was just not "right" with your young one, a very strong (and unexpected) emotion is likely to sweep over you when you learn that your child is really deaf: relief.

Before the widespread advent of newborn hearing screening in the past decade, many cases of deafness were undiagnosed until the child was one or two years old when they normally should start to vocalize. Parents may have strong suspicions for a year or more about their child's inability to hear. During this time, they struggle to keep hope alive, doing their best to suppress their fears. Every now and then, the intuition that their child is deaf surfaces. They ask their doctor, but the response is always, "Oh, all children develop differently, some are late bloomers," and the parents begin again the battle against believing their child is deaf. This kind of emotional tug-of-war is exhausting. A definitive answer, even if it confirms the parents' worst fears, is bound to be a relief.

Alternatively, although some parents interviewed for this book were grateful to have learned early that their child was deaf, thanks to newborn hearing screenings, others were not so sure they would have wanted to know. They felt it ruined their idyllic world of having a happy baby for a while instead of dealing with all of the reactions and stress right after recovering from giving birth.[5] As we can see here, there are differing views about when there is a "good time" to learn about it, but nonetheless, shock is a typical reaction to the news.

Shock can continue for a long time, merging into the zone of emotional protectiveness called *denial*. Denial is a psychological defense mechanism that screens out painful knowledge from conscious awareness. But eventually reality sinks in, and the process of recognition begins.

Consider Nancy, the wife of Terry (described earlier) and mother of three-year-old Ted, who lost his hearing from meningitis. When the doctor gave her the news, Nancy left the boy in the hospital, leaving Terry to cope as best he could. She flew to her parents' home and stayed there for more than six weeks, unable to push past the inertia that overtook her. Far from feeling overwhelmed by emotion, Nancy was dulled. She couldn't understand her inertia and couldn't shake it off.

Nancy had been raised in a wealthy family that placed high value on the medical establishment. Her parents could afford to consult specialists for any medical problem, and Nancy had grown up believing that virtually every symptom had a cure. When told that her boy was deaf for life and that no one could restore his hearing, Nancy was flabbergasted. Not only her son's future but also her whole belief system was called into question. Had shock not screened her emotions, she could have been overwhelmed by confusion and despair at the shattering of her reality.

Eventually, though, with time for the change to sink in gradually in the security of her parents' home, Nancy was able to acknowledge the situation for what it was. After six weeks, she returned to Terry, and they began to share their mutual grief and to care for their son. (For a continuation of this story, see "Ted: An Update" on page 32.)

Nancy's story brings up a sensitive issue that applies to all stages of grief. People do what they can to get through the grieving cycle, and frequently—much more so than is generally acknowledged—what they must do is *socially unacceptable*. Nancy risked heavy criticism from the hospital staff and doctor, from her husband, even from her own parents when she walked away from the situation and went home to nurse her shock.

As another example, Jenny, a friend of one of the authors, went to Disneyland the day her mother died. She had been sitting at her mother's bedside throughout the woman's sudden and unexpected illness and watched her pass away. Then she walked out of the hospital, got into her car, and drove six hours to Disneyland where she stayed for two days. Jenny's family and friends had varied reactions from shock to empathy, but she knew she needed a change of venue to get over her initial reaction to the loss of her mother.

Edward, a young academic, left his family and friends reeling with confusion on the night his daughter Melissa was born. When he discovered that the infant had no left arm, he too walked out of the hospital—and headed straight for a liquor store. Edward rarely drank, even at parties, but on this night, he bought a bottle of bourbon and drank it all. He wept, pounded the walls, bellowed his anger, and finally passed out, leaving his wife to cope with her feelings alone.

In the morning, although suffering from a terrific hangover, Edward was able to confront the situation clearly and do what needed to be done. Most important, as we will see, he began reaching out to his wife. Healthy, productive grieving that moves from shock toward acceptance is accomplished by *sharing*, not by trying to get through the experience in isolation.

After the period of shock—the calm before the storm—comes a time of deep and painful, raw emotion. You realize that your child is deaf. He or she cannot hear and will never be able to hear. Your mind is awhirl with questions, confusions, sudden fears, and insights, like the following.

"All this time I thought I knew my child, and I don't even know what her world is about. Having a deaf child is a part of our lives *forever.* This is something I never asked for, never thought about. I *hate* this."

"What will this do to our finances? We can't afford any extra medical or professional help. And what about special schools? How will we ever cope financially?"

"I'm a single parent and the sole source of support for my children. I can't quit my job. Is this child going to require constant attention or home schooling? I was counting on raising some pretty independent children who could look out for each other. Who's going to give this child the special care he needs while I'm out earning a living?"

"What kind of a future can I expect for my baby?"

"Why did this happen to us? Could it happen again?"

"What information do I need? Where do I turn—to a doctor? A teacher? A social worker? A speech therapist? An audiologist? Where should I call first? Should I try to find a clinic? A special school? Should I look into hearing aids? Cochlear implants? Should I learn sign language? What is sign language, anyway? Will I be able to learn it?"

Many parents are appalled at themselves for even thinking about practical matters at such a time, when they should be worrying about the welfare of their child. If you feel this way, rest easy. With the first shock fading, confusion and overwhelming emotions are natural. Not only is it all right to feel these things, it is certain that the passage of time and especially the communication of your concerns with others who understand, either personally or professionally, will bring relief.

For a child, being deaf is a complex issue with four interrelated aspects: the physiological, the social (which includes communication with both deaf and hearing people), the educational, and the emotional. Try to remember that you will have time later to become informed and make decisions. Go slowly, one step at a time. First and foremost, focus on making the lifeboat strong and seaworthy.

Anger

Of all the stages of the grieving cycle, anger—or its more intense form, rage—is perhaps the most disconcerting for parents to feel and live with. Consider the following examples of angry thoughts. You may recognize yourself in some of them.

"How am I supposed to work things out for the family now? We were just beginning to feel financially secure, and now we'll have special medical expenses, special counselors, and special schools. I've been working as hard as I can, but we're never going to make it now."

"I didn't even want to have another child, but my husband kept pressuring me. And now look what happened. *He* won't be the one doing the extra work. My life is ruined."

"Why can't things go the way they're supposed to go, just once?"

"I'm walking around anxious and exhausted all the time. When am I going to get a break?"

"Why didn't my mother tell me what I was risking when I started a family? If I'd known something like this was going to happen, I would never have had children."

"Who does that doctor think he is—God? How does he know my child will never hear? I won't stand for that kind of dictatorial attitude."

"This child is too needy. Everybody's got to pull their weight in this family, and somehow or other she's just going to have to shape up."

Parents are not the only family members who may feel angry. The hearing siblings of a deaf or hard of hearing child may also experience anger and resentment, but their feelings are often lost in the larger picture. Typical reactions include the following:

- "Why does *he* get all the attention?"
- "Mom and Dad haven't come to one of my Little League games all season."
- "Why do they have to treat him like he's special when he can't even hear?"

Perhaps all of these examples express the single lament we humans most often raise in the face of difficult, life-changing events: *"It is just not fair! Why did this have to happen to me?"* Everyone has a personal sense of fairness, of justice that defines how the world should be. When our sense of the way things should be comes into conflict with the way things are, our whole understanding of reality is called into question. We need time—as much time as it takes—to match our sense of justice with the new reality we face.

The need to revise our understanding is the key to the function of anger. In the short run, our anger—at ourselves, at our spouses, at the professionals we encounter in dealing with the news, even at our deaf children—affords us a bit of relief from the frustration we feel at being unable to change the deafness, to make it go away or fade into insignificance. And in the long run, anger can provide a sense of self-reliance or self-assurance that serves us in reconstructing a new personal philosophy of fairness, a philosophy that will help us understand and cope with the world as it really is. It is important that you deal with your anger in a healthy way, as repressing it can lead to depression and health problems, and definitely does not help your child.

Think of Melissa, the child born missing an arm. During the first year after her birth, she was also found to be deaf. Melissa's mother, Ellen, was a nurse, and her medical knowledge only reinforced her sense that the family was now sentenced to a lifetime of living hell. Melissa would live a "handicapped" existence, and Ellen herself, as the working mother of a severely disabled child, would never again have a moment to herself. Ellen's anger was so intense, it scared her, and she spent months attempting to suppress her thoughts and feelings, which she considered inappropriate for a mother and nurse.

Slowly, Ellen began to collect the resources necessary for constructive action. And beneath the surface of practical activity she began, as she later realized, to reassess her entire value system. It was a bumpy journey at first. But as the years passed, after Melissa had developed into a highly sociable and active young lady (she became the pitcher on her Little League team, among other things) Ellen saw that even anger had played a positive role. "I thought Melissa's being deaf and her lack of an arm meant the end of the world—for her and for me. For months, I was looking for somebody or something to blame. What I found instead—gradually, not all at once—was a whole new way of living. And now I wonder if we

Melissa: An Update

Melissa finished the eighth grade at her spoken language school for deaf students and mainstreamed into her local high school, making use of the interpreters provided for the six or seven deaf students enrolled there. She did well and formed strong friendships with other deaf students. After graduation, she married Jonathan, a deaf classmate, and got a job as an auditing clerk at the post office. Melissa never had any desire to go to college, and after working for a few years, she had two children and became a full-time housewife. This decision left her quite contented and her parents, Edward and Ellen, quite disappointed.

Melissa's parents had cherished great expectations for her and pressured her to set her goals high. All through her school years, they had been very much involved in her life and had made a special effort to meet deaf adults, contact other parents of deaf children, and keep up on the educational research. In short, they were thinking all the time about how to help Melissa grow up to be independent and successful. When she expressed modest ambitions and showed little drive, they blamed it on her being deaf. In fact, Melissa had found ways to express her sociable nature all through high school. She communicated incessantly with her friends, took trips on her own, and loved to sit with her parents in the kitchen and fill them in on her life.

It took a long time for Ellen and Edward to admit to themselves that Melissa was just a regular person with interests different from their own, and that it wasn't that she was deaf, but rather Melissa's whole identity that they were struggling with. They did not begin to enjoy visiting Melissa and Jonathan until after their grandchildren came along. "It is who she is," they were finally able to say. "It isn't the life we'd choose for ourselves, and it isn't the life we hoped she would have. But Melissa is happy as a clam the way things turned out, and that's the important thing, isn't it?" Absolutely, we would say. Raising happy children who can make their own choices and live out their desires is certainly the most important thing. ❏

would have accomplished so much or even been so happy if we had remained the people we were when Melissa was born."

Guilt

If anger is the most disconcerting of the grief stages for parents, it is the guilt parents sometimes express that often bothers the professionals who counsel them. In general, guilt manifests itself in three ways when parents learn their child is deaf.

1. *"I caused this to happen."* The parent feels directly responsible for the deafness—"I refused to quit my job when I got pregnant, even though my husband wanted me to; I was run-down and exhausted, and then I was exposed to rubella—this would never have happened if . . . ." This is the most logical but the least-common form of guilt expressed by parents.

2. *"My child's deafness is a punishment for my own misbehavior."* The parent thinks that somehow he or she deserves the crisis for their past deeds.

3. *"I must have been bad, because that's the way the world works: Bad things happen to bad people."* The parent assumes he or she deserves the crisis but doesn't know why, so reasons that the deafness couldn't have occurred otherwise. In the words of Kenneth L. Moses, "Such a general belief leaves the parent feeling guilty simply because the impairment exists."[6]

Professionals are likely to react against guilt expressed by parents of deaf children, seriously doubting that such a distressing, blame-assigning emotional response can have a positive role in promoting growth and adaptation. But in the context of the grief cycle, as Moses points out, guilt is the vehicle "that allows parents to reevaluate their existential beliefs."[7]

Some of us hardly know our beliefs, or are unable to articulate them fully. Only when they are tested by experience do we come to question them fully—and find, often, that they haven't evolved and matured as we might have expected. A father who believes that his marijuana smoking in college has caused his son's deafness, or a mother who attributes her child's deafness to the fact that she was less enthusiastic about her pregnancy than she let on, may come to see, in talking about these beliefs, that parents are not responsible for everything that happens to their children.

Experience has taught us that the key to such a perceptual change is *sharing* with someone who understands the enormity of the impact of discovering that your child is deaf. For this reason, it is important that the professionals you deal with view guilt not as a pathological condition, but as the starting point for as much supportive conversation as you need in order to explore this new development. If a counselor or other mental health professional dismisses your expression of guilt with comments like "That's outrageous! Ridiculous! Absurd!" think about finding another source of support. (For more on this subject, see "Communicating with Professionals" on page 28.) It may take some time, but it is of course necessary that you do learn to address and process your guilt feelings. Parents who are guilt-ridden and have not had the opportunity to work through their feelings tend to overprotect and hover over their child. Neither of these behaviors is conducive to a good outcome for the child.[8]

DEPRESSION

Surprisingly, although depression is the feeling most often associated with grief, many people view this emotional state as a problem rather than as a normal stage in the process toward readjustment. One of our objectives in writing this chapter is to give grief a new, improved reputation—not as a horrible state similar to mental illness, to be gotten through as quickly as possible, but as a normal process as you and your child transition through life.

As we recounted earlier, Terry, father of Ted, experienced a long period of depression after learning that his son was deaf. When he tried to express how completely tragic he viewed being deaf to be, he wept uncontrollably. He couldn't see the deaf children in his classroom without welling up with emotion, and daily after school for a period of weeks, he went home and simply sat, staring at nothing.

Depression arises from the feeling of impotence. In common parlance, it is "anger turned inward," and this is a good way of describing parents' frustration with themselves at their inability to make life perfect for their children. But just by coming face to face with your frustrated desire to change the unchangeable—to make your child's deafness go away and get back that fantasy child you

Communicating with Professionals

Professionals play a key role in helping parents make decisions about their child. Therefore it is important that you be able to communicate with them comfortably and be satisfied that they have your best interest in mind. In the coming years, as your child grows, you will meet many professionals—pediatricians; ear, nose, and throat (ENT) specialists; early intervention specialists; audiologists; speech therapists; teachers; parent-education counselors; and psychologists—whose lifework relates in one way or another to working with deaf individuals. Many of these people, by virtue of their particular form of training, may be extremely biased toward one or another mode of communication, style of education, and overall approach to dealing with deaf children and their parents. Parents who are emotionally vulnerable when they meet someone with an axe to grind or a philosophy to sell can be swayed from making their own well-informed choices—and the results can be tragic.

In addition, there is the risk of falling into the "experts-are-gods" syndrome that our culture often reinforces and supports. We have seen too many people who believe that it would be downright disrespectful to question a professional like a doctor, teacher, or school principal, and who politely follow the first piece of advice they are offered. The wiser and safer alternative is to cultivate a healthy skepticism and become an informed consumer. The way to do that is to network, learn, study, talk to other parents, ask questions, and do anything and everything you need to do to understand what's best for your child.

In the process of becoming informed, it is crucial to meet deaf adults, particularly deaf adults with children, and to talk frankly with them. You may find comfort in the discovery that deaf parents often celebrate the birth of a deaf child. In the same way that hearing parents may say of a hearing child, here is a child whose inner world we can understand, so deaf parents feel instant empathy with a deaf infant—and possible dismay at the birth of a hearing child. In fact, ironically, we know of deaf parents who grieved because their child was born hearing. If that seems absurd to you, remember grief is a result of the loss of expected and cherished outcomes. We all want our children to be like us and fully a part of our own world. This perspective can be a source of comfort and greater understanding for hearing parents.

Above all, in learning from other people, trust your instincts. Here are a few sample questions to guide you in assessing your feelings about any given professional.

- Does the person see your child as someone who happens to be deaf or as a deaf child who is simply a case to be dealt with?
- Does the person offer clear, up-to-date information or heavy-handed advice, even dictatorial "shoulds" and "musts"?
- Is the person thoughtful and considerate of your feelings or cold, clinical, and aloof?
- Does the person ask if you have any questions and invite you to call back with questions later or cut you off and end the meeting after delivering his or her message?
- Does the person encourage open discussion of all aspects of the issues, including the controversial ones, or is there a feeling of "one right way and its mine"?
- Is the person experienced and comfortable with children?

All of this suggests a pretty safe general criterion for choosing a professional to work with your child—Is this a person you would like to see again, or were you relieved to get out of there? Remember, *you* are the decision maker. No one has "the right answer" regarding what you should do for your child. It can be easy to give in to the temptation during this vulnerable time in your life to let professionals take over the decision-making. What the best professionals have to offer is guidance, information, and support. Don't settle for less than that.❏

thought you had—you have the opportunity to reassess your sense of competency and discover what you can do in the real world.

Learning that your child is deaf is a direct challenge to your faith in your ability to keep your child safe from harm. Although it is not inevitable that you will suffer self-doubt, this emotion, along with a general sense of insecurity surrounding your competency as a parent, is likely to come up and is completely normal. Depression is a response to this loss of confidence.

You may not be able to change the fact your child is deaf, but you can take action by educating yourself, learning about the decisions to be made, and putting the resources you have to the best possible use. Depression begins the act of facing your limitations, so that your competencies and realistic options can slowly come into focus.

By first questioning your competence as a parent, you begin to take measures to restore your confidence in yourself. This may not be comfortable—but change always brings emotional pain. Terry, contemplating his and Ted's shared fate, foresaw no end to the tears and the paralysis. But as he considered his personal resources, he began to see things he could do, steps he could take, people he could call, and questions he could ask. The depression became a window through which he discovered a fresh view of himself and his relationship with Ted.

ANXIETY

If depression is a necessary part of reassessing our competencies, anxiety is the means by which we mobilize and then focus our energies in order to change. Anxiety is the normal and natural response to a radical change in the environment; it is the set of physiological and psychological adjustments that permits us to take action in the world.

In the context of physical danger, this set of responses is called the "fight-or-flight" syndrome. The discomfort we feel in an anxious state—the increased heart rate, shallow and quickened breathing, sweaty palms, shaky muscles, and so on—is itself a great motivator to action. In a sense, anxiety feels terrible *in order to* goad us into action, so that we will respond effectively to the change in our environment and achieve a new balance. Our urgent feelings that we must do something are the forerunners of constructive action. As Moses observes, "It is not helpful at all to give a parent an injunction requiring that he 'calm down.' This is a period when calming down is not only impossible, but maladaptive, for the anxiety itself facilitates a restructuring of one's attitudes concerning responsibility."[9]

Feeling the weight of the responsibility of your child's being deaf is a first and necessary step toward shouldering that responsibility and taking necessary actions. If you seek professional counseling, it is important to find someone who recognizes the value and appropriateness of anxiety at this time in your life. Choose a counselor who will support you as you go through this process, at your own pace. (For more guidance on interacting with professionals and monitoring their usefulness, see "Communicating with Professionals" on page 28.)

Coping

It is all very well to understand our feelings. But how do we *act*, how do we *behave* in order to gain stability, focus, and the heart and spirit for constructive action? Let us respond to this question in two parts. The first part, like the preceding sections, is purely descriptive. The second is a discussion of concrete steps you can take in the real world of action and experience.

First, a definition: *Coping* is the expression through behavior (as opposed to feeling) of the various stages that make up the grieving process. In the same way that the emotional stages of the grieving process occur in no particular order, so can the behaviors that constitute coping occur in no particular order.

CONTAINMENT OF THE LOSS

Unless you had some reason to expect it, the discovery that your child is deaf is a *core-level loss*, a loss that affects the most fundamental aspects of your life. In responding, you will sort through all these aspects: your hopes and dreams for the future, your job, and your personal relationships—with your child, your spouse if

Ted: An Update

The first few years after Terry moved Ted to a nearby non-residential school were not easy ones. The school was a big disappointment, but even more disturbing were the unarticulated, unaddressed problems in Terry and Nancy's marriage. Everything seemed to get jumbled, and Terry and Nancy fell into despair. Without being aware of it, they projected their dissatisfaction with their marriage onto the issue of Ted's education, blaming themselves, in serious bouts of recrimination, for Ted's problems in school.

Luckily, on a summer trip full of emotional outbursts, Terry's parents stepped in. "That boy isn't really doing so bad," said the grandfather. "If you don't mind some advice, I'd look a little closer to home plate. You and Nancy can't seem to get through an hour without having some kind of a spat. Don't you think it is time you paid some attention to yourselves?"

That was it. The two entered couple's counseling, where they were able to reflect a little on their interactions. They isolated some conflicting patterns and their possible roots: Nancy had grown up having problems solved for her; Terry had been raised to solve problems himself. Neither was having much luck solving Ted's communication problems in school. In addition, Terry, who had always been a popular instructor, a father figure for students at his school, found that Ted resisted his attempts to help. As Ted grew older, he made it clear that he didn't want Terry's interventions.

Ted mainstreamed into a public high school and made full use of the support services available to him by law (see Chapter 12). With this new independence from his parents, he began to do quite well. Still, crises arose, and most of them were related to the fact that Ted and his parents had little contact with deaf adults.

There were huge arguments about whether Ted should get a driver's license. Had Nancy and Terry been in touch with deaf adults, they would have seen them driving just like anyone else. Had they been keeping up on the literature, they probably also would have known that hearing drivers are twice as likely as deaf drivers to be involved in accidents. When Ted did get his license, there were struggles over when he could take the car.

These were typical arguments for families with teenagers, but Terry and Nancy often made the mistake of attributing the stress to Ted's being deaf rather than his adolescence. Similarly, they considered Ted's problems with grades and homework to be related to his being deaf rather than the normal ups and downs of life with a teenager. Such misinterpretations led Terry and Nancy to seek solutions that had no real link to the problems' root causes.

When Ted brought home deaf friends who signed, Terry and Nancy couldn't communicate with them and felt left out. Instead of adopting the philosophy "better late than never" and making the attempt to learn sign language, the two castigated themselves for never having learned to sign.

When Ted fell in love with Elizabeth, a young deaf woman, Terry and Nancy worried about how they would manage together, and especially how they would raise children. But the marriage took place, and seemingly overnight, the tension in the family vanished. Terry and Nancy became friendly with Elizabeth's parents, who had faced similar issues but whose marriage had been much more stable. Talking about the issues gave Terry and Nancy great relief, and after the wedding, they were finally able to see that they had mistakenly focused their lives on Ted's deaf status, rather than on Ted himself, who happened to be deaf. ❏

you have one, your friends, your coworkers, and your neighbors. As you assess the actual impact of having a deaf child in each of these arenas, you will begin to perceive the effects of the loss to be narrower and less global than you thought at first.

REASSESSMENT OF "NORMAL" STANDARDS

Society is rife with cruel stereotypes. What it calls "normal" is as exclusive as the most discriminatory, snobbish, unconstitutional country club. Everything outside the picture of a fresh-faced white family of four has been treated as abnormal in our society, including people who are members of various ethnic groups and races, non-English speaking, poor, divorced, children of divorced parents, deaf-blind, nonspeaking, wheelchair bound, and overweight.

Without even making an effort, you will find that constant exposure to the reality of your child's being deaf tends to normalize what you once considered abnormal. You will find that your sense of what is normal includes life as a deaf person (and perhaps a great many other traits that you once considered abnormal).

ENLARGING YOUR SCOPE OF VALUES

Although people's value systems may narrow as they grow older, your child's identity as a deaf person, like any conflict between ideal and reality, can enlarge the lens through which you view and judge the world. We have heard statements like the following countless times:

- "I feel that I have a purpose, that my values are much, much better since we've had this child."
- "I would have been a bored suburban housewife, entertaining myself with coffee klatches and card games. Now I know what's important."
- "I never would have believed how much joy there could be in having something that scared me so much. Everything my child accomplishes is a milestone, and we all delight in it."
- "If just one person had come to us to tell us that despite our initial sadness, there was hope, that this was not the end of the world, but rather a challenge and a uniting force that could bring out the very best in each member of the family, how much more bearable our grief would have been."

Be assured that, in the end, the very conflict between your experience with your child and the standards of the "normal" world will greatly enrich your life.

SHIFTING FROM "COMPARATIVE" TO "ASSET" VALUES

Coping with life-changing events not only enlarges but also refines our values. By this, we mean that coping moves us from a place where we judge our own value by comparing ourselves with others to a place where we value ourselves by assessing our own assets alone.

So, again without making an effort, the experience of learning that your child is deaf can deepen your appreciation for what you already have and what you can do. If, before, you were struggling to keep up with the Joneses, eventually you may find that the child you have is so interesting, engaging, delightful, and *different* from the child you thought you had that competition simply drops out of the picture.

Coping Strategies

In focusing on the important function of grief and in attempting to reassure you, we risk seeming to diminish the impact of finding that your child is deaf. Therefore, it bears repeating that news of a child's "sudden" status as a deaf person is always a core, life-changing event, one that will continue to have some impact on your family throughout life. Still, over the last few decades—with being deaf coming out of the shadows, where it used to exist under the horrible label "the invisible disability"—we have accumulated anecdotal, clinical, and empirical evidence that certain concrete actions work to ease parents out of grief and into constructive action. Here, in a nutshell, are the coping strategies that will help you through the grief cycle.

1. *Share your experiences with others.* The danger in grieving is that the experience will isolate you. In the days when grief was considered a problem that needed fixing, that danger was greater than it is today. If isolation is the danger, sharing with a concerned and empathetic person is the prevention. Simply realizing you are not alone and then learning about others' perspectives on having a

young deaf child will not only ease your personal distress but also will expose you to possible constructive action you may wish to pursue when you are ready.

2. *Network!* Anyone who has attempted to learn everything there is to know about a new subject knows the importance of networking. You are a parent with a busy household. If you try to depend on yourself alone to do the necessary research, you will consign yourself to unnecessary hours of study and legwork, hours you could be spending with your family or at work. Moreover, with regard to certain decisions about communication modes and education, time is of the essence. For all these reasons, it is important to assemble a support network composed of both professionals in the field and lay people who have had personal experience in dealing with deaf children.

3. *Wait until you're ready.* Before you begin networking, it is important to feel perfectly comfortable about seeking out other parents and deaf adults. You almost certainly will feel better and even pleasantly surprised when you start making contacts. But if you want permission not to spend every waking minute focusing on your child's needs, you've got it. Remember the lifeboat idea: You need to be rested, not exhausted and overwhelmed, in order to be strong. When you do feel ready, here are some people to seek out:

- Other parents of deaf or hard of hearing children—parents who will have experiences to recount and resources to tell you about, as well as warnings of what or whom to avoid.

- Deaf adults—people who can help you understand the realities of life as a deaf person and the way it shapes the perspectives of deaf people. Meeting deaf adults will acquaint you with the world and culture of deaf people, and it will bring role models into your child's world—a factor whose importance, right from the start, cannot be overstated.

- Medical professionals, including audiologists and ENT specialists, people whom you trust and with whom you feel comfortable asking questions.

- Educators—people who are trained to work with children who are deaf. Note that we say *educators*, plural. It is important to learn about all the many options open to you before you head down a particular path, and researching these options means meeting people who are expert in the various education styles and modes of communication. More will follow about this complex subject; here, suffice it to say that you, as well as your child, are about to receive an education. For the sake of your child, and for the sake of your own peace of mind as a parent, it is important that this education be thorough and unbiased.

4. *Remember that grief can still come and go during milestones.* Let it happen and let go. You will recover your energy, good spirits, and confidence in your parenting skills. Although the emotional stages you are going through initially are intense and all-encompassing, you will regain a sense of normality in daily family life. Have faith in the quality that, above all, we can count on as human beings: resilience.

5. *Give to others; get involved.* This strategy is a preventive against the debilitating isolation that can inhibit the grief process. But

Two Families

There were two families who had deaf daughters. When the girls were little, the families met in a deaf program and became friends. Over the years, the parents have grown very close, exchanging information and talking in depth about all their concerns, especially those related to having deaf children. These four parents have the habit of discussing with each other everything they hear from professionals, and they've found that their shared testing, brainstorming, and analysis have served them better than a thousand consultations with specialists. They are involved, they respect each other's experience and perspective, and they don't feel they have to take every message from the professional world as gospel. With all four parents participating, each can afford to be skeptical sometimes without fear of disregarding something important.

This openness is a sunny contrast to the impulse of some families to "work this out alone." ❑

there's more to it than that. By meeting people, joining organizations and support groups, and making yourself available to others who may be just behind you on the path, you will be widening your own support network and keeping yourself tuned in to the information channel. No point of view is more healing than the recognition that "we're all in this boat together." Make sure, however, that you're really ready to interact with others. Throwing yourself into a new world can be a form of denial, a distraction from your own shock and screened-out emotions.

6. *Keep your sense of humor.* As you read this book at the beginning of a new journey with your child, you may not be able to come up with too much that strikes you as funny about being deaf. However, as the shock recedes and the coping mechanisms kick in, you may be surprised at your restored ability to smile or make a joke or two about it. After all, now you can vacuum in your child's bedroom without waking her up! Let us urge you from the heart not to censor yourself. Laughter is always appropriate, perhaps most appropriate, in response to the greatest life challenges. Humor brings us momentary relief from the weight of our most consequential decisions—and it may be that, with so many new concerns to think through and act on, temporary relief is all we want or need.

7. *Pay attention to yourself.* Remember the lifeboat concept: Nobody is going to benefit if you sink under the weight of your new concerns and responsibilities. Throughout this book, we offer suggestions for breathers and ways of regaining perspective, but one in particular may be worth all the rest: Have regular date nights. Arrange childcare for two or three hours on a specific night, make a regular dinner date with your spouse or a friend, and *keep it!* Yes, your child will be fine with a babysitter. Trust us. There's no better antidote to burnout than slipping away from your regular life just for a few hours, eating a meal—be it pizza or haute cuisine—and talking grown-up talk on every subject under the sun. This sort of minivacation may represent a financial strain, but as every parent of young children knows (whether the children are deaf or hearing), it is well worth it.

A final word—and we've kept it for last in the hope that it will stay in your mind: Parenting is always a matter of trial and error. Babies do not come with manuals; even this book can only go so far. You will make some mistakes and some great decisions. By the time your child walks out the door as an independent young adult, you may have figured out exactly what you wish you had done. Hindsight is always 20/20, as we all know, and is a great teacher of wisdom. We hope you will pay it forward to other parents just like those who will help you in the coming years. There is much to learn from these lessons. Children are quite resilient, so overly criticizing yourself and your performance as the parent of a deaf child will only add to the burden. Above all, be gentle with yourself. That's important enough to put up on your refrigerator, so you can read it every day.

Notes

1. Janet DesGeorges, "Family Support and Cultural Competence," in *The NCHAM E-Book: A Resource Guide for Early Hearing Detection & Intervention (EDHI)*, ed. L. Schmeltz (Logan, UT: Utah State University, 2015): 6.

2. Emily Perl Kingsley, *Welcome to Holland*, (1987). Available online at www.our-kids.org/Archives/Holland.html.

3. Kenneth. L. Moses, *The Dynamics of Transition and Transformation: On Loss, Grieving, Coping and Growthful Change* (Evanston, IL: Resource Networks, 1990): 5.

4. Ellen Kurtzer-White and David Luterman, "Families and Children with Hearing Loss: Grief and Coping," *Mental Retardation and Developmental Disabilities Research Reviews* 9, no. 4 (2003): 232–35.

5. Elizabeth Fitzpatrick, Ian Graham, Andrée Durieux-Smith, Doug Angus, and Doug Coyle, "Parents' Perspectives on the Impact of the Early Diagnosis of Childhood Hearing Loss," *International Journal of Audiology* 46, no. 2 (2007): 97–106.

6. Moses, *Dynamics of Transformation*, 90.

7. Ibid.

8. Kurtzer-White and Luterman, "Families and Children with Hearing Loss," 232–35.

9. Moses, *Dynamics of Transformation*, 98.

2 *The Family Garden*

3 *A Healthy Family Environment*

WE BEGIN with scenarios of three families. In each case, the parents are preparing to get away for the weekend.

The parents are standing at the door with their suitcases, saying good-bye to their six-year-old son and their caregiver. The boy is subdued but not unhappy. He gives his parents a farewell hug, apparently resigned to his immediate situation.

The parents are clustered by the door of their house. They have hired a babysitter to stay with their child. The consternation and anxiety on the parents' faces are clear. They leave but immediately return to reassure themselves that, yes, their child understands what's going on and to tell the boy that, yes, they really will return in two days.

The family has traveled together to the paternal grandmother's house. It has been a long time since the two boys, aged six and eight, have seen their grandmother, and the younger boy has no memory of her at all. The parents are not so much clustered as struggling by the door. Although the older boy plays on the floor, apparently happy and unconcerned, the younger realizes suddenly that his parents are leaving him in the care of this gray-haired stranger. While Grandmother holds him from behind, the boy attaches himself to his mother's legs. A full-blown tantrum ensues, and the parents regretfully disentangle themselves from the child, grab their suitcases, and flee.

In the first family, where everyone appears relaxed about the impending separation, both the parents and the child are deaf, and all use American Sign Language (ASL) as their first language. The child, now eight, began responding to sign language and even began making his own prelinguistic gestures at about six months. The parents hired a deaf caregiver, also a native ASL signer, brought her in early to get to know the child, and made it clear that they will be returning from their weekend holiday on Sunday night. The boy and the babysitter seemed to take to each other easily, and everyone is happy.

We have two possible explanations for the second family. In one, the child is deaf and the parents are hearing, as is the hired babysitter. This child became deaf as a result of meningitis at age three, and since that time, both parents have been taking night classes in sign language and learning ways of communicating that rely on vision rather than hearing. The child has learned sign language in school and is quite fluent; however, neither parent is fluent, and communicating abstractions is challenging for them. The babysitter has had a little training in sign language and is enthusiastic about practicing.

In the second possible explanation, the child is deaf, the parents are hearing, and the hired babysitter, also hearing, has had a little exposure to deaf and hard of hearing children. The child became deaf as a result of maternal rubella, which the mother contracted during the first trimester of pregnancy. Because the child was identified as deaf, the parents have been studying ways of communicating through speech, speechreading, and auditory skills.

In both cases, the immediate question for the parents is whether the child really understands who the babysitter is and what is happening. Have the parents completely conveyed the fact that they will be returning Sunday night, that the child will be safe with this woman, and that they are going away voluntarily, to have fun, not because something terrible has happened? The child's anxieties circle around the same issues: Are my parents really coming back? Who *is* this person? Can I trust her? Why are my parents leaving me? They seem to want to go—is it something I've done?

In the third family, although the older hearing brother seems content, chaos reigns in the mind and behavior of the younger brother, who was identified as profoundly deaf at the age of five months. Both parents work full-time, and they have been hard-pressed to keep steady childcare, let alone learn sign language. They have developed a homegrown language of gesture and expression, but this has remained simplistic and inadequate to the task of conveying abstractions. Happy as they are to be on the brink of two days of R&R by themselves, these parents have been unable to explain to their deaf son where they are going, why they are going, how long they will be gone, when they will come back, *that* they will come back, whose house this is, and who this gray-haired person is. Without answers to these questions, any six-year-old would be alarmed. This child may be deaf, not blind, but he is being called upon to operate in the dark.

A Clarifying Word

Through this book, we hope to reach the families in the second and third examples above. Deaf parents of deaf children may have little or no need for a book like this; hearing parents of deaf children need all the information they can get as quickly as possible—and that includes a quick course in communication, whether spoken and/or signed. Adapting to having a deaf child will involve changing your family's point of view toward its existing communication patterns, and this means making a fundamental change away from the dependence on hearing exclusively and toward a new dependence on vision. This is not a simple task, but perhaps not so daunting as it may seem at first.

At the outset, we'd like to make it clear that in discussing your family environment, we are not suggesting that you dismantle or abandon your particular ways of doing things. And we're not passing judgment, sight unseen, on the ways you and your family members interact and communicate. Your habits of living, your insights and intuitions, your judgments and preferences, your likes and dislikes and eccentricities—in short, the uniqueness of your family—all hold weight. Our point here is not to criticize or judge but rather to give you the benefit of our experiences as deaf individuals and the experience of many parents in solving a single, multifaceted problem: how to convey information to a young deaf or hard of hearing child.

The most important problems that stem from being deaf are not related to restrictions on hearing but to restrictions on communication.[1] Time and time again, deaf people have told us stories of their worst experiences, and all have been related to being left out of conversations at the dinner table and family events and during the family's daily interactive patterns. As deaf people, one of the most despised and upsetting responses we receive when we inquire as to what is happening is "We'll tell you later." Quite frequently, people forget, and we *never* are told anything later. This chapter offers some general guidelines for shifting your perspective to guard against this sort of unintentional communicative neglect. The next chapter, "Some Gardening Tips," offers more concrete suggestions for making sure your child feels "plugged in" and included in the family unit. And Chapter 5 looks at the family from a slightly different point of view—that of the hearing siblings of deaf children.

Making Changes

Almost invariably, when parents learn that their child is deaf, they want to make the necessary changes in the household as quickly as possible. But what are these changes to be? In the old days, in what we think of as the Dark Ages, before the world began to see being deaf for what it is, many educators encouraged parents to treat a deaf child as they would a hearing child of the same age. We don't disagree with this general concept in terms of expectations for behavior and achievement; but the fact is, children who are deaf *do* differ significantly from hearing children in the ways they receive and transmit messages. The task becomes not dismantling your family patterns and starting off fresh, but finding new ways to *visually* include your deaf child in those patterns and provide him or her with the same information, guidance, and emotional support available to your other children. In other words, if it is auditory, make it visually accessible where possible.

Remember, being deaf is not about sound, but about communication. If information is not reaching the brain via the auditory pathway, does that mean it will never find its way in? Not at all. The objective is to find a new route for the information to travel—if not through the ears, then through the eyes. We know now that the auditory tissue in our brains responsible for processing spoken language also responds equally well to visual sign language input and even better to both.[2]

Interpreting the World

How often have you said or heard parents say, "Now, where in the world did she pick *that* up?" If you've raised children, you know how much children learn simply by absorbing what they hear. This is known as *incidental learning*. It starts early; hearing children learn by listening almost from birth, and parents are often surprised and amazed at how much their children seem to know about the world when they begin speaking. Above all, children absorb, as if by osmosis, the special knowledge that forms the particular culture and personality of your family—the beliefs, customs, opinions, myths, jokes, and understandings that give your family unit its uniqueness.

Children who are deaf, unless given access, will not have spontaneous input from the casual conversation, dinner-table talk, bedtime question sessions, and other auditory activities in which such family information is exchanged. This does not mean that they do not make sense of their realities. Just as hearing children do, deaf children pick up clues about their environment and put them together into a meaningful whole for themselves. However, without the running commentary that hearing parents and hearing children, or deaf parents and deaf children, indulge in together, the deaf children of hearing parents are often completely on their own—and sometimes wide of the mark in their attempts to figure out what's going on.

As many writers and researchers have made clear, deaf children without any guidance at all and without language access do manage to sort out and understand the meaning of things to an amazing degree. They are no less intellectually or cognitively capable than their hearing peers.³ However, most of what deaf children learn must be made accessible to them. Unless parents make sure the information keeps flowing to their deaf children and that its meaning is made clear, the accuracy of the children's interpretation of the world is bound to suffer. One of the most serious problems deaf children have is a lack of prior knowledge, also known as *background knowledge, world knowledge,* or *schemata,* when they start school.⁴ Let us repeat that thought and suggest that you meditate on it. Let it sink in, because it is the foundation for the approach detailed in this book: *Keep information flowing to your deaf child, or the child will not gain an accurate understanding of his or her world that is critical for academic and personal achievement.*

How does your child's continual need for commentary and explanation relate to your home environment? Isn't the important thing, you may ask, to provide a loving and safe refuge for the child, leaving the teaching to the experts—the teachers at school? It is true that young children learn many social skills and the rudiments of academic skills in preschool, but parental involvement and positive expectations for achievement are more influential.⁵ Therefore, although you are not a school teacher, you will be called upon to serve as their first teacher of the meanings of the world; the alphabet, numbers, shapes, colors, objects, and so forth. These are the more visual concepts to teach but there are also the not-so-obvious and abstract notions like social skills. Everything that happens in your household has meaning, but much of that meaning will be unavailable to your deaf child until you consciously make it available. Consider some of the following mundane facts of life, and try to imagine how your child could discover them without being taught:

- Aunt Florence is Daddy's twin sister, and Grandma is their mother.
- It is rude to burp during or after dinner and absolutely forbidden to play with your food.
- In many households, the children come first; but in our family, the old people are considered first.
- Interfering with someone's work project is a cardinal sin—and that includes losing someone's place in a book.
- In our household, the truth rules. Even little white lies are forbidden. If we can't believe you, we can't trust you.

- In our house, everybody does a part. If you don't pitch in, you don't get to share in the rewards. If you stay in bed during a family cleanup, you won't get an ice cream sundae with the rest of the family at the end of the day.

Each family's rules and realities are different, but every family has them. If you don't take it upon yourself to convey such information to your deaf or hard of hearing child, who will?

Remember the three families described at the beginning of this chapter? The first family, which consisted of deaf parents and a deaf child, had a fairly easy time with the pending separation, despite the fact that the parents were taking their first trip since the child had been born. From day one, these parents, without thinking about it, had immersed the child in communication within the family. Both they and the child lived in a world of vision, not of sound, and the parents had ways of conveying all necessary information—abstract information, subtle information, gossip, sympathies, jokes, and values—through the eyes, not the ears—all without thinking very much, in many cases, about what they were doing or why.

You are facing the same task but with much less preparation and practice. As hearing parents of a deaf child, you are being required to shift, quite consciously, your whole communication style. We urge you to remind yourself, as you think about this, that you are not shifting from good to bad, from able to disabled, from healthy to pathological. You are shifting from one point of view to another. Again, a list of examples may help. Consider the contrast in attitudes implied in the following phrases:

"My child can't hear anything clearly" vs. "My child receives information through his eyes, not his ears."

"My child can't communicate normally" vs. "My child can communicate about anything."

"My child is language-delayed" vs. "My child is in the process of acquiring language."

"I have a deaf child" vs. "My daughter, who is ten and a strong reader, who writes poems and has trained her dog to heel without a leash, who loves to swim, who sometimes fights with her brother, happens to be deaf."

If your experience with deaf people has been very limited, the positive expressions in this list may seem like empty words to you. This is just hogwash, you may think; Pollyanna stuff that tries to put the best face on things. Research shows that parents' childhood experiences are significant factors in determining how they raise their own children.[6] A lack of exposure to deaf people in your own life could put you at a disadvantage in assessing the needs of your child at home. If you feel uncomfortable with the idea that being deaf is simply different from hearing, not worse than hearing, take heart—thinking and learning more about the role of communication in deaf lives almost certainly will change your mind.

Special Communication Needs

Being deaf is about communication, not sound. In the deaf world, this is a common way of summing up the challenges of being deaf, but what precisely does it mean? To try to feel rather than figure out the answer, let's look back at the third family at the beginning of this chapter. Jimmy, aged eight, and Charlie, aged six, are going to stay at Grandma's house. Let's flash back in time to when the boys first found out about the trip.

Jimmy, a hearing boy, has been anticipating the trip for weeks. He knows he'll fly on a big plane and that when he gets to Grandma's, his parents will leave on a trip of their own. A week before the journey, Charlie, who is deaf, begins to see that something unusual is going on. He notices that the family routine has been disrupted; clothes are being washed and piled around the living room and stacked in strange brown boxes with handles. He gets the idea, on the day of departure, that the family is going somewhere, but he doesn't know where, for how long, or why—and no one attempts to clear up the mystery. Both of Charlie's parents regard his being deaf as a barrier to any sort of communication; they stopped trying to reach him shortly after learning he was deaf. Although Jimmy includes Charlie in his games somewhat, dragging him in as if he were a doll, he pretty much follows his parents' example and never actually talks to Charlie or tries to help him understand what's going on. Jimmy can barely contain his excitement when the family reaches the airport. He presses his nose to the plate-glass windows to watch the big jets arrive. But Charlie doesn't recognize the silver giants as the tiny dots he's seen flying in the sky. He has no idea what they are and is frightened by the tremendous vibrations he feels from their engines. The farthest thing from his mind is that he might enter one and fly. Even when he is five miles up in the sky, he fails to understand where he is. All he knows is that the thrum of the engines and the bumpiness of the ride are uncomfortable and that his ears feel peculiar.

When the family finally reaches Grandma's house, Charlie has no idea who this gray-haired woman is. He certainly doesn't expect his parents to leave him and his brother with this stranger. But after much hugging and kissing, which vaguely reassures Charlie, his parents walk out the door.

Charlie is inconsolable. He is afraid of his grandmother. He has never met an old person before (except when he was too young to remember), and Grandma's gray hair reminds him of a scary picture of an old, gnarled woman he once saw in a book. Also, he's never been left anywhere overnight. He's afraid that his parents will never come back, and after a day and a night, he's certain of it. He drifts from anger and loneliness into depression. No one can make him come away from the door, where he lies by the hour with his cheek on the rug.

Charlie's reactions all make sense. He has picked up clues about what's going on; but to come to the right conclusion, he needs all the information that is available to Jimmy through auditory messages. Deaf and hearing children do not differ in their ability to process the content of communication; they differ only in the means of communication. Whatever parents discuss with their hearing children, they should also discuss with their deaf children, and no less thoroughly.

In the ideal home setting, Charlie's parents would have conveyed the following information to him: We're going on a wonderful trip to Grandma's house. Grandma is Daddy's mommy, and she loves you and Jimmy very much. We're going on a big, loud airplane that flies high in the sky. After a while, Mommy and Daddy are going away, and you're going to stay with Grandma. You'll have a lot of fun; maybe even go to the zoo and the circus. After that, Mommy and Daddy are coming back to take you home again.

How parents can convey such information (i.e., what mode or modes of communication they can use) is the subject of Part 3 of this book. Here it is important to identify the most serious danger deaf children face: *that they will be left out of the communication process altogether.* You alone can protect your child from becoming isolated. You are the guardian of your child's right to communicate with others. As such, it is your role and responsibility to create a family atmosphere in which communication includes your deaf child.

You, as a parent, will spend more time with your deaf child than any other person he or she may encounter, particularly in the pre-school years. You are the key to the child's healthy emotional development and will play a central role in the development of his or her communication skills. As parent, advocate, and "ambassador" to and explainer of the outside world, you will be the most important teacher in your child's life.

Foundations of Language in a Nutshell

By its very nature, the inability to hear limits access to sound and speech. Deafness itself is actually a socially constructed concept due to the fact that in the hearing world, sound and speech are considered the "normal" means to ends; they are the typical and expected communication routes to other people. By blocking access to these socially expected connections and without a good intervention approach, the inability to hear can have a profound impact on your child's language and social development. This will interfere with the relationships that otherwise would form naturally and grow in complexity as the child matures. It is in this area—the fostering of healthy relationships—that you will function most importantly as a teacher and gateway, informing your child about the ways people interact in our culture; in other words, the wheres, whats, whys, whens, and hows of communication.

You will begin preparing your child for the social world from the day he or she is born. The primary developmental task of infancy is to bond and gain a sense of trust with the primary caregivers. Although seemingly helpless and completely dependent on its caregivers, the infant is not simply a passive recipient of their attention. From the beginning, human development is a reciprocal process. The biological attributes and behaviors of human infants draw caregivers to them, ensuring that they receive what they need. So these little, apparently helpless beings are actually their parents' active interactional partners, equipped to obtain from them the very experiences they need in order to develop.[7] Two of the earliest interactions involve eye gaze and vocalizing.

The gaze of the infant up into the face of the down-gazing parents is a means of establishing a bond; gaze triggers gaze, and the result is the beginning of the infant's first social relationship. This process, which is crucial to the development of infant–parent bonding, is called *gaze coupling*. Vocal interaction carries the bonding further. In the first few months of life, the child learns that his or her cry brings an attentive, need-filling parent. This discovery will eventually provide a bridge to language. The predictability of this interaction marks the growth of trust; if a parent does not respond to the child's cries, trust is slower to develop. And the back-and-forth of the exchange—first I make a sound, then you respond—establishes the pattern for the basis of verbal interaction in the years ahead: conversation. Conversation is a dance of turn-taking, and the first taking of turns is the cry and response.[8]

While a deaf infant is still going to learn that crying or vocalizing might produce a physical response when the parent comes and picks them up, what happens if they are not going to be able to take solace in hearing a vocal response from parents or caregivers from across the room or if they cannot see them? The answer is, not only the communication process but also the relationship can be affected. The deaf or hard of hearing infant may never make the association between vocalizing and a seemingly reliable response from the caregiver. Thus they may be slower to gain trust in the parent and in the environment. The parents may find that their own vocalizations have little or no effect in calming an agitated infant, which then undermines their confidence and their pleasure in the early experience of parenting.

So a natural, reciprocal process is disrupted. But it doesn't have to be, at least not completely. If you are fortunate enough to have learned that your child is deaf very early, you can substitute your close visual presence and touch for the soothing vocal sounds that calm a hearing infant. And you can respond to your baby's agitation by picking the baby up and making sure your face fills his or her visual field. Although you won't be able to rely on the sound of your voice to comfort the baby before you make it to the crib, you can use your gaze and physical presence as the reassurance your infant is signaling for in order to foster trust and predictability and begin to build a relationship. It can take a lot of trial and error trying to figure out what your child wants, but the key thing is to keep trying, because it teaches him how important he is to you.

By ten months of age, the human baby learns to use gestures as well as vocalizations to attract attention or make demands, and can even enjoy simple games (give-and-take-the-object, hide-the-object). By thirteen months, the baby usually shows signs of more elaborate communication patterns—babbling, singing, cooing— the first level of speech. Even deaf babies do this; but to keep this process going, they need patterned visual and tactile input that only comes from language.

Parents need to find a way to offer visual alternatives to the sounds hearing babies depend on. It is not hard to do; what's hard at first is to *remember* it. As we have learned from deaf families of deaf infants, babies whose parents express their attentiveness, interest, and dependability visually through expression and gesture learn manual dexterity more quickly than other babies. Deaf parents also emphasize certain kinds of communication behaviors that are particularly helpful for babies. Adopting these behaviors will help your child pay attention better and learn language earlier.[9]

How does a parent use vision rather than sound to communicate with a very young infant? In part 3, we describe the developmental process we all go through to acquire a means of expression, particularly the nonverbal cues that add meaning, whether speaking or signing. But the following list outlines some of the ways to establish and deepen the infant-parent bond through vision alone.

1. *Hold the child's attention through eye contact.* Here are some tips learned from deaf parents to encourage eye contact:

   a. Place your hand or body, so the baby can see your communication while still looking at a toy or activity.

   b. Move objects or toys in front of the baby and then move them up toward your own face to encourage tracking. When the baby can see both your face and the object, communicate about it.

c. Tap on an object, perhaps several times, before and after you communicate something about it. This helps the baby know what your communication is about.

d. Tap on the baby to signal, "Look at me." Repeat the tapping signal or combine it with moving an object if your first try isn't successful. *Be patient while the baby is learning the signal.* It takes time. Avoid the temptation to put your hand under the child's chin to redirect their attention.

e. You do not have to fill every moment with communication and language. It is more important to follow up on the baby's interests and make sure he or she can see your communication.

2. *Use signs from the very beginning.* Children begin to process and comprehend some aspects of language long before they speak their first sentence.[10] So it makes sense for you to use signs from the start as the parent of a hearing child would use words. Although we do recommend using ASL, it is not necessary as long as the gestures have meaning; as with spoken baby talk, your gestures, bits of body language, and homegrown signs will gain their own meaning in the context of the relationship and the experiences you share with your baby. The important thing is *expressiveness.* Paul's interviews with deaf adults raised on spoken language revealed a universal wish that their parents had used more facial expressions, mime, gestures, and so on, to supplement speech, speechreading, and listening modes.

When parents gesture, sign, and talk to their children from the very beginning, the result is a positive one. The babies begin to absorb the rudiments and patterns of language, a foundation for the subsequent development of their communication skills. As a rule, these babies, including those brought up with spoken language, begin to respond to signing or gesturing parents with signs at about six months of age—even earlier than hearing children speak their first words.[11] This gesture exchange is similar to the vocal exchange that begins between parent and hearing child in very early infancy. Pay attention to the baby's arm, leg, and body movements, as deaf babies tend to do this more often than hearing babies, and deaf parents often respond to these movements as meaningful communication attempts.

3. *Talk, talk, talk, using sound and gesture.* Right from the beginning, the point is to engage in communication and to use it to reinforce and deepen your relationship. The terrible consequence of parents' losing heart and failing to communicate with their infant is that the child is left out of the communication loop, without the resources to develop language. But if you hang in there, using body language, facial expressions, sign language, and, yes, sound, vocalization, and vocal talk, you will succeed in laying the groundwork, both for trust and for the acquisition of language. Because most deaf children make some use of their residual hearing in communication, the control of background noise in your home is crucial to your child's language development. (See pages 221–22 for some tips on noise management.)

4. *Respect your child's communication wishes.* Nobody likes to talk all the time and especially not if it is something in which they have little interest. Babies are no different. Children whose mothers often respond or follow the children's interests, develop language more quickly than children whose mothers change the topic frequently. Take note of what has your baby's interest and respond to it. If the child is looking at a toy or object and grabs it, you can respond and communicate about it. Connecting communication with an object or activity that the child is already attending to will help the child learn new words to identify that object or activity. Parents should avoid the temptation to constantly drill or work on communication with their children. They can get tired or "bored" with conversations, start to look away, and lose their happy faces. Let them rest and have some downtime. Some may do this more than others.

Are you feeling the weight of great responsibility for meeting your child's needs early? Are you afraid that learning later about your child's deaf status or delaying your response could already have had a serious impact on his or her social and language development? Try to relax with the knowledge that, once it begins to flow, communication is an unstoppable river. In fact, wholly out of instinct from the first moment you hold your infant in your arms, you two communicated in the most fundamental ways through touch and sound vibration between your bodies, through gaze and imitation. With imagination and freedom from the prejudice against deafness that has often blocked parents from continuing to develop visual communication techniques, you can create a home environment in which ideas and information flow freely by whatever means are necessary to get them across. This early awareness and practice of gesture and sign with a deaf child can open up powerful channels of two-way communication.

Besides being a pet peeve of many deaf individuals, no one needs to be told how harmful it can be to leave a child out of a family, unable to participate in a simple dinner-table conversation, a family joke, a group decision, or even a family argument. Self-esteem, self-understanding, the child's belief in his or her ability to contribute to the family and, eventually, to the world all depend on the inclusion of that child in the communication loop. But there are other, even more fundamental, consequences of leaving the child without a foundation for language. From the beginning, language has a social function—accompanying actions and serving as a means of social contact. Gradually, though, language begins to serve an internal as well as a social function, helping to give form to thoughts. This language development, in turn, fosters cognitive development (i.e., the development of thinking patterns), which is critical to academic achievement.

Conversation: The Social Building Block

As your baby grows into toddlerhood, gaze coupling and reciprocal body language give way to the beginnings of conversation. Conversation is humanity's principal means of informal communication; a means of interacting that involves much more than merely the give-and-take of dialogue. A whole range of social and cognitive skills governs conversation and gets exercised there. By participating in conversations, children learn "when to speak, when not, and . . . what to talk about with whom, when, where [and] in what manner."[12] Family conversations give children the practice they need to learn and apply the rules of social interaction. The sooner your deaf or hard of hearing child becomes an active participant in conversations, *whatever communication method is used,* the better equipped he or she will be to participate in all the arenas of social life in the world at large.

At first, whether your child is hearing or deaf and whether you have begun in your child's infancy or later, you will find yourself straining to provide and sustain conversation. You will have to take both roles in the conversation to cue the child in responding. To be effective, you'll be acting out the structure of a conversation in order to show the child how it works. Most of us do that quite naturally. By the same token, it is important that you begin your own learning program. *Now is the time to commit yourself to visual communication.* We encourage you to be creative and to get your messages across in any physical, visible way you can. Here is a real-life example of one possibility.

Jean and Frank

Jean and Frank did indeed take sign language classes when they learned that their daughter Maggie was deaf. Jean became extremely fluent in ASL, but like many fathers, Frank was always pressed for time and never really mastered it. He got along fairly well, but as Maggie grew into adolescence, he became aware that much was lost between them. His signing was the equivalent of baby talk in spoken language; consequently, conversations between father and daughter were superficial.

Frank knew that Maggie was a smart girl—he could see the lively conversations she had with her mother—and he felt that he was getting only second-hand knowledge of his daughter's best qualities. He signed up with a well-known teacher of both ASL and Signed English, because in addition to gaining fluency in ASL, he wanted to coach Maggie in the subtleties of his spoken language. Signing about English became a kind of hobby between father and daughter.

Frank once reduced Maggie to tears by using the ASL sign for "TOO BAD" when she broke a mirror. What an overreaction, he thought, until he understood that for Maggie, "TOO BAD" meant "nah, nah, *too bad*, who cares?"—a taunt she had experienced on the playground. Frank perceived that this sort of semantic misunderstanding (a misinterpretation of the use and intent, not the phrase itself) caused Maggie a tremendous amount of emotional distress. He took it upon himself to minimize that through a recreational approach to studying and playing with language.

The Importance of Books

Children who are deaf can benefit enormously from an early introduction to books and written language. Like all children, if they are comfortable with books from babyhood, they are more likely to become strong readers. This enables them to gain tremendously from the written word, even to pick up information they may have missed during their younger years. Chapter 10 contains specific information on choosing and reading books, but here we want to emphasize the importance of introducing your child to English print as soon as you can. And don't forget the pictures!

Jean and Frank talked about how appalled they were by the low expectations of teachers of deaf children and other professionals, with regard to deaf children's reading skills. From their perspective, many teachers have been trained to expect no more than a third- or fourth-grade reading level from deaf adults (for the general population, the average level is tenth grade). Those figures tend to be burned into the brains of many educators and counselors, even when they meet people like Jean and Frank's daughter, Maggie, who is an excellent reader. In our experience, deaf adults who read a lot and who depend on their reading for self-education and pleasure are generally grateful for parents who sensed the importance of reading early and fostered reading skills in their children even before elementary school. As an added incentive, you might want to keep in mind that the authors of this book, who are successful deaf adults with PhDs, are both avid readers. Need we say more?

Taking the Necessary Time

You will soon realize, if you haven't already, that few people outside the family have the patience and sensitivity necessary to communicate fully with your child. One of the realities of being deaf is that regardless of the method used, and often regardless of the child's age, communication requires a tremendous amount of energy, far more than communicating with a hearing child of the same age. Getting your point across to a deaf child takes at least twice as much time as with hearing children, and capturing a deaf child's message accurately can involve many minutes of guessing and puzzling. In fact, communicating involves more than merely responding. No matter what the child's age, from infancy and into adulthood, it requires that you do the following:

- Keep your face to the child at all times.
- Maintain steady eye contact and focus your concentration completely.
- Repeat back what you saw or heard to make sure you have picked up the original message accurately.
- Avoid the use of "yes/no" questions and ask wh-questions (who, what, where, how).
- Use your whole face, body, and often creativity to get the message across.

Maintaining this kind of attentiveness is draining, no doubt about it. With a hearing child, you can often converse while doing other things (e.g., preparing a meal while hearing how the day went at school). But with a deaf child, communication always takes precedence over other activities. When you and your child are communicating with each other, nothing else can—or should—be going on. Few outsiders will have the stamina or commitment to honor that necessity. Therefore, another aspect of the refuge you provide your child will be the total attentiveness required to communicate by visual means. Rest assured that these initial efforts will pay off in the long run, and communication will become more fluent.

Deafness in Daily Life: Anastasia's Story

A whole level of experience seems to have escaped the attention of most educators and theorists on deafness—the kinds of experience that arise unexpectedly in the course of daily life. Being deaf has its impact in unexpected ways, requiring of parents a practical kind of problem solving rooted in empathy and imagination. We offer the following story as an example of how one family has handled these experiences.

Gail and Steven

Gail and Steven have two daughters—Anastasia, who is deaf, and Annemarie, a year younger, who is hearing. They discovered that Anastasia was deaf when she was two and a half years old. At that time, both parents had an egalitarian attitude toward child rearing, believing that they should spend equal time and give equal attention to each of their children. Over the next few years, however, they came to realize that, because Anastasia was deaf, communicating with her took more time than it did with Annemarie. They agreed that it was only fair to give Anastasia the extra time and attention she needed, finding ways to compensate for the imbalance when Annemarie was young. As the hearing girl grew older, they made sure she fully understood that they gave more time and attention to her sister, not because they loved Anastasia more, but simply because she was deaf.

During all the years of the girls' childhood and adolescence, Gail and Steven realized that an important consideration in shaping their home environment was making sure that Annemarie didn't feel left out or neglected. Their strong sense of fairness led them to understand that compensating in time and attention for Anastasia's deafness threatened their hearing child with the possibility of feeling overlooked.

They decided on the spoken language method of communication, and Anastasia responded very well to training in auditory skills, speech, and speechreading. In fact, both child and parents seemed well suited to the method, because the parents were willing to go to great lengths to enunciate carefully when Anastasia missed something. Annemarie and her parents are very expressive people, who don't hesitate to use their faces and bodies to get a message across. They express what would be intonations, inflections, and voice clues in conversations between hearing people through movements of their faces, shoulders, hands, and torsos. The whole picture is one of active, visible exchange—nothing is held back, and the resulting communication stew is rich, nutritious, and enjoyable.

Both Gail and Steven love rock concerts, and they took their little girls to these events. Anastasia couldn't hear the music well, but she could still experience the excitement and visual stimulation; she could feel the resonant beat, and she loved the crowds and the colorful atmosphere. Sometimes, though, Anastasia seemed bored and irritable at the concerts, and her parents wondered whether they were expecting too much of her. It seemed the only alternatives were giving up their own fun or leaving Anastasia out of the experience; instead, Steven gave some deep thought to how he could increase his daughter's enjoyment.

He hit upon the idea of showing Anastasia how to discriminate among the various vibrations she was hearing through hearing aids and feeling from the music, and how to relate them visually to the individual instruments. First, he would act out particular sounds by duplicating their rhythms with his hands; then, moving as close to the stage as possible, he would show Anastasia which musicians' hand movements matched his. Once she caught on, Anastasia loved to stand up close and watch the musicians. She was able to enjoy not only the crowds and atmosphere of the concerts but, visually, the music as well.

We applaud Steven's sensitivity in realizing that Anastasia had been unable to make the connection between the instruments and the vibrations on her own. Many hearing people would have assumed that the connection was obvious. Others would have assumed the girl was incapable of discriminating well enough among the various vibrations to associate them with individual instruments. Steven followed his hunch, and it paid off. (One trick we would like to add is that holding an inflated balloon will help your child feel most of the frequencies of sound and music.)

Gail and Steven's sensitivity to the special circumstances deafness creates extended into the sticky area of discipline. They were firm in their belief that both girls needed to be respectful of limits; but over the years, they discovered that in some cases, they had to think about disciplinary matters carefully to make sure that Anastasia's being deaf was not influencing the situation. Many deaf children learn to use their deafness to worm out of unpleasant responsibilities. "I can't do math. I can't understand the teacher"— in a lenient family, such a complaint might make math magically disappear. Gail and Steven stuck to their resolve that no such thing would happen in their house.

Some things are more difficult for deaf people. For example, Anastasia joined the junior high school swim team, but once she began to compete, she consistently lost races even though she had made winning time in practice. She complained that she was losing time at the start of each race, because she couldn't hear the starting gun and had to wait for a visual clue. She became very depressed and seemed to be losing confidence in herself. Because she was so upset, her parents wondered whether her complaint about the gun was just a rationalization to excuse her losses. But after watching several races, they concluded that Anastasia did indeed lag behind the others in entering the water, and they arranged for a red flag to be dropped when the starting gun sounded.

While acknowledging that deafness could cause difficulties in particular situations, Gail and Steven fostered independence and self-reliance in both their daughters equally. From the beginning, there was no suggestion that Anastasia would have fewer responsibilities than Annemarie. The parents' emphasis on self-reliance and their unswerving confidence in their daughters paid off. Both girls went on to have successful careers, and both married and had children, taking on the difficult juggling act that has characterized the lives of working mothers.

We've described this family in detail, because it embodies a concept that is central to this book—a concept that is necessary for parents of a deaf or hard of hearing child to build into the foundation of family life: *Deaf and hearing children are different in their ways of communicating.* And from this difference, other differences emerge. Gail and Steven realized early that Anastasia's deaf status made her different from Annemarie. They understood that to begin with, the difference lay in Anastasia's powers of communication. And they understood that the communication gap could affect her inner life as an individual. They knew they could never ignore the fact that their daughter was deaf and always had to consider it in making decisions, analyzing every situation to determine whether special steps were necessary to communicate information to her and enable her to express herself.

We see child rearing as analogous to gardening. Think of Annemarie and Anastasia as occupying different parts of the family garden, each with its different varieties requiring different kinds of care. To keep your family garden robust and flourishing, remember that your deaf child is bound to require particular attention from you with regard to communication and the forging of solid relationships.

Notes

1. Kathryn P. Meadow-Orlans, Marilyn Sass-Lehrer, and Donna M. Mertens, Parents and Their Deaf Children: The Early Years (Washington DC: Gallaudet University Press, 2003): 12–13.

2. Laura-Ann Petitto, "What the Eyes Reveal about the Brain: Advances in Human Language Acquisition," Webcast (Washington, DC: Laurent Clerc National Deaf Education Center, 2014). Available online at www.gallaudet.edu/clerc-center/learning-opportunities/webcasts/what-the-eyes-reveal-about-the-brain-webcast.html.

3. M. Diane Clark, Marc Marschark, and Michael A. Karchmer, eds, *Context, Cognition, and Deafness* (Washington DC: Gallaudet University Press, 2001).

4. Patricia L. McAnally, Susan Rose, and Stephen P. Quigley, *Reading Practices with Deaf Learners* (Austin, TX: PRO-ED, 2007): 11.

5. John Hattie, *Visible Learning: A Synthesis of Over 800 Meta-Analyses Relating to Achievement* (New York: Routledge, 2008): 68.

6. Kathryn Meadow-Orlans, Marilyn Sass-Lehrer, and Donna M. Mertens, *Parents and Their Deaf Children: The Early Years* (Washington DC: Gallaudet University Press, 2003): 11.

7. Susan Rose, Patricia L. McAnally, and Stephen P. Quigley, *Language Learning Practices with Deaf Children* (Austin, TX: PRO-ED, 2004): 8–11.

8. Jeanne Machado, *Early Childhood Experiences in Language Arts: Early Literacy* (Boston: Cengage Learning, 2015): 4–11.

9. Patricia E. Spencer, *A Good Start: Suggestions for Visual Conversations with Deaf and Hard of Hearing Babies and Toddlers* (Washington DC: Laurent Clerc National Deaf Education Center, 2001).

10. Jeanne Machado, *Early Childhood Experiences in Language Arts: Early Literacy* (Boston: Cengage Learning, 2015): 4–11.

11. Susan Goldin-Meadow, *The Resilience of Language: What Gesture Creation in Deaf Children Can Tell Us about How All Children Learn Language* (New York: Psychology Press, 2005): 4–7.

12. Dell Hymes, "On Communicative Competence," in *Sociolinguistics: Selected Readings*, ed. J. P. Pride and J. Holmes (Baltimore: Penguin Books, 1972): 6–12.

4 Some Gardening Tips

CHAPTER 3 STRESSED the importance of a safe, secure family life in which your deaf child will find not only refuge but also explanations of the world's invisible mysteries. Here are some specific tips for raising sturdy, healthy, forthright deaf children capable of realizing their potential when they leave the family garden.

You may have noticed that Gail and Steven, mother and father of Annemarie and Anastasia, were not only good parents of a deaf child but also good parents, period. A healthy family environment for a deaf child doesn't differ in kind from that for a hearing child; it differs only in degree. Whereas both hearing and deaf children need to have the world explained to them, deaf children's parents must make their explanations more explicit, never assuming that the child will "just know," never inadvertently leaving the child out of the circle by failing to communicate necessary information. Such failures are almost inevitable when parents lack the tools to communicate with their deaf children.

Virtually everything that can be assumed or taken for granted in raising a hearing child must be made explicit for a deaf child. So, to supplement the first golden rule of this book (that you keep information flowing), here is a second, simpler rule: *In your explanations of the world, assume nothing. Be explicit.* We can take a cue from the observation that deaf adults are often explicit with children in their daily explanations and during book storytelling, when inferences need to be made from the text. The sections that follow cover circumstances of family life in which this rule is particularly important.

Making Your Love for Your Child Explicit

Most parents are aware of how very sensitive children are to their parents' feelings for them, especially in the early stages of life. Even so, children are much more psychologically vulnerable than adults sometimes acknowledge. We have all seen what happens when even the toughest preschooler on the block suddenly senses that his or her parents disapprove of an action. The face crumbles, the eyes fill, and play is forgotten as the child struggles to regain the lost sense of security. Children who are deaf need the same feelings of safety, security, and affectionate support that all children need. In this perhaps more than anything, the rule to be explicit applies.

Do you remember to say, "I love you" to your son or daughter to reassure the child that he or she is safe in your affections no matter what? It is easy to express anger through body language; but some people have less fluency of gesture and expression in conveying love or delight in the company of another. Don't forget the simple power of a hug, a smile, a pat of reassurance, and a lightness of spirit that takes the seriousness out of inconsequential mistakes. Remember that from babyhood on, your deaf child, like all children, is constantly reading your face and body for clues. They are very sensitive to your body language. It is as if every five minutes, the child were looking up and asking, "How am I doing?" Make sure you are conscious about providing the necessary feedback through body language, expression, and signing: "You're doing fine" or, clearly, "There's something I need to show you."

Parents convey their approval to a hearing child in many ways that a deaf child cannot benefit from. For example, in the course of a conversation, most people "back-channel" and give little hums of interest or assent to encourage the speaker to continue. A hearing child telling you of the events of the day at school can take encouragement from these nonverbal sounds; but deaf children have no access to auditory clues. Therefore, parents must make their interest and approval very clear visually. Otherwise, even in this seemingly minor way, they risk communicating indifference.

Frank and Jean (the parents of Maggie discussed earlier) explained to the authors how easy it was to forget that they had to face their deaf daughter when discussing things. With their other daughter, Libby, they could talk from any part of the family room; but to make sure that Maggie was included, they had to make a conscious effort. This was especially true in giving Maggie praise and encouragement. They had to train themselves to stop the flow of conversation or activity and face Maggie or reach out to her, so she could get the benefit of their approval.

Frank and Jean also had to make explicit not only the subject of a conversation but also its "shape." "Libby had no trouble entering and exiting from family discussions," they explained, "but it was difficult for Maggie to know when to interject a comment or statement. So from very early on, we had to make sure she got a turn in the exchange. The extra work, for some people, of understanding a deaf child or communicating something to that child means you have to build it in, or it tends to get ignored."

Dealing with "Differentness"

Deaf children with deaf parents generally become aware of differences when they meet hearing children and notice the mystifying ways in which those children relate to other hearing people. The following anecdote about Sam captures the dawning of this realization. Sam and all his family are deaf. When he was young, Sam became friends with the hearing girl who lived next door.

> One day, Sam remembers vividly, he finally understood that his friend was indeed odd. They were playing in her home, when suddenly her mother walked up to them and animatedly began to move her mouth. As if by magic, the girl picked up a dollhouse and moved it to another place. Sam was mystified and went home to ask his mother about exactly what kind of affliction the girl next door had. His mother explained that she was HEARING, and because of this did not know how to SIGN; instead she and her mother TALK.

They move their mouths to communicate with each other. Sam then asked if this girl and her family were the only ones "like that." His mother explained that no, in fact, nearly everyone else was like the neighbors. It was his own family that was unusual. It was a memorable moment for Sam. He remembers thinking how curious the girl next door was, and if she was HEARING, how curious HEARING people were.[1]

Deaf children of hearing families are generally later in coming to the realization that they are different from many, if not most, people they meet. From his interviewees, Paul found that they come to this awareness anywhere from age four to age ten. The later the realization comes, of course, the harder is the adjustment to this new and startling vision of the world. Our advice to parents is to discuss being deaf and "differentness" with their children as close to age four as possible (before that age, the concept of alternative modes of communication may be too abstract for the child to grasp). Of course, this assumes an expertise in communication that you and your child may not have acquired by this time, but we urge you to use every means you can—speaking, signing, speechreading, gestures, facial expressions, drawings, *anything*—to address the subject and convey to the child that, yes, he or she receives and expresses information differently than most people, but that difference itself is normal.

Easier said than done. Undoubtedly, you will need to sort out your own feelings about deafness. One step toward resolving any ambivalence you may feel is to make sure you are not confusing the child with being deaf. As we hinted at the beginning of this chapter, your child is not merely a "deaf person." He or she is a full human being with an identity and personality that are distinct from deafness. Being deaf is as impersonal as brown hair or blue eyes. Yet many parents think of deafness first when considering their child, as if that quality defines the whole individual. At first, it may strike you as a mere word game to insist on this, but try hard to rid yourself of the phrase "I have a deaf son" or "I have a deaf daughter," and practice using the construction "my son or daughter, who is deaf."

Linda

Linda's story demonstrates the effects of a parent's confusion over this issue. Linda's father is a doctor and has a professional understanding of Linda's deafness. Still, he has always treated Linda differently from his other children. When the children were growing up, he spent money lavishly on Linda while giving more freely of his time to the others. Despite his medical knowledge, it seemed clear to everybody that he viewed her as damaged goods. As an adult, Linda likes attention and expects it all the time. Her self-esteem is very low, and she never feels secure in her social relationships. She is like any spoiled child, hearing or deaf. She is short-tempered, inconsiderate, and self-centered, and all the while uncertain of others' true feelings for her. She believes her father has always seen only a deaf person when he looks at her. Whether Linda's father truly confused her with the disability or only appeared to, the effect is the same. The real source of the damage is her father's failure to convey affection and respect for Linda as a person, apart from her deafness.

Another concrete solution to the question of "differentness" is to normalize deafness. Your child may be the only deaf person in your family, but that doesn't mean he or she has to be the only one in your social world. Making the effort to get to know deaf adults as well as other deaf children will broaden the horizons and understanding of everyone in your family. Slowly, with exposure, your sense of your child's being deaf as different may fade away completely.

Bringing deaf adults into your world serves another purpose as well. It will help both you and your child understand his or her future. Many deaf people the authors know have told them about misconceptions they had as children—that adults could not be deaf and that they themselves would grow up to be hearing adults, or that adults could not be deaf, because all deaf children die before adulthood. These ideas may seem absurd, but, if you stop to think about it, such ideas can be a logical consequence of sending a child to a school for deaf students staffed primarily or exclusively by hearing people. Between the 1890s and 1970s, schools for deaf children avoided hiring deaf teachers, so it was not unusual for deaf children to never have contact with deaf adults. These students struggled to interpret the world on the basis of what they perceived, and they naturally formed the belief that deaf children either grew up to be hearing adults or died.

All too common in families of children with differences—not just being deaf but any traits outside the norm—is the overvaluing of the appearance of fitting in and being just like everybody else. There was a profoundly deaf child named Peter whose parents behaved very coolly toward him unless he kept up the pretense of being "normal." They sent him to a spoken language program where he was trained in speech and speechreading. They wanted so much for him to succeed that they unconsciously withheld their love and made it conditional, setting it up as a reward for doing well in speech skills. Commonly, parents who withhold their affection do so without knowing it, and the complicated system of reward and punishment goes on below their awareness—but not below the awareness of the child.

The first prerequisite for success at learning is a strong family base from which to work, one that includes a secure sense of acceptance and of being well loved. This is not to say that children who doubt their parents' love for them will not reach their learning goals, but it does hint at problems down the road—as anyone will encounter who has misgivings about his or her worthiness as a person.

The Household vs. the Outside World

There's no getting around it: Leaving your protected home and entering the more social business-as-usual world will not be easy for your child. Yet holding back and living behind walls could result in even greater pain for your child in the long run. Here's where the role of ambassador to the greater world comes in. Without your explicit coaching, your child, like most children who are deaf, will have difficulty in understanding social and cultural matters, such as the following:

- other people's feelings,
- other people's social roles,

- the reasons people do what they do,
- the consequences of behavior,
- the meaning and significance of a social event—a birthday party, a wedding, a first day at school, a graduation, and
- the rules and cultural expectations that allow communal life to run as it does: We stop at a red light; we arrive on time; we leave tips at a restaurant; we stand in line for a movie; we listen politely when someone speaks to us; we don't interrupt.

The responsibility for teaching right and wrong goes further than simple courtesy, of course. To a great extent, moral values are learned within the family, whether or not the children interpret their parents' beliefs accurately. The story of Maria demonstrates the importance of fully explaining the abstract concepts that relate to daily life—of assuming nothing and being explicit.

Maria

Maria, deaf from birth, was raised in a strict Catholic family that followed the Catholic code of values to the letter. Maria's mother imposed the faith on Maria from birth but never explained anything about Catholicism, the meaning of the rituals, or the relationship between the religion and the way the family lived. Maria went to church and confession every Sunday.

Maria never knew what was being said in church or how the words related to her life and behavior. She simply went along with everything, because she knew she would be punished if she didn't. As she grew older, she began to hate everything connected with Catholicism, because it seemed to her a system of arbitrary punishments. Now in her thirties, Maria believes she might have appreciated the church as a source of moral guidance and spiritual sustenance had she known it could provide these things. Not until she went to college and began to read about religion on her own did she understand the meaning of Catholicism.

Without clear communication from parents, matters of spirit and conscience are confusing to children. Particularly for a child who is deaf, parents need to make explicit whatever religious or ethical understanding they wish to convey. It is possible for a deaf

child to live within a system of beliefs without even being aware
of it.

Fostering Independence

The point of imparting social skills to children and giving them
a firm emotional base is to enable them eventually to leave home
and operate as independent, productive individuals. Parents can
take an early first step toward fostering independence by seeking
some form of childcare. When you do, try to find a sitter or play
group leader who will take the time to fill in for you as an ambassador to the social world.

Viola and Joseph

Viola and Joseph, who have four children, settled on a
wonderful solution. Antonia, their eleven-year-old daughter,
was deaf; the rest of the children were hearing. Viola and
Joseph advertised at a local college for a student in a teacher-
preparation program, and they found a hearing student to
hire as a nanny. She provided babysitting services in exchange
for room and board. Not only did she learn and use cued
speech with Antonia, but also she was a wonderful role model
for everyone.* Having this young woman live at the house was
an eye-opener for the whole family, and under her influence,
two of the hearing siblings became proficient in cued speech.
Everyone was much more comfortable with communicating
with Antonia, and in the process, the home environment became completely communication accessible for Antonia.

Parents are bound to have mixed feelings about the process of instilling independence in their deaf child. The key to
letting go is to separate the notions of closeness and dependence. You can be intimate and helpful without encouraging
your child to continue relying on you for everything. You can
be loving without being overprotective. You can allow your
child to do things and instruct him or her in how to do them,
without actually doing them yourself. As the child grows older,
you will be expressing your love by allowing him or her the

---

*Cued speech is a visual-gestural supplement to speechreading, and it should
not be confused with a sign language.

opportunity to make mistakes. Without this chance, learning cannot occur.

An essential aspect of this process is the parents' confidence in their child. Without confidence, even parents who value independence can cheat their deaf children of the right to make their own mistakes.

Robert

Both of Robert's parents, Rose and Michael, work full-time. They live on a ranch and have always placed great importance on raising their three children to think for themselves. By the age of six, Robert, deaf from infancy, wanted to be a veterinarian.

In keeping with their rugged ranch life, the parents gave each of their three children ten head of cattle and a horse, and by age eleven, each child was expected to assume full responsibility for the animals. As Robert grew up, he began to notice that his parents were less strict with him than with the other children. They punished his siblings more harshly and repeatedly found excuses for poor, deaf Robert. "Oh, Robert couldn't hear the alarm clock." "Let Robert enjoy what he's doing—his pleasures are so limited. I'll exercise his horse." Strangely, the older Robert grew, the more frequently his parents excused his lapses, blaming them on his being deaf.

After Robert turned sixteen, his parents let him take the car whenever he liked, although they strictly limited his brother's and sister's use of the car. Rose and Michael felt that Robert needed the car more, because he couldn't listen to music or enjoy conversation as easily as the others. They carried this laxness into his academic life as well. Although Robert's sister and brother were given four-year deadlines for finishing college (both got through on time and did well), Robert was allowed to dawdle and took seven years to finish his undergraduate degree. He grew up with almost no self-discipline and never did fulfill his childhood ambition to be a vet. Now, as an adult, Robert resents the deferential treatment he received and thinks it produced a self-indulgent streak in his personality. He has a steady job and makes a fair living but knows that with prompting and learning self-discipline, he could have achieved more.

Without realizing it, Robert's parents were intent above all on protecting their son from failure. In the long run, this deprived him of the chance to succeed. Something in their laxness said: "Look, Robert, you may as well not even try to be self-sufficient. You'll never make it. Let us give you a hand."

Children who are deaf have the potential to live rich, varied, and productive lives, pursuing the goals they choose. Overindulgent and overprotective parents can easily quash that potential and instill in their deaf children dependency and defeat.

The Importance of Playing

This and the preceding chapter have covered some weighty topics. At this point in your reading, you may find the responsibilities you face overwhelming. But there is no need for grimness or discouragement. Raising any child entails work in the sense that there is much to be accomplished. As for how to do the job, that's where play comes in. For preschoolers, and for older children as well, play and work are the same. Both deaf and hearing children build and cement their knowledge of the world through fantasy, interaction with their playmates, and storytelling. Both learn by freely exploring on their own. This sort of play has critical and positive effects on the cognitive and social development of your child. Children remember an idea they have stumbled on during play long after they have forgotten a tiresome explanation or demonstration imposed for educational purposes.

In this case, what's good for the children is often good for the adults. A game, a story, even a messy try at making pancakes together may ease the strain of your responsibilities in a way that a serious attempt at teaching your child to share toys would not. Making a game of button sorting or coloring teaches color discrimination faster than a lesson after dinner when everyone is tired. Even the frustration of blocked communication can be lightened by an old-fashioned game of charades, once the child is five or six. Such activities involve the whole family, giving you a chance to share the burden of total attentiveness. In time, as you and your deaf child explore and learn together, perhaps the distinction between work and play will fade for you as well.

Note

1. Carol Padden and Tom Humphries, *Deaf in America: Voices from a Culture* (Cambridge, MA: Harvard University Press, 1988):15–16.

5 *Your Deaf Child's Siblings*

WE BEGIN this chapter with the story of Rebecca, who has been deaf since birth. She is married to Ken, who also is deaf. Rebecca has made a wonderful life for herself as an adult. She is cheerful, contented, active, and busy with her two sons, Matthew and Mark, who are also deaf. When Rebecca and Ken received an invitation to the wedding of her older brother, Moses, she went into a serious depression. There was no avoiding the wedding, yet she and Ken knew what was in store for them: that left-out feeling that had defined Rebecca's early years at home, a feeling she hoped one day to forget.

Still, Rebecca felt that family was family, and she was not about to miss such an important day in her brother's life. It required a lot of effort to get to the wedding, because Moses lived in the family's hometown 800 miles away. At the first party, a large gathering of the bride and groom's families, all of Rebecca's worst premonitions were confirmed. Moses greeted Rebecca, Ken, and the boys but then returned to the party without introducing them to anyone. This was no surprise; Moses' means of coping with Rebecca's being deaf had always been to ignore it—which meant pretty much ignoring Rebecca. Later, his habit of failing to include her extended to her husband and then to their sons as well. Aaron, Rebecca's younger brother, rescued them from the sidelines of the party, where they had stood smiling uncomfortably like wallflowers at a junior high dance. Dragging Rebecca by the hand, he took it upon himself to introduce her and her family to everybody in the room—but grimly and negatively, explaining with an expression bordering on tragic that his sister, her husband, and both children were deaf. "These people can't hear you at all," he would say to the guests. "You have to look at them when you talk to them. They can talk by sign, but I don't know sign. We just always have to try our best." To Rebecca's extreme discomfort, Aaron was doing what he always did: treating Rebecca and her family as a group of poor, sad deaf people. She knew that both Moses and Aaron feared that she and Ken eventually would become dependent on them. All of this showed on Aaron's face as he dragged Rebecca from guest to guest at the wedding party.

Rebecca's parents had died some years earlier. For them, too, Rebecca's being deaf had been an embarrassment, which they had never dealt with in a straightforward way. They left her brothers to cope with it as best they could, never explaining her needs as a deaf sibling and related issues and never seeming to notice how Rebecca's being deaf affected the family. As soon as she was identified as deaf, Rebecca's parents enrolled her in a private school—and from that point on saw her education and upbringing as the responsibility of the school personnel. It was an unspoken rule that when Rebecca was at home, the brothers would take her around and watch out for her. Moses and Aaron grew up knowing they were responsible for their sister, feeling that responsibility weigh heavily on their shoulders, and longing for a time when they wouldn't have to worry about her anymore. They also felt that Rebecca was more vulnerable and therefore more special and important than they. Although they often felt guilty about it, resentment was the strongest emotion Rebecca inspired in the brothers. And this resentment persisted even after their parents' death.

Typically, although Moses and Aaron had worked out every detail of the wedding party and communicated closely with the bride's family about the wedding service, they had forgotten to hire a professional sign language interpreter. This was a serious oversight, as the matter had been hashed out years earlier before their father's funeral, when Rebecca had insisted on hiring an interpreter for the funeral service. Moses had blown up: "You've had a very good education, and that means you can function fine in hearing society—just like everybody else. Why do you want to seem helpless? Why do you need an interpreter—just to draw attention to yourself? It is important for our parents' friends to see how great you can be in hearing company. Our parents worked hard to get you the education you had, so that you could function in hearing society. I don't want people thinking they failed to take care of business with you, Rebecca."

At that time, Ken, who spoke clearly, had stepped in to argue on behalf of his wife. It was true, he explained, that Rebecca could speechread, but she was good at it only with people she knew well. At large social events, she and Ken and their sons needed an interpreter to feel a part of things. But the brothers did not give in.

For the wedding, Ken and Rebecca wound up hiring their own interpreter, just as they had for the funeral. Some years later, Rebecca and Ken had occasion to invite their brothers to the bar mitzvah of one of their sons. The service would be conducted in sign language, because most of the family's friends were deaf. Now Moses and Aaron and their families were in the minority. The weekend was a revelation for the brothers. They attended a crowded, high-spirited barbecue at their sister's home and found themselves amazed at the great good cheer. Since childhood, they had considered their sister's being deaf as a tragedy that had ruined her life and threatened to spoil their own. At the barbecue, because neither brother signed, they found that they were the ones left out of the animated conversations, except when someone remembered to shift into spoken English and act as an interpreter. Even then, things weren't easy for the brothers; in the lively party atmosphere, they found it difficult to concentrate and understand some of the speakers.

On the day of the bar mitzvah, as Moses and Aaron were about to leave for the synagogue, Ken exclaimed, winking to his wife: "Uh-oh! I forgot to get an interpreter. Oh, well. You don't need one, right? You'll be able to follow."

"What!" sputtered Moses. "You mean the bar mitzvah is going to be in sign language? How are we supposed to follow *that?*"

Ken and Rebecca burst out laughing. "Only kidding," Ken said. "I was just pulling your leg. We've already got somebody lined up!"

Rebecca gave her brothers a big hug. She had forgiven them long before this, realizing that their well-meaning parents had simply tossed her brothers the responsibility for keeping her safe without teaching them the skills and sensitivity to understand and live with her. Rebecca has truly forgiven her parents as well, but it will be a long time, she tells me, before she can forget the loneliness and hurt she endured in her family.

The Family: A Living Mosaic

Rebecca's story seems really terrible, and surely none of us would want that sort of dysfunction happening among our own children. The good news is that the most current research shows siblings of children with disabilities, including those who are deaf, have experiences not much different than the positive and negative emotions as siblings of children without disabilities. Some siblings may be more tolerant, helpful, caring, and responsible, and may serve as role models. However, other siblings may have fears, may overcompensate, or may struggle with guilt or embarrassment about having a sibling with a disability. The siblings' level of adaptation will depend on your attitude and response to the disability, the extent of your availability, and their own level of maturity and understanding.[1]

If you focus only on the deaf child and not on the complete family, you will surely sacrifice something in the development of one at the expense of the development of the other. Although having never met Rebecca's parents, the authors feel confident in assuming that the parents failed to take a holistic view of their family. To see the whole of the family rather than isolated aspects, the parents would have had to pay careful attention to their own psychological and social well-being and to that of each of their children separately. They would also have needed a clear view of the relationships among all five family members. Understanding a family this way, as a network of relationships each affected by the others, sounds like a tall order—and it is.

Family life, in general, is already formidable enough for parents. In the authors' experiences and in that of most other professionals in the field, parents who get very wrapped up in a child's being deaf and the extra attention he or she requires often overlook their relationships with their hearing children, frequently tending to let them evolve as they may. We have asked you to pay close attention to your own well-being. We have asked you to consider your deaf child's special communication needs within the family environment. Now we ask you to turn your attention to your other children, attempting for the moment to see and experience the family from each of their individual perspectives.

As you consider all of this, try to remain neutral, open, and above all, accepting of things as they are. Our aim is not to alarm you into searching for potential trouble spots. The idea is to see your family as a kind of mosaic, with each piece adding to and affecting the whole. Together, the pieces form a unique and complex pattern, no part of which is independent of the others. The mosaic pattern is not determined by family members alone. Other people, outside events, societal forces—all have an influence. And of course, the pattern changes over time as everyone grows and matures.

The Impact of Having a Deaf Family Member

You don't need to be told that the presence of a newborn in the family changes the dynamics among all its members. Suddenly, for example, the three-year-old is no longer the baby of the bunch but finds himself referred to as "a big boy," receiving much less attention than the little bundle in the blanket. A similar impact is felt when a child is identified as deaf. Suddenly, the hearing children notice that their parents may be devoting much more attention, energy, and time to the deaf child. An older boy feels slighted when his father misses four of his games in a row. An older daughter plays basketball with no family members in the bleachers. Suddenly, the hearing children have to "pitch in" by walking home from school when Mom takes the deaf child to the clinic. They find themselves getting their own after-school snacks while Mom helps the deaf child with homework, then doing their own homework without help as their parents stare at the television set, exhausted after hauling the deaf sibling from one appointment to another.

To parents, these may seem like small adjustments, but children experience them as significant alterations in the only reality they have known. Without your realizing it, your children may interpret the changes as signals that they are no longer as important to you as they once were. Perhaps they find confirmation of their erroneous interpretations in the fact that every dinner-table conversation has become a nonstop brainstorming session between you and your spouse about what has been done, what ought to be done, and what might be done to compensate for their sibling's being deaf.

Granted, these perceptions of changes in your behavior may be exaggerated, as children's perceptions often are. But they can happen as borne out by some of the research on the hearing families of deaf children.[2] After diagnosis, parents can be measurably more attentive to the deaf child and more inclined to let their other children fend for themselves. They also can be more lenient and protective toward the deaf child, even becoming impatient with the needs of the others as their energies are sapped and their resources strained in the effort to adapt.

We give here an example of Lucy, an older sister of a deaf sibling. At the age of nine, she sensed all of these things and more when her three-year-old brother was identified as severely hard of hearing as a result of a brief illness. A highly sensitive and anxious child, Lucy adapted by becoming a little mother, looking out for everybody but especially her little brother. She also began having serious nightmares and waking up frightened. Lucy was too young to be motherly and far too young to bear the burden of worrying about her whole family's well-being. When her wise parents arranged for short-term family counseling, Lucy admitted to them that she felt responsible to make up for their having a "not-so-good" child. This opened the way for her parents to reassure her that her brother was in no way diminished by being deaf. Learning of her feelings alerted them to the need to find ways to make her feel special in their eyes—as special and deserving of attention as her younger brother.

In Rebecca's case, her parents transferred to her brothers the responsibility for seeing her through the social world outside the home but offered no hints about how to do that in a positive way.

To the parents, Rebecca's "differentness" was a form of diminishment. So the brothers were left not only with a heavy responsibility but also with the erroneous perception that this burden was a negative one—a highly undesirable situation they had inherited from their parents.

Even when children are not made to feel responsible for their deaf sibling, it is inevitable that they will find themselves in situations where they need to explain and clarify the needs of deaf people to confused outsiders. Don't leave your hearing children to fend for themselves in such situations. Anticipate the questions and teach them what to say and how to say it, so they'll be comfortable in the explainer's role. As a great reminder of how you do *not* want them to act, remember her brother Aaron's consistently negative, depressed explanation that "these people can't hear you." Make the following clear to your children:

- Their sibling's being deaf is not the end of the world—and not the end of family life as they know it.
- It is not the child who has changed since the diagnosis but rather your understanding of who the child is, and your experience of the child, which is becoming fuller and more comprehensible.
- Being deaf means the child does not hear. It doesn't mean the child can't think or communicate in other ways, as some hearing people believe.

With that foundation, you can begin coaching your children in specific ways of bringing this information to people, especially peers, outside the family. Try to be thorough in anticipating the responses they may get in the outside world. Here are some examples of things you can tell your children.

"Many people are afraid of differentness. Even adults are afraid of differentness. In their fear, they may seem shy or even angry. Be prepared, and don't take it personally."

"Lots of people will think that Tommy is too young to use sign language. Let them know he can sign, and show them a sign or two. And let them know that Tommy will feel more included if they smile at him and look directly into his eyes."

"If somebody makes fun of Tommy, you don't need to respond unless you feel comfortable doing it. If the person is an adult or bigger than you, we'll all understand if you don't want to say anything. It will probably make you feel angry and uncomfortable to stay there, so the best thing to do is leave. Of course, if you do feel comfortable about responding when a kid is mean to Tommy, use your words, not your fists."

The "be explicit" rule applies to all of your children. Whatever your family philosophy, convey it to your hearing children clearly in a way they can use. Do you think that asking your deaf child's siblings to explain their communication needs to other people is burdening them with too much responsibility? In the authors' view, it is not the explainer's role that is a burden; rather, it is the lack of parental guidance that makes a sibling's deaf status overwhelming for some children. Remember Rebecca's lifelong suffering at the hands of her brothers, who were not bad people but had received no help—no coaching, no explanations, and no support. It is essential that parents help children find a positive way to relate to their deaf siblings and to be positive advocates for them.

When Enough Is Enough

Siblings who accompany a deaf child into the wider world of children often have a great deal to teach their own parents and professionals about being deaf. But there is a limit. Pressures can build on these good Samaritans, and what parents consider to be a healthy level of participation may actually be an unhealthy burden. There are certain kinds of pressures that siblings—even teenage brothers and sisters—should not be expected to cope with alone. Try to adopt a neutral observer's stance in considering whether your children suffer from feelings like the following:

1. Powerlessness to protect the deaf child from others' ridicule or impatience. Ask your hearing child whether the deaf child is being mistreated, and if so, step in and put a stop to it yourself.

2. Fears that the deaf child's special needs will absorb all the family finances, forcing the hearing child to make serious sacrifices. If this is a danger, discuss it frankly.

3. Feelings of isolation caused by constraints on the family's social life. Parents may be unwilling to attend some public

events, such as Little League games or Back to School Night. Perhaps they are too tired or are worried what people will think of the deaf child. They may not allow the siblings' friends to sleep over, because they view having a deaf family member as a negative part of their life that they don't want to reveal or explain. It takes no magic wand to show how truth and openness are the antidotes here.

4. Diminished self-esteem. Hearing siblings may suffer from the sinking feeling that they are not special and valuable in their own right—or at least not as special or valuable as the deaf child. However, children are easily reassured; simply drawing attention to their special talents or contributions to the family will do wonders for children who harbor a secret suspicion that they are less than special in their parents' eyes.

5. Confusion about the needs of deaf siblings. Sometimes children want information but have trouble formulating questions. The cure for this is easy: Ask, "Is there anything about Randy's being deaf that you don't know? Are there things about it that bother you?"

6. Extra pressure to succeed in school. Hearing children may feel they should be exceptionally good students to compensate if the deaf child is having difficulties. Reassure them: "You know, everybody is different. Randy is struggling to learn how to understand hearing children; you're struggling with algebra. Both of you will find a way over your particular mountains, and guess what you'll find on the other side. More mountains!"

7. Resentment about serving in the role of interpreter. It can become tedious and annoying for the hearing child to be constantly relegated to the interpreter's role. Almost inevitably, owing to developmental differences and the fact they are in constant communication, your hearing children will learn to sign more quickly than you do. Make sure that you don't rely too heavily on your hearing child to represent the deaf child to the outside world. The hearing child may begin to feel like a mere go-between, as if his or her own part in conversations were secondary to the task of conveying messages back and forth.

The fundamental danger is that responsibility for the deaf child will limit the hearing child's development and love of life. This can happen in families with one deaf child and one hearing child. However, hearing siblings of deaf children often learn positive lessons of kindness, consideration, and equality at an early age and show patience, increased tolerance for differences, altruism, and creativity in communication. They are often described as "mature beyond their years" and "more serious" than other children.[3] Be alert to these siblings' positive qualities, but be careful to protect them against becoming solemn little adults with the weight of the world on their shoulders.

Monitoring the Family System

Stephen Bank and Michael Kahn describe the sibling bond as a complex connection between two selves, functioning on both intimate and public levels. The relationship between sister and brother, sister and sister, or brother and brother is nothing less than the living, breathing process through which two people fit together their identities—two people who, at least in their childhood, are in constant contact as they grow and change. The nature of the bond varies greatly, determined not only by the individuals' personalities but also by countless other variables within each family.[4]

Dale Atkins, a child psychologist, listed the following as factors in a family that shape the relationships between siblings: family size, birth order, age spacing, sibling genders, economic status of the family, marital status of the parents and level of harmony in their relationship, expectations, roles within the family, individual temperaments and physical attributes, family values, degree of presence of family caregivers and strength of the internal support system, number and intensity of stresses, both acute and chronic, level to which feelings are expressed, distribution of responsibilities among family members, efficiency of time management, similarities and differences between siblings, rivalries, styles of communication, perceived or actual favoritism, parenting styles, and level of involvement of all family members.[5] Some of these factors are obvious, and some operate below conscious awareness.

The length of the list, which is not meant to be comprehensive, suggests how very complex this system is that we call *the family.*

When a deaf child enters the dynamic, evolving network of family relationships, it changes everything—perhaps subtly, perhaps immeasurably. How can you hope to control these myriad influences? It is as if a great wave has swept out of nowhere to shake up every pebble on the beach. Reassuringly, research and experience suggest that staying alert to certain critical areas of family life does give parents a measure of control. You can exert a positive influence on sibling relationships in your family by applying the following two concrete principles.

1. *Commit yourself to creating an environment that is conducive to communication.* Language links people; walls of silence separate them. Make sure that your deaf child acquires language, signed and/or spoken; learn sign language yourself and make it available to your hearing children. Encourage everyone in your family to communicate with everyone else. Discuss being deaf openly.

2. *Stay alert to the possibility that unfair burdens have shifted to your hearing children.*

Listen for complaints like "I have to take her everywhere"; "I always have to stay around and interpret, even for Daddy"; "At school, I always have to explain, even to the teachers, that she's not stupid—and I have to show everybody how to communicate with her." Hearing children who continually perform such functions need to be relieved of them. They are too young to be the deaf child's ambassador. That's *your* job, along with making sure that the growth and development of your hearing children are not neglected.

The second edition of *The Silent Garden* included an informal survey of parents and professionals, asking them what "golden rule" of family life they would like to convey to readers, especially those with both deaf and hearing children. Here is a list of their responses:[†]

[†] Thanks to Lita D. Aldridge, Dale V. Atkins, Lisa Binswager-Friedman, Marilyn Cassidy, Linda Daniel, Mary Elsie Daisey, Mal Grossinger, Irene Leigh, and Ginny Malzhkuhn.

- First and foremost, recognize, value, and appreciate each child's individuality.
- As a general rule, arrange special times to spend with hearing siblings.
- Be alert for signs of stress not only in your deaf child but also in hearing siblings as well.
- Praise the efforts and accomplishments of hearing siblings.
- Don't expect the siblings to be saints—remember that the added pressures are affecting everybody, not just you.
- Take active steps to provide opportunities for siblings to express their feelings. Don't wait for your children to give voice to any resentments they may feel. They may hide their feelings out of guilt or a wish to protect you. Find a way to encourage them to tell you the truth (e.g., "I know you must be wishing you didn't have to explain Betsy's communication needs to everybody—I feel the same way myself. Am I right?")
- Teach siblings how to express their anger and frustration without physical fighting or verbal abuse. If you are unable to come up with strategies that work, consider outside counseling.
- Admit that you don't have all the answers; that the most you can promise is to stay alert to changes and problems that need to be solved.
- Provide your hearing children with books, videos, and websites about deaf people. They may have questions they don't want to ask or misperceptions that you don't know about.
- By modeling (i.e., providing an example in your own behavior), teach siblings to take pride in the deaf child's difference rather than considering it a problem.
- Look for special sibling support groups in your community. If you can't find any, consider starting one.
- Reassure all of your children about their importance in the family by asking for their input and advice in family discussions.
- Insist within your extended family that no favoritism be shown to the deaf child.
- Avoid making comparisons among siblings.
- Make sure you never tolerate behavior from your deaf child that you wouldn't tolerate from your hearing children.

- Acknowledge and reinforce the positive interactions you observe among the siblings (e.g., "I love the way you and Eddy laugh together at cartoons." "You're really terrific at noticing if Eddy gets left out. I appreciate that and I know he does, too").
- If decisions must be made that inconvenience the siblings in favor of the deaf child, discuss them openly in advance. That way, even if children do feel resentment, they won't have the additional emotional burden of feeling steamrolled.
- Allow the siblings to watch and participate in activities designed to help the deaf child.
- To balance the flow of give-and-take, provide opportunities for the deaf child to be of help to the hearing siblings.
- Participate as fully as possible in the school-related activities of all your children.
- Whether your deaf child attends a special school or is mainstreamed, you'll see endless opportunities to contribute and participate in his or her education. Be fair to your other kids and to yourself. Prioritize and do what you can for each one.
- Schedule quiet time with each child alone. Otherwise, you may wind up having private conversations only with the deaf child (perhaps in the course of special activities or on the way to appointments) and relating to your other children only in the group.
- Take time periodically, as your children grow, to update and educate them on the issues surrounding the needs of their deaf siblings.
- Share your concerns about the deaf child with your other children—as friends and teammates.
- Role-play or provide suggested responses for difficult situations that the hearing siblings may encounter: "If people ask what's wrong with your brother, here's a good way to put it: 'He's deaf, so he gets his information through his eyes instead of his ears. Make sure he can see you clearly, and you'll be amazed how well he understands you. I'll even teach you some signs.'"
- Play games and watch TV as one of the group, not always in an authoritarian, facilitator role.
- Invite your hearing children's friends over to have fun with your family, so they'll get to know the deaf child as an individual. Your

children may not tell you that they feel uncomfortable about having friends over; they may need you to break the ice.

- Bottom line: *Within your family and with other people, be open and honest about your deaf child's communication needs.*

The Gibbs Family

That's a long list of guidelines, perhaps an overwhelming list. To show that all these pieces of advice can coalesce into a doable approach that fosters growth and free-flowing communication, we introduce the Gibbs family.

The Gibbses

The Gibbses are great talkers. When their second daughter, Meagan, was born with a severe hearing loss, the news came as a big blow. The parents had talked to their oldest daughter, Mandy, from the day she was born, naming, explaining, and enjoying the opportunity to share the world with her. How, they wondered, could they give Meagan the same opportunity to learn and communicate?

The Gibbses decided almost immediately to learn Signing Exact English (a manually coded English system) and encouraged everybody else in their large extended family to learn it, too. They enrolled Mandy in signing classes, involving her from the beginning in their decision-making and explaining every issue that came up in a family forum.

By the time Mandy entered the first grade, she had been coached to respond with age-appropriate explanations when children and teachers asked about Meagan's hearing loss. The parents picked up any and all storybooks that included deaf characters. One of their deaf adult friends, whom they had met at a support group for parents of deaf children, happened to be a librarian. "Perfect!" said the Gibbses, who were becoming excellent networkers, as they learned the value of community support.

A year after Meagan's birth, a third daughter, Miriam, was born. The Gibbses made it a priority to reassure Meagan that, although she was different and in the minority with two hearing sisters, she was just as valuable and interesting as the other girls. The hearing sisters agreed; both became fluent signers and, thanks to their parents' early emphasis on teaching Meagan to read, developed into voracious readers themselves.

Meagan was never left out. The parents saw her special needs as enrichments for their family, not handicaps. They encouraged the three daughters to watch television with the sound off sometimes in order to experience Meagan's way of seeing the world and looking for clues to its meaning. Watching television or a movie together (with the sound *on* and captioned for Meagan) became an important ritual for the Gibbses. At the same time, however, the parents made sure that each of their daughters felt special and that each had her own toys, friends, activities, and time with them. They kept their home open to all the girls' friends, confidently depending on their hearing daughters to explain Meagan's communication needs. As a result, in the Gibbses' immediate and extended family and in their whole lively social circle, deafness occupied an appropriate place.

All three girls and many of their friends became fluent signers. Although some of the extended family members enrolled initially in a signing course, they dropped out after a while, as frequently happens. Mr. Gibbs, too, cut class a lot and never found the time to practice enough to be fluent, but he manages to communicate effectively within the family by signing and talking simultaneously. Mrs. Gibbs, on the other hand, became so fluent that she is now a full-time interpreter for the local school district. "Meagan's being deaf gave me a new career," she says. "Far from being negative, having a deaf family member brought things into our home that we never would have known about at all."

The Gibbses have problems and very bumpy spots like any family. But being deaf is rarely a major issue in their home—it certainly doesn't slow them down. They're still a family of marathon communicators, and now they're comfortable and fluent both in English and in sign language.

Notes

1. Renuka Sundaram Raghuraman, "The Emotional Well-Being of Older Siblings of Children Who Are Deaf or Hard of Hearing and Older

Siblings of Children with Typical Hearing," *The Volta Review* 108, no. 1 (2008): 5–35.

2. Dale V. Atkins, "Siblings of the Hearing Impaired: Perspectives for Parents," *The Volta Review* 89, no. 5 (1987): 32–45.

3. Lynne Koester and Kathryn P. Meadow-Orlans, "Parenting a Deaf Child: Stress, Strength, and Support," in *Educational and Developmental Aspects of Deafness*, ed. D. F. Moores and K. P. Meadow-Orlans (Washington, DC: Gallaudet University Press, 1990): 229–320.

4. Stephen Bank and Micheal D. Kahn, *The Sibling Bond* (New York: Basic Books, 2003): 134.

5. Dale Atkins, "Siblings of the Hearing Impaired: Perspectives for Parents," *The Volta Review* 89, no. 5, (1987): 32–45.

3 Communicating

6 *So Much More than Words*

MOST OF the world communicates, to a large degree, by means of sound. Being deaf limits your child's access to sound but not the instinct to communicate. Your deaf child's desire and need to transmit and receive information are as great as anyone else's. Furthermore, although being deaf can affect the ability to develop speech, it does not rob the body of the power to communicate. Deaf people still have their hands and arms, their faces, their postures, their gestures, their expressions, their lips, and their tongues. They also have their eyes, which they use to read the gestures, postures, expressions, and often the speech of others.

We don't mean to undervalue speech or to dismiss the significance of being deaf in limiting access to spoken language by focusing on the importance of nonverbal communication. Nevertheless, most people often overvalue speech by viewing it as the only means of transmitting information face to face. They are surprised to learn that in social conversation, only a small portion of the total communicative energy is expended in the verbal utterance of words.[1]

Nonverbal Communication

Back in the days before captioning of video material, many people were surprised to learn that deaf people would watch television and go to the movies. "How can you tell what's going on?" they asked. "How can you follow the plot?" The answer is that most television programs and movies, especially those that tell stories, show people in action. Everything in these shows, not just the script, is designed to communicate information relevant to the story, including the costumes, sets, and pace of action. All the great actors are trained experts in body language, facial expressions, gestures, and movement as well as the use of their voices. People who are used to scanning the visual world for information have no trouble following a cinematic story visually, and deaf people can watch action-oriented video programs without missing much.

Because most people rely on auditory input, though, they usually have difficulty fully following a video without the sound on. People do send and read nonverbal messages. In fact, it has been estimated that 65 to 70 percent of the meaning is carried by nonverbal means. The exact percentage is not the issue as much as the fact that nonverbal communication is *very* important to our messages.[2] In conversation or watching a TV program or movie, people may focus on the spoken words, but they are also subconsciously reading the visual messages that all great actors have learned to convey.

To picture how these unconsciously transmitted messages work, imagine meeting a friend on the street. You might ask how he's feeling today and hear him say he's fine, just great, thanks. You take him at his word at first and go on your way, but you have a nagging feeling that something is wrong. If you saw a video of the exchange, you would notice that throughout your conversation, Joe's eyes darted around, and he pulled at his tie as if it were choking him. You would recognize that his eyes conveyed a message of their own, and knowing that Joe is an unusually direct fellow, you might interpret his tie pulling as symbolic choking on a lie. But without the benefit of a video replay, you dismiss your nagging feelings. A deaf person experienced in consciously observing body language might be more prepared to treat the eye darting and tie pulling as part of Joe's message.

In this sense, your child's deaf status will motivate you to read body language and to learn to use your body to convey information. You will need to become like the great actors and sharpen your perceptions of gesture, posture, and facial expression, and loosen up and use all of these elements when communicating with your deaf child.

CHILDREN'S BODY LANGUAGE

Our initial "conversations" are those first wonderful exchanges of touch and gaze between infant and parent. Extending our "great actor" idea, Jean Piaget, the developmental psychologist, described children's early communication experiences with others as "acted conversations."[3] An example given was that of a discussion accompanied by gestures and demonstrations with the fingers along with childish talk: "That does that, and then it goes there, and it goes like that," and so forth. The messages may seem cryptic at times, but more often than not, preverbal children (hearing children who have not yet learned to speak well) manage to get their points across much more so than by verbal means alone. So, even with reference to hearing children, we need to shed the common misconception that nonverbal communication is not real communication. Consider the following scenario.

Two twelve-month-old children, a girl and a boy, sit side by side in a sandbox. Each has a colored cup and is absorbed in filling it with sand. Suddenly the little boy glances up, notices the girl's red cup, drops his own yellow cup, and brushes it aside impatiently. He then reaches out to grab the red one. The boy's face registers a series of emotions: delighted interest as he spies the red cup, impatience as he casts his own cup aside, and knit-browed determination as he fastens his grip on the rim of the red one. A struggle ensues, and as the little girl loses her grip on the prize, her moan of irritation grows into a shriek of fury. Suddenly, she stops screeching and savagely bites the hand of the interloper. He lets go of the cup and begins his own wail of pain and surprise. As the scene closes, the chastened boy is stretching out his arms to his mother, and the girl, having prudently turned her back to the boy, is tranquilly filling her red cup with sand.

Who can say communication has not occurred here? True, these hearing children are too young to speak. Ten-month-old babies understand many words and even say a few, but they do not use them to express themselves. Still, these two have managed to make their feelings about their cups quite clear. They have clearly expressed happy desire, determined acquisitiveness, possessiveness, fury, hurt, territoriality, and smug satisfaction, all without using language.

Katherine Bridges, a child psychologist, discovered in her research with hearing children that by the age of two, regardless of family background or sex, children are capable of communicating nonverbally at least twelve different emotions, including elation, affection, excitement, anger, jealousy, joy, distress, delight, and fear.[4] "But wait a minute," you may object. "Is conveying feelings really communicating? Isn't communication concerned with information?" The fact is that many messages we send have to do with feelings. Where children are concerned, it is fair to say that the majority of their messages relate to how they feel, and this is true even after they learn to talk. If you don't believe this, survey the content of the communication that passes between you and a hearing child over a period of a few hours or days. Here is a verbatim transcription of a typical morning conversation between one mother and her three-year-old son:

"Good morning. How are you feeling today? Did you sleep well?"

"Mommy, I'm hungry."

"What would you like for breakfast? How about some eggs?"

"Yuck, I hate eggs. Let me have some, um, uh, um—you know what? Jason at school said I was a dumdum, and I cried."

"Oh, that's awful. But you're not a dumdum. Did you tell him you weren't? Calling names is terrible. Now, what do you want for breakfast?"

"I'm not hungry."

"But you have to eat. Otherwise you'll be too hungry when you get to school."

"But I don't want to go to school! I want you to stay home and let me stay home with you."

"But I thought you loved school! Why don't you want to go to school? I think you'll feel better about it when you have something to eat. What do you want for breakfast?"

"I don't want any breakfast. I hate breakfast."

The child's side of this conversation is almost totally emotional—how he feels, what he wants or doesn't want, and so on. Much of what children talk about, and much of what they need to get across to their parents and others, has to do with their feelings. So denying the importance of the emotions in children's communication is denying their most important subject matter.

Of course, most parents do respond to their hearing babies' expressive behavior. As the parent of a deaf child, you have a special reason to concentrate on the vocabulary of gestures, expressions, and postures that the child develops over time. By learning to read your child's body language, you'll be taking a step closer to participating in an ongoing conversation every bit as valid and informative as a signed or spoken exchange. Research has shown that deaf children in the absence of spoken or signed language input will fashion a gesture system that, if one observes carefully, looks like natural language at the word and sentence level and actually functions like a natural language. It is also known that if adults respond appropriately to these gestures, it helps children develop critical language skills.[5] This flexibility, or resilience, of the human brain to adapt to circumstances in order to communicate is truly amazing!

Eventually, you and your child will develop a system of signs and signals together. For the moment, don't worry about trying to be perfect with sign language. Concentrate on the child's natural movements and expressions. After all, as far as the child is concerned, gestures and facial expressions are what communication is all about. Enter into the pleasure of invention the way your child does. Until the child begins to realize that he or she is different from others, being deaf is simply the way things are, and nothing is missing from the world. The child is prepared to go along as she or he has been since birth, communicating through body movement, facial expression, and posture.

Importance of Gesture in Language Acquisition

David McNeill, in his now classic book on gestures, gave strong evidence of a speech-gesture system that all children develop. He recommends that we speak of language-*gesture* acquisition instead of only language acquisition. Speech and gestures develop parallel to each other, are the components of a single system from the earliest periods, and are inseparable after the age of two.[6] Given all children's natural talent for nonverbal communication, it is doubly sad when parents fail to perceive their children's efforts to express themselves. Although the children persist in the only way they know, a way that has great potential for conveying information, all too often, their parents remain unaware of their efforts and never discover how effective the gestures could be were the parents to learn to decode them.

Unfortunately, this kind of situation is common in the families of deaf children, even after infancy. Sometimes the parents' ignorance of their child's nonverbal communication skills is a manifestation of an intense wish for the child to be "normal." It is that old self-deception: "If she could only learn to speak, she wouldn't be deaf anymore." In this single-minded hope, parents focus on the spoken mode of expression to the total exclusion of other modes. "Learn to talk, learn to talk" is their consistent message. Very often, what they are really saying, although perhaps subconsciously, is, "Forget about other ways of communicating. Just learn to talk." Consider this example of the effect of a speech-centric approach to language learning on a deaf child.

Marie

Four-year-old Marie has lost her ball somewhere in the house. She goes to her parents, who are talking together in another room, and begins gesturing for them to come help her look for her ball. "What is it?" her father asks. "I think she's lost something," her mother says, adding with careful enunciation, "What are you looking for, Marie?" The girl gestures again excitedly, but her parents are stumped. They look at each other and exchange a puzzled glance, and then the father loses his temper. In the past, he has had some success in teaching the girl to form words, and he is furious that now, when she really needs to communicate information, she is relying on gestures. "Come back when you can tell us what you're looking for!" he shouts angrily, and turns his back on the girl.

Having failed to get her message across, enlist her parents' help, and find her ball, Marie is on the verge of a full-blown tantrum. However, much worse for her than the frustration of all this failure is the hurtfulness of her father's reaction.

As we advocated in Chapter 3, children's sense of safety and security grows out of trust that when they signal, their parents will respond. To grow strong and independent, a child needs to feel safe and unconditionally accepted. Parents who discourage their deaf children from relying on nonverbal communication unknowingly threaten the children's development and sense of security by making expressions of parental love and acceptance conditional on the children's success in communicating through speech. The children may feel that only when they learn to speak will their parents truly love and accept them.

Parents who are aware of this danger and prepared to acknowledge their child's natural skills at nonverbal communication will react very differently from Marie's father when confronted with something like the lost-ball situation. They will drop everything if the moment calls for it and focus on the child. Instead of brushing aside the child's attempts to explain what she wants or needs, the parents will persist in the effort to understand the child by gesturing, speaking, questioning, and following hunches; when the message becomes clear, they will help the child find the ball. Look at the following benefits of such an approach.

1. The child successfully conveys the problem and enlists the parents' help in problem solving.
2. True communication—of feelings *and* information—takes place.
3. The child experiences the satisfaction of initiating a successful exchange, whether or not the ball is found.
4. Above all, the child feels secure about the parents' interest and concern and has no reason to question their love.

The impulse among some parents of deaf children to discourage the use of natural gestures in favor of spoken communication has another serious consequence: It inhibits children's natural impulse to learn as much as possible about their environment and their own place in it. Observe a hearing two-year-old, and you will realize how much simple body motion means to that child in terms of being alive and participating in the world. Babies do not sit still passively in the middle of a room or a landscape. They roam, seek boundaries, and feel textures. They look at people, coo at them, crawl to them, and touch them. From a child's point of view, loving and existing are synonymous with moving and reaching out.

Deaf children, of course, have as much need to be physically free as hearing children—perhaps more, because they have one less sense through which to receive information about the world. Therefore, unless discouraged, the deaf child will move, move, move—seeking knowledge of the world and stimulation for his or her active senses. At the age of four or five, when a hearing child begins to give up some motor activity in favor of spoken communication, the deaf child will develop gestures that are more refined, subtle, and capable of conveying specific meanings.

To summarize: Although your child is deaf, he or she is not without communication. This communication consists of blinks, nods, sweeping arm movements, tiny finger movements, wrinkling of the nose, baring of the teeth, changing angles of the head, specific attitudes of the spine—in short, an infinity of gestures, expressions, and postures. Among many communicative acts, this self-evolved communication may not be as precise or explicit as a formal language, such as English or American Sign Language (ASL). You will have to sharpen your sensitivity to learn to read it, and even then, interpreting it will give you many moments of confusion and frustration. As long as you try, however, you will be confirming the value of your child's attempts to reach you and let you know what is going on in his or her mind. To turn away from the gestures of preschool deaf children is to plug your ears to the messages they are sending. If you want to discover how much your deaf child has to say, open your eyes!

Developing Your Own Communication Skills

Being receptive is only half of the communication equation. The other half, of course, is transmitting messages. As noted earlier, many hearing people are so dependent on speech that they fail to recognize how important nonverbal communication is in their own lives. Perhaps the easiest way to realize the significance of nonverbal communication is to imagine an exchange without it. Visualize a meeting with a very dear friend you haven't seen in years. Can you imagine greeting this person in words alone, without at the very least breaking into a happy smile and extending your hand in greeting? In reality, you would probably make a great many more movements—depending on how expressive you are naturally—and you would doubtless be unaware of most of them. Were you to greet this long-lost friend merely by speaking, even while raising your voice to indicate your excitement, very possibly your friend would feel snubbed. "Hmm. No handshake? No smile? Just standing there with her hands at her sides? She must not be very glad to see me."

One of the most powerful forms of nonverbal communication is eye contact. Our eye movements and expressions, most of which occur without conscious control, communicate messages of excitement, pleasure, grief, anger, sorrow, and so on. Truly, the eyes are the windows to the soul. The shades of meaning conveyed by eyes can be extremely subtle. So the first rule in communicating with your deaf child or any person who is deaf or hard of hearing is to *maintain eye contact at all times*. If you make it difficult for the child to read your eyes, he or she may get the gist of your message without gaining a sense of your personal feelings about it. You will be withholding the visual equivalent of the tone of your voice. If parents consistently fail to meet their deaf children's eyes, the children may begin to feel that they don't really know their parents at all.

Supremacy of the Spoken Word: A Fallacy

Sadly, the same impulse that leads some parents to discourage nonverbal communication in their deaf children, because of a desire to make them concentrate on oral skills, often leads them to suppress their own nonverbal communication. So intent are these well-meaning parents on helping their deaf children acquire spoken language skills that they mute their facial expressions and gestures and deprive their children of physical clues to the meaning of their spoken messages. These parents don't want to distract their child's attention from words. They forget, or don't know, that by suppressing their natural forms of expressiveness, they are stripping away a large percentage of the content of normal social conversation. This explains why many deaf people with hearing siblings complain that their parents are more expressive with the hearing children in the family than with them.

Nonverbal communication does not replace spoken words or signed language; it complements to make meanings clear. Most deaf children learn a formal language much later than their hearing peers, so in their preschool years, they need to be encouraged to develop other ways of conveying and receiving information. Communication feeds curiosity and sparks self-awareness. To delay a child's ability to communicate until the child can learn language, whether signed or spoken, is to risk inhibiting the development of these very basic qualities.

GETTING YOUR MESSAGE ACROSS

If you have relied all your life on speech as your primary communication mode, you may not be fully acquainted with your body's potential for transmitting messages. You may find it useful to spend time in front of a mirror to observe the messages you are sending and to devise gestures and expressions that match what you want to convey. If you initially find this difficult to do, you are not alone. One of the interesting things we have noted in adults learning sign languages is that they have the most difficulty, not with the vocabulary or syntax, but with making appropriate facial expressions and body movements.

Nonverbal communication is not a complex system that has to be studied and learned. The meanings of specific facial expressions and physical gestures are fairly universal, at least within a given culture. Therefore the purpose of focusing on specific techniques is not so much to "teach" you to use your body as to help you to use it consciously. It is like learning to ride a bike or other new skill; you have to constantly be aware of your movements at first. But once you get the hang of it, it becomes a subconscious part of yourself, just like bike riding.

As you cultivate your skills in nonverbal communication, keep in mind the following points, which apply specifically to communication with children who are deaf:

1. As an overall guideline, imagine yourself communicating across a language barrier. How would you interact with someone from another country who knew no English whatsoever? The analogy is not as odd as it may seem at first. By imagining yourself as "stretching" to reach across the language barrier, you may think of ways to convey your meaning that hadn't occurred to you before.

2. Be sure to use your gestures and facial expressions at your child's eye level. It does no good to shake your head and scowl to mean "No!" if you are standing at your full height far above the child's line of sight. Kneel down and make direct eye contact with the child before trying to get your point across.

3. Remember that all eye cues are important and that they carry the more subtle aspects of your message. For this reason, too, maintain eye contact at all times. Stay conscious of your head movements, and make it as easy as possible for the child to see your eyes.

4. Be as responsive as possible with your face and body to all of your child's messages. Do not restrict your use of gestures to the very active, message-sending function of communication. Remember that the child will be unaware of the sounds people ordinarily make to encourage a speaker to continue. Without visual cues or feedback to encourage them, deaf children have no way of knowing whether their listeners are still interested and engaged.

5. Whenever you're with your deaf child, use normal gestures as much as possible. Neither restrict nor exaggerate your gestures and expressions. Be aware that it is through you that the child will learn how gestures and expressions are used among hearing people generally. You will be teaching your child to read and send nonverbal messages, naturally, to people in the environment.

6. As your child grows older, be prepared to refine your nonverbal communication and use it at a more sophisticated level. The older the child, the subtler and more complex will be the meanings conveyed nonverbally.

7. Be alert to the fact that every child, whether deaf or hearing, is a mimic in early childhood. This phenomenon usually is quite strong between the ages of three and five, once the child has learned to understand others and has realized that he or she can get messages across. At this point, the child is excited by the newfound power to communicate and starts imitating and repeating every gesture that evokes a response. It is during this period that some parents begin to fear that their deaf child is becoming too attached to gestures and will never learn a more formalized mode of communication, such as spoken English or signs. Be reassured that your child's early, whole-hearted exercise of nonverbal communication represents a passing enchantment with the newly mastered communication tool; it is analogous to a hearing child's fascination with the telephone. Eventually, things will even out, and nonverbal communication will become a supplement to the child's formal language, as it is for hearing children.

8. Whatever mode of formal communication you settle on— spoken language, cued speech, Signing Exact English, Signed English, or another manually coded sign system (all these methods are explained in detail in the next three chapters) —be sure to *stay flexible* and continue using gestures and facial expressions to express your feelings. Far too often, parents and professionals are so intent on reinforcing a child's use of the chosen mode of communication that they tighten up noticeably, conveying anxiety to the child. Let yourself go! Your child will be reading your body language no matter what, so you may as well use it for all it is worth.

HONING YOUR SKILLS

Common phrases with nonverbal equivalents are often used successfully with children aged one to four years. We've included some examples in Table 6.1—not only to teach you how to convey a sentence nonverbally word for word but also to show you that nonverbal communication is natural and that most nonverbal messages are instantly recognizable. Because children learn to handle

TABLE 6.1. NONVERBAL FORMS OF COMMUNICATING SPOKEN PHRASES

English Phrase	Nonverbal Behavior
"Open your mouth."	Open your own mouth and point to it, holding your face directly in front of your child's. In all nonverbal exchanges, take advantage of the child's natural urge to imitate your expressions and gestures.
"Are you sleepy?"	Show your droopy eyes, yawn, raise your eyebrows in an interrogatory way, and then point to the child. The child will soon learn that a querying expression coupled with a pointed finger means that a response is expected.
"Are you hungry?"	Pretend to place a spoon in your mouth, chew, rub your stomach, smile, query with your brow, and point to the child.
"What's wrong?"	Show a worried face, squint your eyebrows, and look at the child intently. Place your hand on the child and incline your body toward him or her in concern. Then assume a querying expression and point to the child.
"Good girl/boy!"	Smile and look pleased. Touch or point to the child to make it clear that he or she is the cause of your pleasure. Do a thumbs-up, high five, or fist bump. Let your whole body (arms, shoulders, back) show your pleasure.
"No! That was very bad."	Look very displeased and shake your head from side to side. Hold your head, neck, and back rigid. The child will soon learn to associate a side-to-side shake with "no" and up-and-down with "yes," just as hearing children do. As you shake your head, touch or point to the child to show that he or she has caused your disapproval, then indicate exactly what the child has done wrong. Act out the misbehavior if necessary.

TABLE 6.1. *Continued*

English Phrase	Nonverbal Behavior
"Go to your room!"	Point to the room, then point to the child. Make a gesture of "no" if the child ignores you or begins to do something else. Be firm and do not smile. Relaxing your posture will undermine your intention.
"Go to the bathroom."	Same as above, but not angrily. It may be necessary to point to the appropriate areas on your body and query the child. Sometimes using the universal gesture of holding your nose for "poo-poo."
"What are you doing?"	Query the child with your facial expression, raise and lower your eyebrows, shrug a little, with your palms up, and point to the activity in question. Be sure to remain attentive after you have invited a response.
"Where are you going?"	Incline your head a little in the direction the child is going, query with your facial expression, and point to the child and the direction the child is going.
"Tie your shoes."	Make a tying motion with your fingers and point to the child's shoes. (This is an example of the need for specificity in gestures. Parents often tend to mouth commands while looking or pointing at something, leaving the child to guess what is being requested.)
"One, two, three, go!"	Translate the tag lines of games into body language. In this case, count off the steps on your fingers, raise your eyebrows, brighten up your expression, and move hands forward for "Go!"
"This is delicious! Do you think so?"	Show your enjoyment of the dish at hand. Then point to the child and query.

TABLE 6.1. *Continued*

English Phrase	Nonverbal Behavior
"Oh, what a terrible mess."	Roll your eyes and show disgust.
"Let's go to a movie."	In proposing plans, work on conveying your attitude toward what you are saying. First present the concept "movie"—this may take some charades. Then work on the subjective side of the question, communicating a feeling such as ambivalence, excitement, boredom, or uncertainty. Then elicit the child's opinion with a query and a point.
"Oh, you silly thing! You do it then!"	Humor should become a solid part of your nonverbal repertoire when the child is sophisticated enough to understand it—typically by the age of three or four. Before then there is always some danger in interjecting irony or affectionate name-calling because the child may take it literally. In this case, you could look comically angry and kind at the same time and give a gentle shove toward the job to be done, crossing your arms, and turning away from it. Then look back and smile.
"I'd like that one. Which one do you want?"	Show the options, show your preference, query the child with your expression, and point to both choices and the child. Then be prepared to negotiate.

more complex messages as they grow older, the table is arranged with the more sophisticated examples at the end.

The complexity and subtlety of nonverbal communication continues to increase with age. The learning of other modes of communication opens up the nonverbal level even further, as nonverbal techniques combined with linguistic methods lend depth to the message. Paul recalls the complexity of the information that can be carried by nonverbal means. When he was about twelve years old, his older brother took him to the airport to meet their parents on an incoming flight. While waiting for the plane, they sat across from a row of doorless telephone booths, all occupied. As the young Paul scanned the line of people talking on the phones, he could tell which ones were enjoying their conversations and which were not, which were talking with people they liked or loved and which with strangers or business associates, and which were nervous about what they were saying and which were talking naturally. Paul could even speculate about who was lying or telling the truth. How much more could he have learned about those people if they had been talking to him while he maintained the same alertness to their nonverbal signals?

CONSISTENCY AND STRAIGHTFORWARDNESS

Your goal in training yourself to communicate physically will be to send clear, consistent messages. Consistency is especially important for the parents of deaf children, because confusion is inevitable when the body and the intended message contradict each other. Sometimes, when we're not in total control of our bodies or when we feel ambivalence, our body movements are inconsistent with the message we want to convey. When this happens, a deaf child may think, "His body is saying 'okay,' but his gestures are saying 'no'"; or, "His gestures are saying 'you did well,' but his eyes are saying 'you weren't good enough.'" Or, in the case of a child who can speechread, "His mouth is telling me to go ahead, but his eyes are saying 'stay here.'"

Perhaps it is too much to ask of yourself to be 100 percent consistent. However, you can learn to eliminate common sources of confusion that arise when your body comes into conflict with your message. For example, when your preschooler has a temper tantrum in the grocery store and hundreds of eyes are turned your way, you may be tempted to smile and subdue your angry gestures as you try to make it clear to the child that his behavior is totally unacceptable. You wind up smiling as you say or gesture, "You bad, bad boy," and your child misunderstands what you really mean. A clearer response would be to ignore the eyes of the world and make it very clear, with no softening of expression or gesture, that such behavior will not be tolerated. Remember, the child is not sophisticated enough to realize that you are embarrassed. He or she will think you actually mean what your physical expressions seem to say.

On the other hand, do not underestimate your child's ability to read your nonverbal signals. Remember, the child has been reading your expressions, gestures, and postures from babyhood and has become well versed in their meanings. Don't fool yourself into thinking you can hide your true feelings by smiling and patting your child on the head. The child will be able to read your unhappiness and will need reassurance—as any child needs reassurance when they perceive a parent, the child's solid rock, to be in danger of crumbling. The challenge here is to acknowledge your feelings and, at the same time, protect your child's sense of security.

PEOPLE-WATCHING

Paul's father was an avid people watcher who had a knack for reading the gestures of strangers. He would point out people and say, "Look at that woman with her arms folded across her chest. She'll never give in. She's protecting her position." Or, "Do you see how that man clings to the arm of that woman over there? He has staked his claim for the world to see. But she's looking off toward the great unknown."

Paul's parents and brothers often took him people-watching, or at least that's what he *thought* they were doing during many excursions. His parents or brothers provided commentary and showed him what to look for. The father was most interested in families, the boys talked about all kinds of people, and the mother, ordinarily the most careful to fill in details minute by minute, showed a ladylike reticence about the behavior of certain couples.

Paul recalls very clearly an incident that took place in New York City when he was nine years old, on an outing with one of his older brothers. They were sitting on a park bench watching a small boy eating candy, when the boy's sister, slightly older, approached him and demanded a share. He refused quietly and went on eating. His calm stubbornness enraged the little girl; she hit him, yelled, stamped off, and returned, again demanding a share, all to no avail. The boy finished his candy and began to play in the sandbox. For a long while afterward, the girl would come every so often back to harass her brother, talking angrily, kicking down a structure he had built in the sand, making a mean face. Paul recognized then the general principle that people's gestures and messages are not always related to what is going on at the moment. This insight represented a big jump in his understanding of the ways people communicate with each other. He was able to see that relationships between people are complex and often unfathomable even for hearing observers.

This example demonstrates how much deaf children can learn about human communication if their parents encourage them to observe. One need not be rude to "eavesdrop" on gestures, only receptive. Movies and television also offer a feast of nonverbal communication for you and your deaf child to enjoy together. By sharing your observations, you can learn from each other.

In conclusion, we would like to repeat that encouraging deaf children to communicate nonverbally will not cause them to lose interest in learning other modes of communication, like spoken language. Nonverbal communication is an *essential* complement to all modes, helping deaf children take part in the flow of ideas that is necessary to their growth and development; it is particularly important in the early years before formal language is learned. Communication in any form feeds the mind. If we silence the language of gesture, we isolate our deaf children from the world, and ourselves from them. By contrast, everybody gains if we take advantage of nonverbal communication as an opportunity to get to know our children.

Notes

1. Heather Mohay, "The Interaction of Gesture and Speech in the Language Development of Two Profoundly Deaf Children," in *From Gesture to Language in Hearing and Deaf Children,* ed. Virginia Volterra and Carol J. Erting (Washington, DC: Gallaudet University Press, 1998): 192–95.

2. Peter A. Andersen, *Nonverbal Communication: Forms and Functions,* 2nd ed. (Long Grove IL: Waveland Press, 2008): 3–4.

3. Jane Johnston and John Halocha, *Early Childhood and Primary Education: Readings and Reflections* (Berkshire, England: McGraw-Hill Education, 2010): 95.

4. Barbara Wood, *Children and Communication: Verbal and Nonverbal Language Development* (Englewood Cliffs, NJ: Prentice-Hall, 1976): 193–95.

5. Susan Goldin-Meadow, *The Resilience of Language: What Gesture Creation in Deaf Children Can Tell Us about How All Children Learn Language* (New York: Psychology Press, 2005): 221.

6. David McNeill, *Hand and Mind: What Gestures Reveal about Thought* (Chicago: University of Chicago Press, 1992): 295.

7 Communication Options: An Overview

DO YOU remember the simple adage of the deaf world quoted earlier in the book: Being deaf is not about hearing; being deaf is about communication? To many parents grappling with the impact of deafness on their child and their family, it can take a long time to understand this observation. Perhaps above all, it takes personal experience with the myriad ways being deaf can make it difficult for information to flow freely across the hearing barrier. Both you and your deaf child will experience frustration, irritation, bewilderment, anger, and loneliness as you develop the skills necessary to overcome the barrier. In the end, the process will enhance your appreciation of the paradox of communication—that it is both the most complex and the simplest of all the things we humans do. The following two quotes together capture the essence of this contradictory truth.

> Communication is at the core of our existence. Individuals thrive on their ability to convey ideas and express feelings. Concepts are formed, vocabulary expanded, values instilled, and educational horizons broadened, all through the channel of communication. For the heart of expressing oneself lies in language—the basic tool which in turn links us to our culture, home, community, and surrounding environment. By being provided with the opportunity to share our thoughts, feelings, and knowledge with others, our lives become enhanced and we are able to transmit our information base to others, thus creating a bond with previous and future generations.
> —Nanci A. Scheetz[1]

Use what language you will, you can never say anything but what you are.

—Ralph Waldo Emerson[2]

Emerson reminds us, as we turn to the subject of communication options, just what the decision is all about: giving our children a means of telling us *who they are*. They will initially depend on the mode(s) of communication we choose for them to express what they need and want to express, ask what they need and want to know, and fulfill their impulses to play, explore, experiment, and innovate. We also want you to know that this should not be an "either/or" decision.

There is no reason to choose just one modality. Many children do quite well with both signed and spoken languages. Some are better at one than the other. Also, regardless of what you as parents choose initially, in the end, it becomes your child's choice. As an example, like a lot of deaf adults who started off with spoken language in their youth, the authors now prefer to use American Sign Language (ASL) in most situations. Of course, we never lost what speech we learned initially. Spoken language is still a communication tool we use as needed with people who don't know ASL.

Deciding on the communication options that suit your child in every way is a challenging process. It requires that you educate yourself, and as you become acquainted with the options, it will be clear to you that you have to take the initiative in the beginning. During the early intervention years (from birth through the age of three), children are far too young to make their own decisions as to which modes of communication and which languages may suit them best. We can't stress enough that the most important thing to keep in mind is language acquisition. Whatever your decision, just make sure that your child is acquiring language! Without language, communication can't take place. Delayed language acquisition can have serious long term consequences for learning.

Deaf children's language expression and use has been described on two continuums: receptive, which is how children best receive it, and expressive, which is how best they express themselves. These continuums range from the fully visual sign language user to the fully auditory spoken language user (See Figure 7.1). Most are

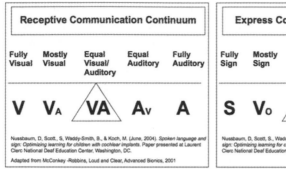
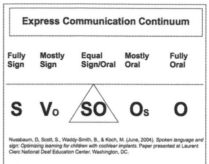

Figure 7.1. Source: From Paludneviciene and Leigh (2011), p. 194.

somewhere in between these two ends of the spectrum. For example, there are children who receive their information visually as *big V, little a,* and prefer to express themselves via sign with some emerging speech, as *big S and little o.* There are other children who may be *big A, little v* but express themselves as *big O, little s,* mostly auditory with visual support and expressive speech, with some signs for clarification.[3] Some deaf individuals, who are *VA* and *SO* on the continuum, are capable of code switching between sign and speech as the need arises. Based on the decisions you make and the resources available, your child may move along the spectrum as they grow and progress into adulthood.

During the information-gathering and decision-making period, your role as your child's ambassador to the outside world is critical. On behalf of your child, you'll need to learn about many options and consider many interacting factors. And you'll feel some very real pressure to move quickly to save your child from losing precious language acquisition time. As you begin the process, keep in mind the following considerations:

1. The communication mode you choose is less significant in itself than how well it suits your child's temperament and native skills, the family's willingness and readiness to learn and work with it, and the local resources available to support child and family.

2. Because the decision carries with it many consequences for your child and your family, it requires a full understanding of all options.
3. The advice and information you receive can be clouded by long-standing controversies about deaf children's education. Knowing about these controversies will help you step back from them and base your decision solely on the match between communication mode and your child.
4. Above all, you are the expert on your child and your family. The choice is up to you.

Our purpose in this chapter is to present you with some important background information as you begin your quest. We would like to start with a brief account of the continuing debate regarding deaf education and communication. You are about to look into a pot that has been boiling and bubbling for a long time, hundreds of years in fact.

The First Controversy

Sorting through the information and conflicting points of view surrounding modes of communication means working your way through multiple issues. Fundamental to them all and to your ultimate decision, which will affect all subsequent decisions, is the ongoing battle in education between what were traditionally known as the *oralists* and the *manualists*. The terms identifying these two approaches to the education of deaf and hard of hearing children are clues to their orientation.

The traditional term *oralists* refers to those who are committed to teaching children who are deaf or hard of hearing to communicate in *spoken language*. There was a time when oralist schools expressly forbade the use of sign language based on unfounded fears that it would inhibit speech development. To date, there is no research that proves the use of sign language inhibits speech. The anti-sign language stance has softened over the past few decades. In fact, the authors are surprised how many of the spoken language specialists today *do* know sign language. The oral approach is now more commonly called *Listening and Spoken Language*, and it promotes the development of speech skills and listening skills via either amplification of whatever residual hearing a child may have using hearing aids or by the use of cochlear implants.

The traditional term *manualists* refers to those who favor teaching children who are deaf and hard of hearing to communicate in a visual sign system. Some believe ASL should be the primary mode of communication and the child's first native language; others promote the integration of visual signs with oral communication and/or written English techniques. Today, they are more commonly identified either as ASL-English bilingual advocates or as supporters of one of the manual English systems. It will probably come as no surprise to you that a lot of deaf individuals, even those who initially started out with spoken language, advocate the use of sign language, particularly ASL.

A third option, total communication (TC), is more a philosophical approach advocating the right of each deaf student to whatever form of communication is most suitable to their needs. TC, which became widespread in the 1970s, was supposed to find a middle ground in the oral-manual disputes. It represented an alternative to the oral approach that had dominated the education of deaf people for nearly a century prior. TC is a combination of spoken language, sign language, auditory training, and visual aids; it includes anything and everything necessary to give the child access to language. Generally, the degree to which each mode is stressed depends on the particular child. One thing we want to emphasize here is that TC is *not* to be confused with simultaneous communication (Sim-Com), which is signing and voicing English at the same time, although Sim-Com is one of the TC choices that can be used.

Because the controversy between spoken language and sign language advocates can be rather intense, you are likely to meet proselytizers for both sides among parents, educators, and clinicians. People will want to convince you that their way—the way their children, students, or clients responded to with success—is the *only* way. Biased professionals may convince parents to keep their child in a program for years and years despite an obvious mismatch between child and program. Remember, keeping children in programs that are inappropriate for their needs actually holds them back from acquiring language, and thus communication, during the language acquisition years. We advise you, for this and a number of other reasons, to steer clear of hard-core advocates who won't budge. We like to think of them as being on the extreme ends of a political spectrum. As you may know, neither end really gets anything done alone as much as the ones willing to meet in the middle of the aisle.

The consequences of persisting in the mistake of blindly following a particular approach are serious. The child who fails to respond to a program but is kept in it year after year loses self-esteem and precious time in acquiring the means of communication that works for him or her. Keeping a child in a program that's not working because a doctor, teacher, or another parent tells you it ought to be working—when it is clearly not—puts the child at risk. Some even go as far as accusing the parents of not trying hard or long enough, and/or blaming the child. These professionals are highly unethical and can do serious harm by setting up a child for self-blame and deep discouragement.

The authors have met many parents who lack the confidence to disagree with their children's teachers, letting them make basic decisions about modes of communication. We've also met teachers who tell of parents so certain of the rightness of their course that they ignore the teachers' suggestions that their child be placed in another kind of program. This can happen especially when parents choose a spoken language program, because it matters to them above all that the child learn to function in the hearing world. Parents who hold this position (and some educators, too) may forbid their children to sign, reasoning that the child who can't take the "easy way out" will concentrate fully on mastering oral skills. There is no unbiased research the authors know of that has backed up this position.

To protect against dogmatic views, which are rooted less in knowledge of the individual child than in a wish for certainty, we urge you to fashion your own understanding of the issues, keeping the following pointers in mind:

1. In the beginning, try to stay open to all views, knowing as you collect information that many of your informants will pressure you to accept their perspective, sometimes citing

impressive but selective research or by parading out only their best students. (Note: When visiting a program, ask to meet as many of the children as you can. If they refuse, it is a red flag.)

2. Remember that there is no single test or assessment tool that can match individual children with the best programs for them. Given the number of variables, it is unlikely there ever will be such a test.

3. Monitor yourself for irrational loyalties to one position or another. Remember, the true test of a program is whether your child is learning to communicate, is happy in the effort, and has healthy self-esteem.

4. Support your child's educational program by fostering a home environment in which communication among all family members, including guests, is valued above everything. In this kind of environment, difficulties arising from a wrong choice, a mismatch with a particular program, or an imbalance among modes of communication are likely to be noticed early.

Inherent in the decision between spoken language and signing is the choice of what will be your child's first language. If you choose spoken language only, you are tacitly choosing English. If you choose signs only, you are choosing ASL, the native language of deaf people in America. The decision you make will have lifelong consequences for your child. Again, the authors see no reason not to try both. Being bilingual has a lot of advantages. As Yogi Berra, the Hall of Fame baseball player, famously quoted in giving directions to a friend: "When you come to the fork in the road, take it." It didn't matter which way you took, it got you to his house.[4] Our point here is that you as parents in the driver's seat are the key to getting your child to his or her destination, not so much the route taken. What is the destination? Yes, communication!

The Second Controversy

If you opt for ASL or manual English, you will need to consider the types of educational programs available to your child, and these may vary depending on the area you live in. Again, you will be faced with options, each of which has passionate proponents equipped with impressive educational philosophies and research literature. You may be surprised that you have choices in this area. After all, how many sign languages can there be? There is only one *true* language—ASL—but educators have also devised manually coded English systems. These systems are referred to with a variety of names, and, in general, they borrow and modify ASL signs to represent the vocabulary and grammar of English. The basis of the controversy here is which approach is better suited to help your child learn to become literate in written English.

Our goal in this and the next two chapters is to articulate all sides of the complex language issue, so that you can make fully informed decisions. For now, set aside the impulse to make a decision. Think of yourself as planning a trip and using these chapters as a map. Each highway leads to a number of roads, and when you drive down one, the others will become the roads not taken. Too often, parents turn impulsively down the first exit ramp without learning about alternative routes. Our hope is that with the terms defined, the various modes of communication explained, and pros and cons for each one laid down as clearly and fairly as possible, you will be ready after you read these chapters to go out into your community and evaluate the options available to you. Then you will be ready to choose and commit to a course of action.

The Options

Let's turn to specifics. We will cover the following six best-known and most widely used types of school programs available to deaf and hard of hearing children in the United States:
• ASL-English bilingual education
• cued speech,
• Listening and Spoken Language,
• Manually coded English,
• Signing Exact English (SEE II), and
• TC.

Each option is explained as thoroughly as possible, together with the pros and cons that have revealed themselves over the years. Although this book is nontechnical for the most part, we're closing this chapter with a glossary of terms. There's a lot of information to absorb, especially at first, and you may find the glossary helpful in keeping it all straight.

Glossary

American Sign Language (ASL). A sign language completely distinct from the English language in grammar, syntax, and all other aspects; it is the native language of many North American deaf people (except in Quebec).

Amplification. The use of hearing aids or cochlear implants to amplify and take advantage of residual hearing in order to give the child an opportunity to learn language through the auditory channel. Through auditory training, it is possible for deaf and hard of hearing children to learn to recognize environmental sounds and speech.

ASL-English bilingual education. A method of education that includes establishment of language foundations and access to learning through two modalities: auditory and visual, and two languages: ASL and English.

Auditory therapy. Techniques for teaching deaf and hard of hearing people to use their hearing aids or cochlear implants, with strong emphasis on visual techniques, to develop listening and speech skills.

Auditory-verbal therapy. A form of spoken language training, also known as *Listening and Spoken Language*, that teaches speech without the use of visuals and relies on auditory training and amplification.

Communication. A process through which living creatures convey information to each other; for humans, the expression of feelings and ideas and the reception of others' feelings and ideas.

Cued speech. A mode of communication that uses handshapes and placements near the mouth in combination with speech to make the phonemes of a spoken language visible.

Fingerspelling. The spelling of words with the fingers by means of manual symbols representing letters in the alphabet.

Gestures. Hand movements (not signs) and body movements used to express feelings and ideas.

Language. A formalized system agreed upon by a community of users to communicate feelings and ideas by use of signs, sounds, gestures, or marks.

Lipreading (also Speechreading). Receiving the meaning of speech by translating the movements of the speaker's lips and interpreting the contextual cues of the conversation intuitively.

Listening and Spoken Language. See *auditory-verbal therapy* above.

Manualism. A traditional term for the use of sign language in the education of children who are deaf or hard of hearing, with various levels of attention given to speech. Today, this is known as *ASL-English bilingual-bimodal education.*

Manually coded English. A system of signs presented in English word order and with special markers to represent specific syntactical features of English, and thus a means of communicating manually in English rather than in ASL.

Oralism. A traditional term for the use of speech and speechreading in the education of children who are deaf or hard of hearing. Today, this is known as *spoken language.* Children taught exclusively by the oral method generally are not permitted to use sign language during their formal educational process.

Residual hearing. The amount of hearing that a deaf or hard of hearing person possesses without amplification.

Signed English. One system of manually coded English.

Signing Exact English (SEE). One system of manually coded English.

Speech. The ability to express thoughts and feelings by the articulation of spoken sounds.

Speechreading. A more comprehensive form of lipreading that includes reading the speaker's facial expressions and posture to understand the message.

Notes

1. Nanci Scheetz, *Orientation to Deafness* (Boston: Allyn and Bacon, 1992): 99.

2. Ralph Waldo Emerson, *Emerson: Essays and Lectures*, ed. Joel Porte (New York: Library of America, 1983): 937–1124.

3. Debra B. Nussbaum and Susanne M. Scott, "The Cochlear Implant Education Center: Perspectives on Effective Educational Practices," in

Cochlear Implants: Evolving Perspectives, ed. Raylene Paludneviciene and Irene Leigh (Washington, DC: Gallaudet University Press, 2011): 194–95.

4. Allen Barra, *Yogi Berra: Eternal Yankee* (New York: W. W. Norton & Company, 2009).

8 Opportunities in Spoken Language

THE EDUCATIONAL approaches referred to collectively as *spoken language*, or by the traditional term *oralism*, teach deaf and hard of hearing children to gain access to English by learning to speak and by learning to listen with their amplified residual hearing or via cochlear implants. In "pure" oral programs, children are usually not allowed to use sign language. There are two popular oral methods, plus a third, which we include here because of its stress on the use of spoken phonemes. Each is distinguished by their emphases on certain aspects of the communication process.

1. *The auditory-oral method.* Children are taught to make maximum use of their residual hearing through amplification (hearing aids or cochlear implants), to augment their residual hearing with speechreading, and to speak. This approach has a strong visual component. The main emphasis is on speaking and comprehending a spoke language via visual and auditory means.

2. *The auditory-verbal method.* This approach is similar to the auditory-oral approach, except it does not encourage speechreading. Children are taught not to rely on visual cues and to rely mostly on their residual hearing via amplification or cochlear implants and auditory training. This approach is based on the observation that many deaf and hard of hearing children have some usable hearing. The degree of hearing they do possess is commonly referred to as *residual hearing*. Residual hearing in deaf

TABLE 8.1. CATEGORIES OF HEARING LEVELS

Hearing Level	Classification of Loss
0 to 26 dB	No loss (normal)
27 to 40 dB	Slight
41 to 55 dB	Mild
56 to 70 dB	Moderate
71 to 90 dB	Severe
91+ dB	Extreme or profound

Source: Adapted from Paul & Quigley (1989, 1990) and Ross (1986). The standards for the hearing levels are based on those of the Acoustical Society of America (1982).

people ranges from little or none (severe to profound loss) to a substantial amount (slight to moderate loss). (See Table 8.1.)

3. *Cued speech.* Some experts consider cued speech to be an oral method, although not all are convinced because of its visual components. Spoken phonemes are an essential part of this approach. Children are taught speech and speechreading, and the latter is supplemented by specific handshapes placed in specific positions to represent the vowel and consonant sounds in spoken English (see Figure 8.1). These signals do not constitute a language, but rather function in combination with spoken language to help the child "see" the pronunciation of spoken English.

In discussing these methods, we cover the first two options together; cued speech, distinguished by its system of hand signals, is covered separately in the subsequent section.

Some Cautionary Notes

Don't get us wrong here: Spoken language programs can and have worked out very well for a good number of deaf children. However, it has also been a tragedy for many others who struggled to succeed way past their critical language development periods. We are here to help you learn to be aware, including balancing your own desires with what is actually happening with your child. Ethical professionals will also let you know if your child is not doing well.

Parents who are inclined to enroll their child in an oral program tend to choose between auditory-oral and auditory-verbal methods based on the amount of hearing the child has and their own desire to have the child communicate with the hearing world. The authors understand that many parents want their child to be like them, to function as a hearing person. We also want them to know it may not be an appropriate or realistic goal for their child. In addition, parents sometimes find it difficult to commit to a mode of communication, like American Sign Language (ASL), that does not come naturally to them. The mode of communication chosen must be what is best for the child—what affords that child the greatest range of communication, matches the child's skills and natural preferences, and reinforces his or her self-esteem. This bottom line may shift as the child gets older, so you'll need to stay sensitive to that possibility. As time passes and your child grows, you may need to change schools, even communication modalities.

To some extent, the children themselves can indicate the proper choice between spoken and visual modes of communication. When children are given the chance at an early age to develop both speaking and signing skills, they usually show a preference for one or the other by the age of three or four. Parents and teachers may try to influence the preference or, in extreme cases, simply impose their own preference by teaching speech exclusively to a child with strong sign capabilities or vice versa. Yes, we have met deaf children who did better using speech than ASL, but they were usually the exception.

From the 1880s until the 1970s, almost all schools or programs for deaf and hard of hearing children in the United States were exclusively oral. It wasn't until the 1970s, after ASL was recognized as being an actual language that people began to recognize that it could help children learn English and serve as an alternative for those who did not benefit from oral programs. Today, many more people—professionals and parents alike—welcome sign language as an option or even as supplemental.

Often the first professionals parents meet in connection with their child's hearing loss are clinically oriented: doctors, audiologists, speech pathologists, and others who are more familiar with the spoken language philosophy than with other points of view. These professionals don't always realize how difficult learning to listen and speak can be for those children with a severe or profound hearing loss. Because deafness in children is still relatively rare, about one in one thousand births, most clinical professionals' exposure tends to be limited to those who have lost their hearing later in life. Keeping in mind that many professionals, including pediatricians, have limited knowledge of communication modes can protect you against undue, if well-meaning, pressure in favor of cochlear implantation and spoken language. At the top of the authors' wish list is the hope that eventually all professionals dealing with deaf individuals will be educated in the full range of communication modes and will pass on to parents their knowledge of all the available choices. Meanwhile, be warned: Many clinical professionals view implantation and spoken language as the best choice. When, in fact, it just may not be right for your child.

With that cautionary note, let's turn to the option of spoken language with clear eyes and an open mind, weighing the pros and cons as evenly as possible.

Auditory-Oral and Auditory-Verbal Programs

About 90 percent of children who are deaf or hard of hearing have hearing parents. The goal of Listening and Spoken Language programs is to give deaf and hard of hearing children access to spoken English and the hearing world. Children who succeed in learning spoken communication skills can participate in their family's native mode of communication, making it unnecessary for the family to learn sign or some other new method. At the same time, the orally trained child learns to participate in the mode and language of the society at large. That sounds like an ideal outcome, and we won't argue against that if it is best for the child. We and a good number of our deaf friends do well with spoken language.

To a certain extent, a child's chances for mastering speech, speechreading, and listening are tied to the amount of hearing he or she has. If the residual hearing is substantial, the chances for success are great, particularly among children who have learned to speak a language before their hearing loss occurred. In regards to cochlear implants, spoken language performance outcomes are usually better for those who are implanted very young. This is the time when the brain most readily masters language. For children implanted later, auditory delays may already present negative results in educational and rehabilitation challenges that are difficult to overcome.

Another crucial factor is the level of the parents' commitment and involvement in their child's program. After getting hearing aids or implants, your child will not automatically be able to hear and process spoken language. There is a big difference between being able to hear something and to make sense of it. For example, one of the authors can hear speech when wearing hearing aids, but even after years of therapy, he still has to focus intently to understand what is actually being said. For your child, it takes a great deal of time, work, and commitment, of which you are an integral part of that team. However, many other sometimes difficult-to-measure variables contribute significantly to a child's speech success (e.g., stamina, emotional stability, intelligence, tenacity, frustration level, and auditory learning strategies).

How much easier things would be if we could predict beforehand which children will truly benefit from the spoken method. Spoken language programs can be very successful for children with significant amounts of residual hearing, children who use pediatric cochlear implants, or children who have lost their hearing relatively late. However, for children with severe deafness experienced early, before basic language skills are established, success rates tend to be lower and much harder to predict than dedicated proponents of spoken language want to admit.

In their hopes for children's attainment of free-flowing spoken communication, spoken language advocates sometimes overlook the importance of healthy self-esteem, good social and emotional adjustment, and a lively social life filled with natural, spontaneous friendships. All too often, the authors have met those who struggled for years to learn speech and ended up with only a very limited ability (if any) to participate in spoken conversation. Moreover, if the program is a strict one where students are not exposed to sign language, the children will have no alternative means of communicating until later years (or until leaving the spoken language program), when they can finally learn sign. By then, they may already have serious language delays that impact their academic achievement and future ability for gainful employment. Clearly, at the core, the risk of isolating a child with no means of communication must be perceived and overcome.

Most current spoken language programs are only from early childhood to kindergarten, with the goal of mainstreaming in classrooms with their hearing peers at the beginning of elementary school. These early childhood programs may sometimes emphasize speech and auditory training at the expense of learning academic subjects. Some adults, successfully trained in spoken language, complained to the authors that their programs left them academically ill-equipped for mainstream classes; others reported that being mainstreamed in regular classes helped them compete with hearing peers on an equal footing, thus keeping them on schedule in reading, writing, and other academics. Whether your child will be ready to successfully transition academically from spoken language to a mainstream program is an issue to keep in mind in determining whether the fit between child and program is a good one.

Another drawback of spoken language programs has to do with parents' inhibitions and reluctance to gesture and to act out messages they are trying to convey. Young children just learning to speechread need their parents and teachers to convey the meanings of spoken messages in alternative ways. Parents often find that they are unable to mime with sufficient freedom along with their speech in order to get meaning across. The effort required is so great in those early years that many families fail to sustain it. Without the support of clear and constant communication, the child is unable to capture the meaning of spoken messages.

An excessive focus on speech can lead to humiliation for children who do not learn it or who achieve functional but not "perfect" speech skills. Like many deaf adults who speak, we do have what we call a nasal sounding "deaf accent." It works for us most of the time, and those around us are used to it, but others meeting us for the first time may have difficulty comprehending us. Parents who opt for spoken language, so that their children will appear to be hearing, may be setting an unrealistic goal—one that will result in a lifelong feeling of failure and shame. Many stories were conveyed to the authors of deaf children and adults who felt compelled and struggled to "pass as hearing" because of the stigma attached to being deaf.[1] Realistic parents know that there are many benefits to be had from speech programs short of achieving the fluency necessary to socialize with hearing people freely and unreservedly. They do not expect the child to become a hearing person—or to pass for one. Many children can benefit simply by acquiring the level of spoken English necessary to make themselves understood in stores and public places.

The Reading Challenge

One more risk, the greatest of all, is that the child, after years of trying unsuccessfully to master speech skills, will pass through the prime language-acquiring stage without learning any form of language. Historically, deaf people as a group have had poor reading skills, and the situation has not improved over time. Most deaf high school graduates read at a fourth-grade level, even today. Why is this so? To answer that question, we need to return to our definitions: *Language* is a symbolic system for communicating ideas and feelings; *speech* is audible language created by the mouth, tongue, voice box, and breath.

For many years, experts failed to distinguish speech from language, thinking that if one does not have speech, one does not possibly have language. Linguists have since disproven this link. Speech is just a means of expressing language—one of several. Sign language is another way to express language, and writing is yet another. A child who learns speech by imitation, or "parroting," does not automatically learn language. Have you ever learned the lyrics to a song in a foreign language that you didn't understand? Or learned English lyrics without paying any attention to their meaning? Your lack of comprehension doesn't necessarily affect how well you sing the song, especially if you are a good imitator and have a good model. The principle here is the same: Deaf children who have never heard spoken language can learn to imitate it without understanding it. However, it is impossible to speechread without understanding the language, because the guesswork requires a working knowledge of vocabulary and grammar; only 50 percent of the sounds we use are visible on the lips and mouth. Language acquisition involves learning the meanings of words and learning the accepted ways of putting words together to make messages that others will understand. Imitating language, then, is a separate activity from learning to speak meaningfully.

Children not properly exposed to language from an early age often fail not only to read and write well but also to speak *and* understand, which are the main objectives of spoken language training. Like a person taught the motions of swimming but kept from the water, these children never quite gain control of the medium. But whereas the swimmer can learn, eventually, to stay afloat, language is so complex, with so many parts and rules, that children not immersed in it early often lose heart. If children are not encouraged, they can remain perpetually bewildered. You need to keep in mind and always remember that every word deaf children learn, if not already naturally acquired, must be taught until they know language well enough to use a dictionary. The same holds true for every rule, every technique for changing forms of words, every tense, every mood, every one of a thousand explicit details that give hearing children headaches in grammar lessons. Somehow these details all must be made clear to deaf children, starting at the beginning of their lives. English is a highly complex language with rules that have many exceptions that many hearing children acquire naturally but still need teaching in its intricacies as they grow older.

So word pronunciation, itself a daily challenge for a deaf child, is only one aspect of spoken communication. The even more demanding aspects relate to understanding language. Learning to read and write is totally dependent on language comprehension. In assessing a spoken language program that you are considering for your child, you must assure yourself that the teachers teach *language* as well as speech. Otherwise, your child may learn to imitate a series of sounds without being able to form intelligible messages. An equally serious risk is that the child will never come to feel at ease with the written word. To a deaf person, the ability to read means independence, the freedom to gather information at will without relying on others for instruction. No matter what program parents choose, they must make sure their deaf children learn to read and write. Think about this: Two deaf individuals who succeeded at literacy wrote the book you are reading.

Irene's Wish List

Paul's friend Irene lost her hearing at the age of ten months when she got chicken pox from her older brother. At the age of eighteen months, she was identified as severely hard of hearing, although, in fact, she bordered between hard of hearing and deaf.

Irene was raised in the oral tradition and mastered oral skills with great success. She was asked to reflect on her upbringing for this chapter, and she wrote the following piece as an open letter to parents of deaf children who are learning to communicate in the oral mode.

> I want to start by identifying the strongest part of my upbringing, for which I'm very grateful: My family helped me develop a strong work ethic. Very early, I learned the importance of working hard and becoming independent and successful. For example,
>
> - I shared family chores and responsibilities from a very young age.
> - I worked part-time in high school.
> - I got my driver's license when I turned sixteen.
> - I opened my own checking account at seventeen.

Although my parents rarely said this in so many words, their fostering of my independence was a means of expressing their love, caring, and confidence. Still, things could have been much easier for me if my parents had had a clearer understanding of the effects of being deaf on communication. My worst dilemma stemmed from the fact that because I had learned to speak and lipread well, everyone, including my family, assumed that I was able to follow group discussions, conversations between other people, and any kind of communication that didn't include me. That put a lot of pressure on me, because those sorts of exchanges are very difficult for me to follow—I never know where to look first. People assumed that I would pick up everything automatically with the help of my hearing aids, but that was far from the case. It was as if I had no limitations. Some members of my family would get very impatient with me when I missed out on some of the conversation. Their impatience hurt me many times.

Because they assumed that I was able to function well, my family didn't see me as a deaf person or a person who has some limitations when it comes to rapid verbal communication. To them, I was a hearing person. It was very difficult for me to deal with such unrealistically high expectations. My family scorned sign language and deaf people in general. Because being deaf was and is part of my identity, my parents' rejection of other deaf people really hurt.

Many deaf children who have been raised using spoken language share common experiences. Here is my wish list for all parents of these deaf children:

1. *Just because your child speaks well, don't assume that he or she will pick up everything automatically in any social exchange or in family conversations.* Take time to explain things and allow your child to ask questions and discuss anything that isn't clear.

2. *Don't try to separate deafness from your child.* Although you may wish you could "throw deafness out" forever, that would be throwing out a central aspect of the child's personality. Encourage your child to have as many deaf friends as possible and make sure there are deaf role models in his or her life. My parents always made me feel that I was superior to deaf people I met—they felt that deaf people would be a bad influence and discouraged me from mingling with them. As a result, I developed a very bad attitude toward deaf people in general. It took me a long time to get over that.

3. *Take active steps to become involved in the Deaf community, and make a real effort to socialize with deaf adults.* Right now, with your child young and impressionable, you have the chance to widen his or her horizons by networking and becoming involved with parent groups. Introduce the child to living, breathing examples of successful, creative, and productive deaf adults. Don't confine your child within the boundaries of the hearing world.

4. *Don't brainwash your child about sign language and Deaf culture, both of which are essential to the identity of every deaf or hard of hearing child.* Although I am not fluent in ASL, it plays an important part in my life. It gives me a cultural identity and cultural pride. The time may come when your child will want

to learn sign language and meet Deaf people. Don't create unnecessary ambivalence in the child by perpetuating biases about Deaf people, sign language, and Deaf culture.

5. *Don't correct your child's speech in public.* Do this at home or in private. I was humiliated every time my father corrected my speech in front of others.

6. *When your family socializes with other people, make sure those others have a healthy attitude toward your child's deafness.* Educate them! Don't leave your child to do the work or to experience their sheer ignorance. This can be painful.

7. *At big social events involving lots of people, don't forget to check with your child to make sure he or she feels included and knows what's going on.* When my extended family gets together for a reunion, they tend to forget that I don't follow everything. For example, when my father tells a joke, he talks slowly at first to make it easy for me to follow—until he comes to the punch line. This he says very fast, and everybody roars with laughter while I'm wondering why I missed the best part of the joke. Then—it never fails—somebody asks, "Why didn't you listen more carefully?"

8. *Don't simplify communication with your deaf child.* I'm always wishing that some members of my family would spend more time talking with me instead of keeping the conversation short and trivial. Every time we get together, I try to carry on an extended conversation, but unfortunately, most of my family members are doers rather than talkers. Deaf people as a group value communication more consciously than hearing people. It is for this reason that I feel so close to them—a line of reasoning my family has difficulty understanding. So I hope you'll spend a lot of time talking with your children and encourage them to ask questions and discuss things with you. It will be a big part of their education.

9. *Help the whole family—including all siblings of every age—to understand and participate in communication with the deaf child.* Otherwise they may feel resentful, envious, or left out. My parents were so wrapped up in my education that they never explained to other members of the family why they spent so much time with me and spent so much effort getting me

private tutors, speech lessons, and so forth. Communication should be a family matter.

10. *Beware of two serious misconceptions about deaf or hard of hearing people who speak well:*

a. *Myth #1:* The child's level of speech clarity reflects his or her command of the English language.

b. *Myth #2:* The child's level of speech clarity reflects his or her level of intelligence. These two myths do incalculable damage. Research shows that there is no relationship among speech intelligibility, intelligence, and language mastery.[2] Parents, teachers, and professionals must monitor each area separately, searching for trouble spots—and for educational solutions that match the child's particular needs and skills. My own experience illustrates this. Because I was bright and my speech was clear, my parents and teachers would not accept the fact that I was having trouble with writing skills and with English in general. Therefore, I never got the special training I needed. ❏

This is not to say that the child will be unable to learn signing later. Many deaf adults told the authors of seeing orally trained children come alive when they finally learn sign language. We had parents tell us they were shocked or amazed how much more information their child was sharing. Often the children become so animated that one wonders what was happening to all that vitality during the course of oral training.

CONCLUSIONS

To sum up, the disadvantages of spoken language all stem from the difficulty of learning speech skills, which many deaf children struggle to master. Parents considering this route need to assess the chances of their child's success based on the following:

• the amount of hearing the child has,

• the etiology of the hearing loss, which may indicate possible audiological or neurological difficulties,

- when the onset of deafness occurred (before or after the child was exposed to spoken English),
- the child's individual learning abilities,
- the child's psychological sturdiness in the face of challenges,
- the amount of parental support and willingness to be consistent with expectations, and
- other disabilities.

The advantages of spoken language when it succeeds are that it enables the child to communicate within the family without requiring the family to learn a completely different language or mode of communication, and it equips the child with the skills necessary to communicate in the language of the larger society.

There's no easy formula to determine whether a child will respond to speech training. Based on the hundreds of conversations with deaf people the authors have conducted, we know it *can* work, and we also know it *can* be a disaster. That's where careful monitoring comes in. The same is true for any route you choose: You'll need to stay attuned to your child's progress, compare it with that of other children of the same age (always respecting and acknowledging your child's uniqueness), network with other families of deaf children to learn from their experiences, and consider whether the chosen program is giving your child better access to the outside world and the best possible opportunity for free expression. And remember, an ethical professional will always be honest with you if your child is not progressing well.

Cued Speech

In 1967, Dr. R. Orin Cornett invented cued speech with the idea of enabling those who cannot hear spoken language to clearly see all of its phonemic components (individual sounds). The desired outcome was proficiency in understanding spoken language and to ultimately provide them with literacy skills needed for academic success. Because cued speech is sound-based and not language dependent, it has since been adapted to work with many other spoken languages besides English.

Cued speech is not a mode of communication in itself but rather a communication tool, consisting of eight handshapes performed close to the mouth, chin, and neck to show the speechreader which vowels or consonants are being spoken. These signals, usually used by adults to help children learn speechreading, serve to make speech sounds (not words or phrases) visible, thereby enabling the children to differentiate sounds that look the same on the lips (see Figure 8.1). For example, think about this for a minute: Without cues, the words *muff, buff,* and *puff* look exactly the same on the lips. With cues, all three words are easily distinguished. Cued speech users say that 50 percent of the information they receive comes from lipreading and 50 percent from the cues.

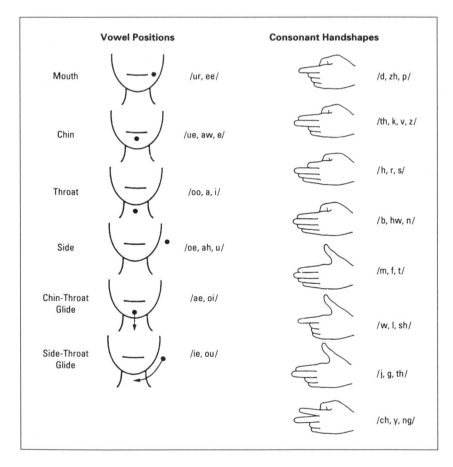

Figure 8.1. Cued speech vowel and consonant code. Source: Adapted from Bornstein (1990), pp. 141–42.

One advantage of cued speech is that it can be easily integrated with other communication modes. Furthermore, because it is based on units of sound (phonemes), not of meaning, it can be adapted to any spoken language or dialect. Because cued speech signals have no inherent meanings of their own (they must be used in conjunction with lipreading), they are useful primarily to help children who know English to learn to speechread English. Cued speech can also be used to represent onomatopoeias (e.g., sounds things make, such as cat "meows" or cow "moos") and to dramatize the rhythm and rhyme of spoken English. With the hand signals supplementing and drawing attention to these qualities, deaf and hard of hearing partners in conversation are more able to appreciate the fun of tongue twisters (known by cuers as *finger tiers*), nonsense words, idiomatic expressions, and plays on the sounds and similarities of words.

Perhaps the most widely appreciated advantage of cued speech is that it is easier to learn for people who know English than is sign language. Most people who grasp the phonetic basis of the language (the sound units the words are based on) can learn the handshapes and positions of cued speech within eight to fourteen hours. This makes it particularly attractive to people who lose their hearing as adults. Because they are long past the years when the brain most easily learns language (that developmental stage ends at about age five), they are likely to have a struggle learning any new language, whatever their general level of intellectual competence. However, as was noted earlier, young children just learning oral skills can also benefit markedly from cued speech both in speechreading and in learning to speak, because the cued speech signals draw attention to speech sounds at the word and phrase levels.

Depending on where they live, children who learn cued speech in special programs and then mainstream into regular classrooms generally have access to cued speech transliterators. These transliterators repeat with cues everything said in the classroom (much like a sign language interpreter), so that the students can speechread, listen, and watch the cues, which give them access to every letter, syllable, and word.

Ryan's Story: Cued Speech

Ryan is a cued speech teacher's dream: He speaks freely and interacts well in the hearing world. He's a successful electrical engineer working for a small business, is profoundly deaf, and seems to be living confirmation of the link some people see between superior oral or cued speech skills and ambition in the workplace (no research has proved this link, however).

But the most significant factor in Ryan's success has nothing to do with cued speech or residual hearing: It is the positive personal and social adjustment that stems from a warm, happy, supportive family life. Ryan's parents took care not only to make language available early but also to foster strong self-esteem in Ryan and reinforce his sense of belonging. After enrolling him in a cued speech program at the beginning of his school years, both his parents and his two older sisters learned to cue with him. His hearing loss was severe, but with cueing, he picked up speech easily. Surprisingly, he also had a natural talent for playing the piano, which his family also encouraged.

In interviews with Ryan, he said he didn't consider cued speech right for everybody. "It was pure good luck that the first program I was in matched my natural leanings. But I'm sure that if I hadn't done well, my parents would have pulled me out and tried something else. They weren't married to cued speech. They just wanted me to be able to fulfill my communication potential. I'm guessing, but I think they would have tried a total communication program next." Ryan asked the authors to caution parents who read this book to watch their children's progress in school carefully and pull their children out of *any* program to try something else if the child doesn't make good progress in the first six months or so.

Ryan doesn't cue any more but does consider cued speech to be the factor that enabled him to catch up with his hearing peers in language development. Without the cued speech program and the support of his family—his mother, in particular, was very dramatic and loved cueing everything that was said—Ryan says, "there's no way I would have absorbed the structure of English. Cued speech helped me to 'see' the speech and environmental sounds that others hear. And it helped build my English for speech and reading, which means it contributed hugely to my whole quality of life. Sure, I caught up—but I also took off. Very early, I learned that if there was anything I needed to know, I could find it in a book. That's a jewel of a lesson that many people, deaf or hearing, never learn."❏

Classroom exposure to cueing can be a great advantage to students who have developed excellent listening skills, either through years of intensive auditory training or through a natural ability to pick up amplified speech sounds. Cued speech in the classroom is also helpful to children in oral-aural programs who are more visual than auditory. The visual cues may serve to convey the speech sounds the children would otherwise miss.

Informal interviews and discussions with successful students who use cued speech revealed that it can help a great deal with difficult phonemes (e.g., *s, g, ch, x, st,* and *g,* and the cluster *m, p,* and *b,* which all look the same on the lips). One student said that, as part of his efforts to develop his residual hearing, he practiced listening skills by taking his eyes off the teacher's lips and watching only the cues. Others said cued speech helped them with reading and spelling through phonics (sounding out).

Older students have said that cued speech helped them become stronger readers whether or not they were confident speakers. Through their exposure to cued speech, they learned to recognize and enjoy the subtleties, humor, and intricacies of the sounds of English—rhymes, puns, vocal imitations, and word jokes of all kinds. They could appreciate a level of spoken language that oral deaf people skilled in speechreading may miss. And those who were strong speakers found cued speech helpful in adding to all their oral skills, allowing them to learn new words phonetically more quickly and easily than through traditional speech therapy programs, discriminate with more certainty among phonemes, and refine the articulations and vocalizations that constitute clear speech.

Perhaps the chief disadvantage of cued speech is its lack of public awareness and widespread acceptance. It is sort of the "neglected stepchild" of deaf education. Not only is it not integrated into many programs where it could potentially enhance instruction and skill learning, but also the number of professionally trained cued speech transliterators is still relatively small. This means that it could be hard to follow up on a cued speech program with the benefits of a transliterator in a mainstream classroom. Equally important, adult deaf and hard of hearing users of cued speech who could serve as role models to show its value are still relatively rare. This could be because cued speech was meant to improve receptive skills, not to be a means of expressing language. Many, like Ryan, who used cued speech in childhood, stop using it as adults. You will probably never see two deaf adults cueing with each other.

On the technical level, although cued speech relies on very few hand signals, plus you have to break every word down into phonemes, some people—both adults and children—find it difficult to learn, because they never quite catch on to thinking phonetically. Parents in this category rarely follow through with the practice necessary to gain facility in cueing; however, many of them continue to send their children to cued speech programs, and the more their children use and rely on cueing, the more the non-cueing parents are left out of the communication loop. Cued speech teachers and transliterators often wind up as the child's key communicators.

Not everyone can think in phonetics, but all parents need to communicate with their children. The point is to open parent–child communication, not to close it. If you think you will be unable to follow through with cued speech, we strongly urge you to choose another option. The children who have trouble grasping cued speech also frequently have difficulty developing spoken language skills. By careful monitoring of children's progress, parents can avoid losing time that might more fruitfully be spent in learning sign language. Here, we'd like to make a special point and underscore it: Never commit to a program of cued speech—or any program, for that matter—without building in frequent evaluations and parent–teacher conferences. Stay alert to your child's progress, and if there is none, reconsider. Making a turn onto a dead-end street with the mode of communication you commit your child to is not an unusual occurrence and not the real problem. It is failing to notice and making the necessary U-turn in your course of action that can cause trouble down the line. *We cannot emphasize this point enough!*

In the cued speech classroom, much depends on the ability of the transliterator. Professionally trained transliterators are hard to come by, so some of the transliterators who claim to be proficient may be less than fully adept. Be sure to ask if they have professional credentials from organizations recognized by the National Cued Speech Organization. Those cued speech transliterators with inadequate training or experience have trouble matching the pace of the speaker whose English they are cueing. If a transliterator falls too far behind, the children become confused. Observers have noted that cued speech transliterators who become overwhelmed by all that's going on in the classroom tend to skip words or even whole sentences. But skipping bits of language defeats the whole purpose of cued speech. The value of the cues is in simply "being there" as phonemic reference points when the children need them.

In the Deaf community at large, there is a lot of skepticism about cued speech and the philosophy behind it. For one thing, although cued speech teachers, transliterators, and parents cue to the children, very few children cue back. In this sense, cued speech is something of a one-way street. Cued speech was developed as a speechreading aid, and it has been used largely in oral programs. Children have been taught how to "read" it, but not to use it when they speak. Also, in many mainstreamed programs—that is, regular classrooms where deaf and hard of hearing students are integrated—their teachers and hearing peers do not cue at all. One young woman interviewee felt that because cueing looks so different from sign language (which the public tends to recognize

Amy's Story: Cued Speech

Amy works for the IRS as an auditor. She signs and speaks in a very calm—and calming—manner, as if she's perfectly content in all she does. She's married to a hearing man and has no children. Her husband is only fair at signing, but Amy is an excellent speechreader.

When she was three, Amy's parents learned about cued speech, which was just emerging as "an alternative to the oral method." They became enthusiasts. "It wasn't easy to learn it," Amy said, "but both my parents and all my teachers cued with and to me all the time. I responded by speaking, lipreading, and listening through the school's advanced amplification system. Off campus, I wore hearing aids."

Even so, things slipped by Amy. "I was a passive learner, meaning I was receptive, I picked things up. But I missed things, too, and couldn't work up the confidence or whatever it takes to be an expressive speaker. Everybody else kept making a big fuss over my progress, though, so I just went along with it, trying my best.

"Sometimes I loved cued speech, sometimes I hated it. On the hate side was the hour-after-hour, day-after-day, year-after-year drudgery of speech and speechreading training. The results just didn't justify the time and energy that went into it all. I'm still self-conscious about speaking with hearing people, especially groups of hearing people. One-on-one I do fine, but groups. . . . What a nightmare."

In middle school, for the first time Amy met deaf students who signed. She felt an instant rapport with them. "I loved learning to sign, especially Signed English. As soon as I started, I knew I was going to like using sign language interpreters instead of cued speech transliterators. My parents took it very hard, but since my speech was good enough for them by then, they let me have my way. The funny thing is, when I look back on those times, I realize that most of the kids I knew who learned cued speech in their early years gave it up for sign language as soon as they reached middle school. It seems so strange to me now, looking back, to think of us all learning cues. I just wish I could have started out from the beginning in a total communication program where I would have learned to sign *and* speak and lipread. All that effort! All that work! It just doesn't seem fair to make kids work that hard.

"And the terrible part, if you think about it, is that I did pretty well at learning cued speech. Lots and lots and lots of kids go through that and never pick it up. Because they aren't allowed to sign—teachers and parents tell them to put their hands away before they'll talk to the kids at all—so the ones who aren't able to learn oral skills don't have *any* way of communicating. That's the awful risk of an oral program."

In high school, Amy met Ronny, who was in the sign language club along with a number of other hearing students. "I fell in love with him for a lot of reasons: He was quiet and hated crowds, he was a man of few words, and he worked to keep up on his signing, so he could interpret for me sometimes when we couldn't avoid being in groups. Seeing Ronny interpret in sign language still flips my parents out, but they're getting used to it now. They just always wanted me to be a complete oral success, and when I was slow at feeling comfortable about speaking, they thought, 'Just one more year at school and she'll be really good at speech and speechreading.'"

What would be on Amy's wish list if she could go back and change her education? "If only my parents had understood that I worked hard, but I didn't really have a flair for oral skills, even with the help of cued speech. I just wish I could have avoided all that and found signing earlier, which seemed so natural to me right away."

Amy's reference to "flair" is consistent with the useful way that some professionals think about oral skills: that it is a natural proclivity, like a talent for playing the piano. Some intelligent, deeply insightful people have no flair for speech skills

whatsoever, whereas some with only a superficial understanding of the world are impressive speakers and speech-
readers. The difficulty, as with piano playing, is that there's
no way to tell beforehand who will have that flair. Some cued
speech advocates suggest that there are criteria for success,
such as the cause of the hearing loss and the age of onset, the
range of sounds affected, the age at which the child is fitted
with an appropriate hearing aid and begins auditory training
to develop residual hearing, and the extent of the family's
support. To date, however, no means of predicting success at
cued speech has proved reliable.❏

for what it is), it should be used in speech therapy programs rather
than in the general population. "It is embarrassing," she said. "It
made me different, which is terrible in school. Nobody wants to
be different. And everybody was always asking me about cueing."

CONCLUSIONS

Although the authors have seen a good number of personal success
stories of cued speech and even shared one here, to date, there is
some, but not much, research evidence showing that cued speech
improves the acquisition of literacy skills in deaf or hard of hearing
children learning *English*. There is good evidence that it facilitates
learning French. It appears that French, Spanish, and Italian have
very regular sound-to-spelling correspondence, whereas English
does not. However, cued English clearly facilitates speech reception and may support literacy subskills for some deaf or hard of
hearing children and especially those with early cochlear implantation; however, the conclusion is that English is simply too irregular
for it to be of use with cued speech for literacy.[3]

Many parents choose cued speech in the hope that it will help
their children speak more clearly, yet there is no guarantee of that
result. The jury is still out on the question of why some children
improve their speech through a combination of spoken language
and cueing and some do not.

Two Stories of Spoken Language

In the following two stories of "oral successes," we leave the conclusions up to you. These are simply two sets of experiences whose outcome depended very much on the individuals involved. Remember: In assessing your options and evaluating programs, it is not your job to determine which approach is most appropriate and effective, period, but which is most effective and appropriate for your child, in his or her uniqueness.

John's Story

John's parents had high ambitions for all five of their children, and John's profound deafness did not alter their faith in education as a road to professional success. In deciding on a course of education, John's parents cared more about academics than philosophical orientation. They wound up choosing a new, vigorous spoken language program at a private school in a neighboring county, one with a stated commitment to academic excellence and the scores to back it up.

John entered the school at age five and stayed there through the eighth grade, when he mainstreamed into the local public high school. Students in the spoken language program were required to communicate with each other solely through speech and speechreading while at school. No sign language was taught—and no signing was permitted, even on the playground. Despite their teachers' vigilance, John and his friends regularly engaged in nonverbal exchanges in addition to speaking; however, by the sixth or seventh grade, they had developed a strong grasp of English and were writing poems on their own, even experimenting with rhyme. Through it all, they never questioned the spoken language approach and, following their teachers' lead, felt "superior" to the signing deaf people they occasionally came across. At best, the oral students felt sorry for sign language users; at worst, they ridiculed and looked down on them as less accomplished academically and socially.

John did well in the public high school. Very often, he missed information in class, but his brother and sisters helped him there, and by and large, he sailed through his four high school years. He chose a hearing college where he would meet the same academic challenges faced by hearing people. There, for the first time, John felt intensely that his communication skills were limited. Most of the classes were conducted as seminars, and John had trouble following group discussions. In addition, the reading assignments were dauntingly long and complex.

Still, with hard work and aggressive questioning, John did well at college. A sociable sort, he was exhilarated by the range of people he met there. He continually sharpened his speech skills with them and then went on to graduate school in Washington, DC, at Gallaudet University, the world's only liberal arts college for deaf people. There, in a surge of concentrated effort, he learned sign language. He then went into business with his father, becoming a well-respected executive. Mostly, he relied on his oral skills for doing business, but in group meetings, he used a sign language interpreter to convey both sides of the conversation by signing to him and speaking to the hearing conversants.

John felt completely at home in the hearing world, enjoying his accomplishments and the role he played as an emissary from the mysterious land of deaf people to his hearing friends and colleagues. He was grateful for his parents' insistence on academic excellence above all things and equally glad that their scrupulous search had led them to an effective spoken language education. He attributed his comfort in the hearing world to a combination of strong speech skills, native intelligence, and hard work. Although he had entered the Deaf community belatedly, as a young man, he considered the trade-off worthwhile and, for the sake of his speech skills, wouldn't have had it any other way.

Sandra's Story

Sandra's parents were committed to spoken language from the beginning. As soon as the doctor confirmed that Sandra was deaf, they enrolled in a correspondence course for the parents of deaf and hard of hearing preschoolers. They strictly enforced a no-signing rule in their home and sent Sandra, at age five, to a residential spoken language school. She was homesick and discouraged from the start, and spent a lot of time watching television with the other young children not advanced enough in their oral training to speak with each other.

Sandra became shy and was slow to acquire speech skills. Still, she wanted very much to please her parents, so she worked diligently at speech and speechreading. Kept from signing, she remained committed to perfecting and relying on her spoken language skills all through school and college.

In her last year of college, Sandra visited Rose, a former teacher at her school who invited her to observe at the school where she was now teaching. This school advocated the total communication (TC) philosophy, integrating speech, signing, and auditory skills. After the visit, the two went out to lunch, and when they were seated in the restaurant, to Rose's great surprise, Sandra began to cry.

"What is it? Have I done something wrong?" asked Rose.

"I resent you so much," said Sandra, after gaining control of herself. "I resent you for denying me the right to be a deaf person."

"What?" exclaimed Rose. "How on earth did I do that?"

"You never let me sign—no one did. You made me believe that signing was a weakness, dirty almost, a symbol of failure. I can understand my parents doing that, because they didn't know. But you—you were trained, you learned what being deaf was about. Now I see you signing with the kids in your school—and they're having such a great time learning and being with each other. It is not the struggle for them that it was for me. They don't feel weak, as if part of them were missing that they were trying to replace by learning to speak. You denied me the right to relax, and I still don't fit in anywhere. I'm not really a hearing person. I miss a lot of what's said; I still struggle hard to understand. I'm not comfortable with hearing people, because I miss so much. And now, though I'm learning to sign, I'm not comfortable with signing friends, because I miss a lot with them, too. I just don't fit in anywhere."

Some might argue, "Sandra will see that the delay was worthwhile, because she'll have the skills to enter both worlds, not just one or the other. Had she been allowed to learn to sign earlier, she might never have learned to speak well enough to explain her resentment to Rose." Others will argue, "Sandra missed out on many learning opportunities, had a miserable childhood, and will probably never be as fluent in ASL as she could have been if she learned early." The authors have seen both sides of this coin, and one interesting bit of research we found out is that children who acquired strong spoken language skills *early* in life and learned ASL later were *almost* as fluent as those who learned it early, but *not quite.* Those who learned language, spoken or signed, after the critical early period of acquisition were generally weak overall in both.[4] We've already made the point, and will continue to do so, that early language success, spoken and signed, equates to success in many other areas of life.

We offer these real-life stories as examples only, not as the only two possible outcomes of a spoken language education. Perhaps their greatest value to you, as a parent at this crossroads of your child's future, is in showing just how significant this first choice can be. Decisions about language made early in a child's life can have lifelong consequences. It is not possible for you to see into the future, but we hope these and the other case studies we present will help you anticipate possible outcomes and reflect on how they might affect your child.

Notes

1. Brenda Jo Brueggemann, *Lend Me Your Ear: Rhetorical Constructions of Deafness* (Washington DC: Gallaudet University Press, 1999), 38–41.

2. Susan Maller, "Intellectual Assessment of Deaf People," in *Oxford Handbook of Deaf Studies, Language, and Education,* ed. Marc Marschark and Patricia Spencer (New York: Oxford University Press, 2003): 451–63.

3. Jacqueline Leybaert and Jésus Alegria, "The Role of Cued Speech in Language Development," in *The Oxford Handbook of Deaf Studies, Language, and Education,* 2nd ed., ed. Marc Marschark and Patricia Spencer (New York: Oxford University Press, 2011): 276–89.

4. Rachel Mayberry, "Early Language Acquisition and Adult Language Ability: What Sign Language Reveals about the Critical Period for Language," in *The Oxford Handbook of Deaf Studies, Language, and Education,* 2nd ed., ed. Marc Marschark and Patricia Spencer (New York: Oxford University Press, 2011): 281–91.

9 Opportunities in Visual Language

BECAUSE THE choices are so fundamental and have such great life consequences for your child, let's briefly review the controversies concerning the *modes of communication* and the *language* or *languages* the child will learn.

Controversy 1: Spoken vs. Visual Modes of Communication

Your first choice is between educational programs centering on spoken or visual languages. Most parents who choose speech are convinced that it is important for their children to learn the preferred mode of hearing society (i.e., spoken English). They want their children to speak, speechread, and use their residual hearing without any dependence on signs at all. In keeping with this point of view, many oral programs discourage the use of the hands (gestures) to convey information and even prohibit signing.

Visual language programs, on the other hand, emphasize the importance of learning language and communication over the modality of speech. The proponents of signed language believe that children who learn sign are able to communicate sooner and more fluently at early ages, because they are learning language, than those who rely only on speech. Further, because speech skills are hard for deaf and hard of hearing people to master, visual language proponents point to the risk that a child who has struggles in a spoken language program will wind up with no real language base. Such a child would have to begin learning sign at a late age, after the critical language-acquiring years, resulting in serious communication and learning delays.

In Chapter 8, you read about the spoken language choices available and the pros and cons associated with each. Here, we will fill in the visual side of the spectrum. But first, let's take a side trip to controversy number two.

Controversy 2: ASL vs. Manually Coded English

Major life choices are rarely easy or straightforward. The road not taken beckons us no matter what we choose, and the road we *do* follow quickly presents us with forks of its own. Such is the case with manual communication. To understand the options it presents, you will need to immerse yourself in what the authors call *the second controversy*. Which particular visual approach should your child learn to sign—Signed English or American Sign Language (ASL)? Each of these choices is supported by compelling arguments and enthusiastic proponents.

First, let's review the following definitions:

- *American Sign Language* is the native language of Deaf people in America, passed down from Deaf adults or parents to children and from these children to their peers who have hearing parents.

- *Manually Coded English* is signing based on English. Systems of manually coded English consist of signs that represent English words arranged according to English grammar and syntax. Manually Coded English is meant to be used simultaneously with spoken English. Keep in mind that Manually Coded English is *not* a true language, like ASL, but is an artificially contrived system of communication. It is modeled on English grammar or syntax, with visual components from ASL.

If you decide that your child will learn to sign English—which, if you are a hearing parent, is likely to be your own native language—then you'll need to choose among several systems for rendering English into sign. The three most widely used are Signing Exact English (SEE II), Signed English, and English-based signing.

Some people consider cued speech to be a form of manual communication. It is important to note that this is a misunderstanding. Cued speech is a visual tool that helps deaf and hard of hearing people learn the phonology of spoken language, not a language itself. ASL and Manually Coded English, on the other hand (excuse the pun!), function through signs.

Choosing a program in one form of signing often means excluding the others (again, some programs teach both ASL and Manually Coded English, with varying emphases). The choice has some important consequences for your relationship with your child. If you choose a manually coded English program, your child will learn the vocabulary of ASL but with the syntax or grammar of the primary language of hearing society. This means that you will also need to learn how to sign in English word order but will not need to fully learn ASL, which has its own vocabulary and grammar.

If you choose a program that includes ASL, it is likely to be a bilingual-bimodal program. In these programs, children learn ASL with spoken or written English as a simultaneous language, with emphasis on Deaf culture and the culture of the American people in general. An essential feature is that each language is recognized as distinct and used differently. English is *not* relegated to secondary status, because Deaf people do value it as a communication tool, especially with reading and writing. With this approach, your child will gain access to the Deaf community and the sense of belonging that it entails, but will also learn English in order to gain access to general society. (We'll return to these programs in more detail in Chapter 11.)

Most deaf children do not learn ASL early in life, because most have hearing parents. It is usually in families where at least one parent is Deaf (and both parents signing) that children acquire ASL from birth, and it is on the basis of this natural process that ASL is understood to be the native language of the American Deaf community. If you decide your child should learn ASL, you will need to start at square one, learning not a system of signed English but rather a complete language with its own vocabulary, structure, grammar, and mode of expression. Having fluent deaf adults as role models for you and your child will facilitate this process.

"What? Another Language?"

It happens all the time: Hearing parents set out with the best intentions to immerse themselves in ASL without fully realizing that it is a complete language *utterly distinct from English.* ASL is the native language of American Deaf people, passed down from Deaf parents to their Deaf children, and spread "horizontally" through the community by social and academic interactions between those native signers and other Deaf people, both children and adults. ASL has evolved within the boundaries of the Deaf community, and simultaneously, as all native languages do, it has become a major defining factor for that community. In other countries, Deaf communities have developed their own signed languages, distinct from the native languages of the hearing populations of those countries and just as distinct from ASL.

Bob Paul, a well-known Deaf professor at a community college in Illinois, describes ASL succinctly:

> It is a visual-gestural language created by deaf people . . . . The units of ASL are composed of specific movements and shapes of hands and arms, eyes, face, head, and body posture. These movements . . . serve as the words and intonations of the language . . . [and] since ASL uses body movements instead of sound, listeners or receivers use their eyes instead of their ears to understand what is being said. And because all linguistic information must be received through the eyes, the language is carefully structured to fit the needs and capabilities of the eyes.

ASL and Manually Coded English: How They Differ

In none of its elements is ASL even remotely similar to English. It even has a different structure and grammar. English-speaking observers knowing only the vocabulary meaning of signs alone would need a tremendous amount of guesswork to sense the meaning in a rapid ASL exchange, much as they would if they had memorized, say, a substantial vocabulary list in Russian and tried to follow a discussion in that language.

Signed English and SEE II, on the other hand, reflect English, particularly English sentence structure. Both follow the structure of the language precisely and use sign markers to indicate such changes as tense and number. SEE II and Signed English use many ASL signs, with the addition of markers and fingerspelling for affixes (additions to base words), such as *-ing* and *-ed.*

ASL itself has few signs for the markers that express tense and condition. Rather, it relies more on certain specific facial expressions, body movements, and contextual cues to convey this information. Facial expression and body language also carry the meaning of modifiers in ASL. For example, to express "I walk carefully," the ASL user signs ME and WALK only, using a specific facial expression, mouth shape, and body position to convey "carefully." Varying any of these three markers could alter the meaning to "warily" or "clumsily," for instance. Finally, ASL users depend on facial expressions and body language to replace voice intonation, which for a hearing person carries the tone and most of the meaning of the spoken message.

For years, the significance of these subtle but meaningful facial and body movements escaped non-ASL-using observers, which accounts, in part, for the fact that ASL was long considered too simplistic to warrant study as a real language. Observers were missing a significant portion of the messages by failing to recognize various movements and expressions as meaningful parts of the language.

Many native ASL users consider Manually Coded English too superficial and quite time-consuming to be adequately expressive. The manual codes use one or more signs per word rather than modulating and shaping messages with the facial expressions and gestures that give ASL its wide range of expressiveness. Thus, in the view of many native ASL users, much of the subtle meaning of ordinary conversation is lost. It can be difficult, for example, to determine when an English signer is being humorous or sarcastic.

Another objection is that Manually Coded English is less precise than ASL. For example, SEE II uses one single sign to symbolize all meanings and concepts of a particular word. In the following sentences, the word *run* is conveyed by the same sign in SEE II (as in moving at a speed faster than a walk), despite the differences in meaning:

I run a fever.

I run a business.

I run for election.

I run to work.

I have a run in my stocking.

I run every day.

I will run to catch my plane!

In ASL, each of these meanings or concepts of *run* is conveyed by a different sign. Many native ASL signers hold that the precision gained through separate signs for separate meanings enriches their language, as compared with the manual systems of English. However, experienced SEE II users who associate several meanings with the sign for RUN are not confused when they encounter them in reading. (But on the other hand, they get into the habit of using the "wrong" sign in their encounters with ASL users.)

A final objection is that structural differences between Manually Coded English and ASL make it impossible to use the two together in the classroom. For example, word order is an important factor in the meaning of a message in English. Often, changing the word order changes the meaning, as when "I work to live" is changed to "I live to work." In ASL, however, word order is somewhat flexible; altering it doesn't necessarily affect meaning. How you modify verbs *does* affect the meaning. For this reason, and because of the other distinctions discussed earlier, the structures of messages in ASL and English rarely correspond. Teachers in the classroom cannot sign in true ASL while speaking in English—that would be a job for a two-headed genius.

American Sign Language

Many deaf people consider ASL to be their own true language, even if they have been in oral or manually coded English programs for years and have come to ASL relatively late. For deaf people, ASL is easier to learn than other systems of sign. Deaf ASL signers often point to its extraordinary suitability as a language for deaf people:

It is so visual, subtle, and comprehensive, so inclusive of gesture and facial expression, so expressive of the barest nuance of meaning and abstractness, that many users consider the language to be *neurologically* attuned to the demands of communication through vision, carefully structured to match the needs and capabilities of the eyes.

For deaf children in particular, advocates argue, it is much easier to express and comprehend complex ideas and thoughts in ASL than in signed or spoken English. For example, it would be very easy for a deaf person to miss the inflections of sarcasm in someone's voice and assume they are being literal. On the other hand, is not difficult to comprehend sarcasm in ASL by seeing the facial expressions that come with it. Also, watching a person sign for a long period in manual English can strain the eyes, brain, and emotions in ways that ASL does not. Because it is a natural language, deaf and hard of hearing children take to ASL so easily that they pick it up almost by osmosis (really by imitation and practice) from other ASL signers—not necessarily in the classroom, but on the playground and in social gatherings.

Because ASL naturally developed in places with large concentrations of Deaf people, many see in it a kind of guarantee that a child who learns it will get an education and gain access to the Deaf community, even if he or she has no one to communicate with at home. Many Deaf people, including those who have no ties with their families, because they never shared a common mode of communication, find it wonderful to be a part of this community. The authors have heard over and over from deaf people that they finally felt a sense of belonging after learning ASL.

ASL proponents argue that children who are not taught ASL may never tap into this rich and vital culture and will grow up feeling like outsiders in hearing society. They offer this argument in further support of teaching deaf and hard of hearing children ASL from the very beginning of their language-acquiring years. ASL proponents generally support a bilingual education program with ASL as the primary language and English as the secondary language (but no less important), emphasized in connection with English literacy. The focus in bilingual education programs is on teaching ASL and English, so that children have the language base to communicate in both the Deaf and hearing worlds.

One major objection to choosing ASL over Manually Coded English comes from parents. For them, ASL is more difficult to learn. They will assess the challenge of learning a completely new language (ASL) along with a new mode of communication (visual) and conclude that it is daunting. They may well decide to commit their child to learning English, either signed or spoken, to ensure that they share a common language. However, let's keep in mind that regardless of which path you take, spoken and/or visual language, it can require just as much time and effort for you and your child.

Even more challenging, perhaps, is the idea that to choose ASL is to commit not just yourself, but your whole family, to learning it. Will the other children in your family be willing to put in the necessary effort? Will there be resentment? Will life intervene, swallowing up the time required to learn and practice? It can come as a surprise to hearing people that if you sign in ASL, you can't speak in English at the same time (this would be like trying to speak English and Spanish at the same time). Using Signed English and spoken English simultaneously is a little easier. It can be done, and hearing people find it much easier to learn. When parents realize that choosing ASL means they can't spontaneously use their own first language with the child, some at this important crossroads take the strictly English path.

Some educators and parents have unfounded beliefs that to teach deaf children ASL as their primary language is to neglect a major goal in deaf education: equipping children with English, so that they can navigate the hearing world. These critics worry that children trained primarily in ASL will be delayed in learning grammatically correct English. Further, they fear that deaf children who have a substantial amount of hearing and strong potential to become clear English speakers will be blocked from practicing spoken English and fall behind in their speech development. Nothing could be further from the truth. The goal of ASL-English bilingual programs is *literacy*: the ability to read and write in English and express oneself in ASL, and, if possible, spoken English (in short, to have a fully bilingual child, who is comfortable in both languages in all its modalities).

Please keep in mind, however, that English is extremely difficult for deaf children to learn. English is a highly irregular language with complex and often contradicting rules that confuse even hearing children. Remember your years and years of English and grammar classes in school? Research on spoken language bilingualism (e.g., English-Spanish or English-French) suggests that children either need a solid foundation in one language before beginning to acquire another or better yet should learn both simultaneously.[1] ASL should either be taught as the first language or simultaneously with English, say proponents, because ASL is a natural, visually based language that deaf children take to easily and can be used to help them understand the intricacies of both languages. This understanding of the process of how a language works is called *metalinguistic awareness.*

Research on school programs for very young deaf children of both Deaf parents and hearing parents shows that the children of Deaf parents frequently enter school with a wider range of experience. Through ASL, these children have been drawn into family communication from an early age, often from day one, and this enables them academically to outperform children of hearing parents. The higher academic scores of children with Deaf parents is consistent with the argument that learning ASL first, before English, is of inestimable value to deaf children. It forms a conduit of communication through which the children's parents can give them early and constant input.[2]

At the time of the last edition of this book in 1995, one problem noted with the ASL option was its relative unavailability. Since then, ASL has won general recognition among linguists and educators as a distinct, complete, and sophisticated language with its own vocabulary, grammar, and relationship to a discrete culture. In fact, as of this edition, it is the third-most commonly taught world language in U.S. universities after Spanish and French.[3] ASL has established its position in the education system (both private and public), and there are a good number of bilingual programs—offering both ASL and English, and access to both Deaf and hearing cultures in most metropolitan areas. If, after assessing all the options, you decide on a bilingual program, the

Matthew's Story: American Sign Language

Matthew was raised in a rural area, and when he was identified as deaf, at age three, his parents weren't used to searching far afield for information. They decided almost immediately to send Matthew to an oral program close to home, although later, they wished they hadn't been so easily swayed. They had tremendous respect—almost reverence—for the educators and professionals with whom they spoke, and they followed the instructions of Matthew's speech teachers to talk, talk, and talk.

Despite all their efforts, Matthew learned very little language in his early years. He was a quiet child but expressed a lot of frustration, impatience, and confusion. Despite their commitment to speaking to him as much as possible, his parents were never really sure he understood them. What they didn't know was that Matthew was an exceptionally bright boy, using his unusual cognitive skills to figure out life. He managed to create the impression of doing well in school, although his language skills hardly progressed at all. And although he *felt* his parents' love, the communication between him and them was mostly nonverbal: The three spent a lot of time in silence, sitting around smiling, hugging, patting backs, and so on, but virtually never exchanging ideas and information.

When Matthew was ten years old, his teachers told his parents that he would never do well in an oral program and recommended that they enroll him in a state residential school that used sign language. The parents visited the school and were astounded by the students' vitality, alertness, and lively communication skills. Regretting that they had waited so long, they enrolled their son.

Matthew took to sign language like ice cream. He told Paul, "It was like waking up in heaven. I felt almost as if ASL were biologically innate to me. It was developed, refined, and kept alive by deaf people, and it *feels* right. It is designed to meet our needs. Not only that, but the people of the Deaf community are my people, my family. Even though I was born to hearing parents, as soon as I entered the ASL community, I felt as if this was *my* family, and I'd been destined to be part of it all the time."

Eventually, Matthew entered Gallaudet University, married, and became a father. Not until his daughter was born (hearing) did he think much about the fact that after enrolling him in the residential school, his parents had never tried to learn to sign. Now, anticipating his responsibilities to his own baby, he was thunderstruck. Why hadn't they gone to the trouble to learn *his* language? He'd put in all that time and effort trying to learn *theirs*. "They never seemed to notice that we weren't communicating. It made me very nervous about being the right kind of father. Thinking about how I grew up, I had a very strong sense of obligation about being communicative."

At one point, Matthew's resentment at his parents' lack of interest in signing became overwhelming, and he realized he needed to confront them. When he expressed his position—and his anger—his mother understood and immediately enrolled in classes to learn sign language; however, she never caught up with Matthew in signing skill.

Nowadays, Matthew tries to be patient but still harbors negative feelings about all the time wasted before he was exposed to ASL. "I really don't think things will get much better between my parents and me, but I think my daughter will fill the void. And maybe she'll help close the gap, so we can forgive each other. I see now how you can love somebody and still make a mistake on his or her behalf. Through my daughter's eyes, I'm seeing that they made their decisions out of love." ❏

Spoken Language vs. ASL-English Bilingual Education: The Cultural Aspect Summed Up

Most strict spoken language proponents contend that in order to understand and participate in hearing culture, deaf people must grow up learning only the communication mode of hearing people, which in the United States is spoken English. These purists argue that deaf people who are not proficient in the majority language are blocked from participating fully in the society.

Proponents of ASL-English bilingual education respond that strict spoken language advocates deny deaf children their identity as natives of the Deaf world and attempt to masquerade them as members of the hearing world. "You may be able to imitate and pass as a hearing person temporarily," a proponent of ASL-English bilingual education might argue, "but whenever hearing people turn their backs on you, you will be deaf again." By contrast, they contend, ASL is the link that binds Deaf people into a true and living culture—just as any shared language is the binding force that gives individuals a cultural identity.

Perhaps no decision is more consequential than the choice of the mode of communication your child will learn in school. When you face this question, no amount of reading will substitute for real-life experience. We urge you, therefore, to make every effort to discuss the subject with deaf adults of diverse educational backgrounds. Don't be content with the advice of educators and professionals, but follow every lead that will take you to someone who has *been there*, someone whose own parents made a decision that set the course for his or her education and mode of communication. Historically, deaf people have had far too limited a *voice* (an ironic term perhaps) in this and other controversies related to deafness. It is time to dismantle the barriers that stand between the hearing and deaf worlds—not just the hearing barrier but the cultural barriers as well. ❏

Bryan and Janette: ASL-English Bilingual Education

Bryan and Janette, a married couple, both grew up in "truly Deaf families." Each had two deaf parents and many deaf relatives in their extended families. Both went to state deaf schools with total communication (TC) programs and then on to Gallaudet University, where they met. Both are now teachers themselves at a state deaf school.

Bryan and Janette describe their academic education as less than excellent. But school life, as a whole, was rich and varied. "What we had was a true bilingual and bicultural experience," they say. Both learned ASL as a first language at home and English at school. They grew up in a Deaf community but learned to feel comfortable in the hearing world. "We got the best of both worlds," says Janette. "A strong cultural identity, which was the source of a lot of pride and self-esteem, and the tools to do well in the hearing community."

For many years, ASL was considered an inferior language, if a language at all, and therefore was banned in many schools in favor of English. In TC programs, which were popular at the time, where English was taught and ASL permitted, students seemed to slide naturally into ASL. True, it was impossible to sign in ASL and speak in English, which is one primary reason educators cited for keeping ASL out of the schools. "But we would never talk about boys and girls, sex, parents, home life, sports, or deafness—anything that really mattered—in English," Bryan and Janette said. "These were topics to be discussed in ASL. Even teachers who knew ASL found themselves shifting into it to explain a story they had read to the younger children in English."

It wasn't long ago that virtually no hearing teachers knew ASL. Few had the opportunity to learn it, because most ASL users communicating with hearing people will naturally tend to code switch into—or at least toward—English, to make mutual conversation possible. Remember, a native language, such as ASL, has the effect of binding members of a community together, but it can also function to keep outsiders out.

Bryan and Janette have seen changes since they became teachers: "There are more textbooks and more classes for teaching ASL," they said. "In fact, there's lots more appreciation of ASL's expressiveness and its potential to boost deaf children's self-esteem." But as ASL supporters gained strength, the opposing side—SEE II and Signed English proponents—were also gathering power. The debate kept growing hotter, but now seems to have settled more in favor of ASL, although there are still plenty of proponents left for the other approaches.

Above all, say Bryan and Janette, children who are deaf need the clear and distinct cultural identity afforded by ASL. They need exposure to Deaf role models, "not training in functioning like hearing people, which is how we and many others in the Deaf community view oral, cued speech, SEE II, and Signed English programs. But critics are still screaming about the research: 'There's nothing to show that the bilingual philosophy really *works.*' We say that's not true. Look at the consistent data showing superior academic achievement and normal social and emotional development among Deaf children of Deaf parents. This is the proof they say they can't find. These children, like us, grow up in a true bi-bi environment."

next step will be locating programs that make geographical sense for your family.

Manually Coded English

When hearing people who are unfamiliar with the Deaf community see deaf people signing, they are likely to assume that they are seeing English rendered into sign. They may also assume that the manual exchange is a word-for-word transliteration and that the

A model ASL-English bilingual program, where early access to and acquisition of linguistic proficiency, in *both* ASL and English, is integral to a deaf or hard of hearing student's overall development, would offer the following.[4]

- early, unrestricted access to language, which is critical to linguistic and cognitive development,
- bilingual development of ASL and English, which is critical to deaf and hard of hearing children establishing early communication with their parents, developing their cognitive abilities, acquiring world knowledge, communicating fully with the surrounding world, and acculturating into the hearing and deaf worlds,
- accessible and consistent ASL and English adult and peer language models, which are integral to fostering language acquisition and learning,
- use of visual language, including ASL, and a rich English print environment, which are critical for access, acquisition, and development of both languages,
- if the child is able to use spoken English, then he or she is valued, encouraged, and incorporated into the environment specific to his or her characteristics and goals, and
- family involvement and competence in facilitating early accessible language and communication, which is critical to a child's cognitive and social-emotional development. ❑

grammatical structure of the signed messages is pretty precisely that of English. In reality, most signed conversations witnessed by hearing people are in ASL. But in classrooms, signing is more likely to be in English. This section describes the three most widely used systems of manually coded English: SEE II, Signed English, and English-based signing. All of these systems were developed to help young deaf children learn to read and write English. All incorporate ASL signs, but modify them in different ways.

SIGNING EXACT ENGLISH

SEE II is a system that renders English into sign.‡ The first SEE II
dictionary appeared in 1972; the latest print edition, which came
out in 1993, contains more than four thousand signs. That was
later followed by a CD-ROM and is now available online as of the
printing of this book. The signs of SEE II represent English words
and affixes (prefixes, suffixes, and tense markers) arranged according to English sentence structure and grammar. Most of the
base signs in SEE II come from ASL signs that have only one English translation. Other signs were created either by changing the
handshape of the base sign to the first letter of the English word,
known as *initialization,* or by inventing new signs based on linguistic principles. For example, in ASL, one sign can be used to mean
beautiful, pretty, and *lovely;* in SEE II, that sign is used for *beautiful,*
whereas *pretty* does the same sign with a P handshape and *lovely* by
using an L-handshape. Because ASL has no signs for the verb *to be,*
signs were invented to represent it in SEE II.

In SEE II, a two-out-of-three rule determines whether only one
sign will be used for multiple-meaning or similar-sounding English
words. One sign is used if the English words meet two of the following criteria:

1. The words are spelled the same.
2. The words sound the same.
3. The words have the same meaning.

For example, the word *bear* satisfies two of the criteria: It is always
spelled the same and always sounds the same. Therefore, it has
only one sign, no matter what it means; in the phrases *bear a burden,*
bear a child, and *the bear growled,* the word *bear* is signed the same
way. On the other hand, if the English words meet only one criterion, different signs are used. The words *right, rite,* and *write* have
only one criterion in common—they sound the same—so different
signs are used for each.[5]

---

‡ SEE II was created a few years after a similar system, called Seeing Essential English, came into being. Because Seeing Essential English came first, it is
referred to as SEE 1 and Signing Exact English as SEE II. Although SEE 1 is no
longer used, the numbers have been retained.

The aim of SEE II is to meet the need to visually represent words fully and accurately and was designed to correspond with the morphemes of English. Morphemes are the smallest meaningful units of language: root words and their affixes. Signs for root words are usually derived from ASL with invented affix markers (e.g., *re-*, *un-*, *-ing*, *-ity*, *-ness*). These root words and any affixes used with them are made visually obvious. The hope for this system was that signing English would increase the language, reading, and writing abilities of children who were deaf or hard of hearing. This concept was explained in the forward of the 1993 editions of the SEE dictionary, explaining that SEE II visually displays figurative, authentic, exact English, which Pidgin Signed English (PSE) cannot.[6]

The invented affixes expand the system's ASL vocabulary to reflect English and are particularly helpful in bringing clarity to the signs. For example, in SEE II, the base sign for *develop* is the ASL sign for that word. SEE II users show the past tense by signing *develop* with the *-ed* affix; the noun *development* is signed by adding the *-ment* affix.

Perhaps proponents' strongest argument in support of SEE II is that it helps the child learn not only the primary language of the society but also, in most cases, the native language of the parents. The first three years of life are critical for the development of language, and children learn language primarily by interacting with their parents, starting at birth. In order to plunge right in and begin the kinds of interactions that foster language development, parents need to become proficient very quickly in a visual communication system. As mentioned earlier, parents have an easier time learning Manually Coded English as opposed to ASL—after all, they *think* in English. So, ironically, the first advantage of SEE II is that it is accessible to the parents; it gives them the opportunity to begin communicating early with their child rather than delaying while they learn both a complex language and a manual mode of communication.

Parents seem to like SEE II, because of its approximations to English. Some parents who were interviewed reported that they were less concerned about which sign system their children would use later in life than about making sure the children learned to

Alyssa and Ashley's Story: Signing Exact English

This is about two college students who shared the story of the coincidental course of their friendship. Alyssa and Ashley had been in the same TC preschool classes for three years. They then went their separate ways and, after similar public school experiences, met again at college. When interviewed, their school and communication histories were eerily similar, almost as if they had been separated twins.

Alyssa told the authors how her mother had chosen the preschool where she and Ashley met. Shortly after Alyssa's diagnosis, her mother visited a well-known oral school of excellent academic reputation and had serious misgivings about what she found there. She then visited the TC pre-school program, which taught SEE II and oral skills; there, she saw Alyssa's eyes begin to sparkle with excitement. Alyssa's mother later explained to her that she had chosen the SEE II program for the following reasons:

1. Knowing that deaf children learn signing more quickly than speech, she believed that if Alyssa learned both, she could begin acquiring information and communicating earlier than in a spoken language program.

2. Alyssa's mother believed the TC approach was a form of insurance. Even if Alyssa didn't learn enough speech skills to interact freely in the hearing world, she would still have a language—a sign language—and so a means to interact. "After my mother visited the oral program, she was intent on guarding against one awful possibility," Alyssa told the authors, "that I might emerge from a school program as bewildered and isolated as when I entered it. She thought she saw evidence of this in some children at the oral school."

3. Alyssa's mother believed that SEE II could serve as a deaf child's bridge to the oral world. Because the teacher signed and spoke every message, Alyssa would learn two modes of communication at once and, ideally, would gain access to both the hearing and deaf worlds.

Alyssa's parents enrolled in SEE II classes, too, and soon felt that they were *really* communicating with Alyssa. A very sociable little girl, Alyssa wore hearing aids in school as part of the TC philosophy and, over the next three years, learned to use her residual hearing to its fullest extent. In the first grade, she entered a regular classroom where her mother served as a sign language interpreter. The girl did wonderfully socially and fairly well academically. Adolescence was turbulent, but with a family willing and able, with good communication skills, to discuss every nuance, things calmed down again when Alyssa went to the community college. After two years, she moved to the state college, and there she met Ashley, her old preschool classmate. They became instant best friends.

Ashley, too, attended public school on the strength of her foundation in TC. She, like Alyssa, had a turbulent adolescence. Both girls dated hearing boys who proved insensitive to their communication needs, and both had unpleasant experiences with other deaf people who had not been exposed to SEE II. "ASL signers look down on SEE users," Ashley told the authors. "They think SEE is an aberration, not *real* signing. It was very painful to be shut out in that way, and to be looked down on by deaf people, even though we were very fluent signers."

"So we decided together to work on the problem," said Alyssa. "We enrolled together in ASL classes—"

"To fulfill the state college's foreign language requirements," Ashley interjected. "Two birds with one stone."

Both Ashley and Alyssa felt they would always understand native signers but, because they had grown up signing English, would never become as fluent as native signers in ASL. However, both agreed that, as a result of studying ASL, they were using more ASL features in their everyday communication. They found the combination more flexible and not so structurally rigid as SEE II.

The story of Alyssa and Ashley should bring some relief to parents who feel a heavy weight of responsibility to make the right decisions at the beginning of their child's education. Remember that options exist and remain open all along the way and that your child may well decide later in life to pursue another course for reasons you did not anticipate. ❏

The Original Ten Tenets of SEE II

These are the principles agreed to in 1969 by the originators of SEE. The SEE committee had five members—David Anthony, Donna Pfetzing, Esther Zawolkow, Gerilee Gustason, and Marjoriebell Holcomb. The original group disbanded in 1970; Gustason, Zawolkow, and Pfetzing joined together to develop SEE II based on the following tenets:

1. It is tremendously difficult for a child born deaf to learn English.
2. The most important factor in acquiring good English is understanding its syntax (i.e., the structure of the language).
3. Normal input must precede normal output—that is, humans must be exposed to language before they express themselves in it. Because aural input is blocked or limited in deaf and hard of hearing children, they must receive English through visual means.
4. The visual cues of speechreading—that is, the lip movements involved in forming spoken English words—are too small and ambiguous to make normal, natural language learning possible.
5. Sign language is easier to see than speechreading or fingerspelling.
6. It is more important for a child to understand the structure of a word than its spelling.
7. The patterns or structure of the English language can be conveyed through sign language with relative ease.
8. It is easier to sign all parts of a sentence than to sign some and spell others—for instance, affixes, such as *-ed, -ing,* and *-s.*
9. Any specific sign should mean one and only one thing.
10. English should be signed as it is spoken, especially with regard to idioms, so that students are exposed to English as it is spoken.[7]❏

read. "My child can learn ASL later, after his English is established," said one. "SEE II enables my child to learn English grammar with signs in the same way hearing children learn it. It is simply an alternative way of learning the same thing—that's what I like about it," said another.

SEE II also exposes deaf children to the idioms and multiple word uses in English that can confuse and slow down a child who has learned English only through books and school. Children who learn English from written sources tend to pick up a more formal version of the language than those who learn it "naturally," through conversation and other kinds of interaction. The conversational learners are much more comfortable with multiple meanings and other complexities of the language.

A final advantage of SEE II is that it allows children to use a variety of modes: sign, speech, speechreading, and listening. Four modes add up to better comprehension and enable the student to communicate with more people. One parent told the authors, "I want my daughter to have choices in her mode of communication, so she can function in different settings with both hearing people and deaf people. I don't want her barred from mainstream society, because she has learned ASL only or ASL primarily. I want her to have her choice, depending on the situation, so she has wider access to the world."

Overall, although limited, the research does show that SEE II can achieve the goals of its originators: English literacy for deaf and hard of hearing children by enhancing their knowledge of morphology. This is if parents, teachers, and students are *consistent* in using SEE II over a period of at least five years.[8] However, it was also noted that with English-based signing systems like SEE II, there is little evidence that they work any better than ASL, which does not easily map onto English. The key to deaf children's academic success is early and effective access to language and being surrounded by it *consistently* whether it be signed or spoken language.[9]

One irony of SEE II, which many people regard as a drawback, is that the more skilled children become in it, the more likely they are to start cutting corners and using ASL-like grammatical features. This is true even if they have never actually been exposed to ASL. They often drop suffixes (*-ed, -ing,* and *-tion*) and articles (*a,*

Kirk: Signing Exact English

Kirk was in a SEE II-based classroom for nine years before being mainstreamed at the age of thirteen. He was never highly skilled in oral communication and preferred to use the signing, rather than the oral, aspects of SEE II. Once he entered the regular classroom, he relied heavily on interpreters. All his sign language interpreters at school used SEE II, and he didn't know ASL at all. This he considered a real detriment.

As Kirk grew older, he found SEE II too superficial to be adequately expressive. "All during my years in public school, I had trouble telling whether somebody was joking or being sarcastic," he told me. "SEE just doesn't let in facial expressions, and there's too much detail in the codes. But when I made friends with ASL signers outside of school, I realized that a lot of the signs I was using were imprecise. I really *got* what they were signing in a way I hadn't all that time in school." Kirk, like many native ASL users and fluent ASL professionals, recognized that in ASL, facial expression and body language replace voice intonation, which for a hearing person, carries much of the meaning of a message. SEE II, which does not encompass facial expression—so the argument goes—is incapable of ASL's subtlety. Also, because SEE II

an, and *the*) in order to increase their signing speed. They may use conceptually accurate ASL signs instead of following the two-out-of-three rule. Having (hopefully) gained a structural knowledge of English, the children end up signing for information content and ignoring the syntax and precision of English. Teachers and parents who sign exact English also tend to omit words and endings as the children's skills increase. So, as children become more proficient in English, there appears to be less need to adhere to SEE II.

Proponents of SEE II respond to this observation by suggesting that it is entirely appropriate for deaf children to sign less strict word order corresponds to that of English, it is, by nature, less flexible in structure than ASL. As Kirk became more familiar with ASL, SEE II seemed too rigid by comparison to allow full communication.

Kirk's fascination with ASL continued to grow. Eventually, he became a teacher of deaf and hard of hearing children, and then an instructor in a community college. The study of language had him in its grip. "I still think about going to graduate school for a Ph.D. in linguistics, and maybe I will someday. But I feel it is my responsibility to teach ASL to deaf and hard of hearing children, so that their communication won't be hampered and limited the way mine was by SEE."

Kirk resents having been educated in SEE II. Unlike Alyssa and Ashley, who value the verbal facility they gained through SEE II for showing them the beauty and richness of the English language, Kirk believes that for many years, the rigidity and inexpressiveness of SEE II cut him off from his potential to communicate fully. (Ashley and Alyssa did agree, by the way, that if their oral skills had been limited, as Kirk's were, they probably would have felt the way he did.) Now Kirk is deeply immersed in the Deaf community, far more so than Alyssa or Ashley ever could be with their limited fluency in ASL. ❏

English as they become more proficient in it, generalizing rules and taking shortcuts as hearing people often do. In doing so, they point out, the children are gradually mastering the language in a natural way, just as hearing children master English.

Many people object to SEE II as being too difficult for young children. The use of special signs for affixes to words (e.g., *-ing*, *-ed*, and *-s*) means that one word may require two or more signs, which adds significantly to the number of signs to be learned and used. This can be hard on the hands and eyes of very young children, and overwhelming to them in terms of what they must learn (there are more than 90 affixes). Further, staying with the structure of English, especially formal English, can make signing a tiring, colorless, by-the-rules experience. SEE II can be very dull and cognitively demanding in comparison with ASL signing.

Some teachers find it difficult to speak and sign at the same time. This means that they may not become skilled SEE II signers, and so may not be adequate English models for their students.

As for the parents, although it is true that SEE II gives them a way to begin to communicate early with their deaf child, many hearing parents learn to use it without any experience in ASL, which leaves their sign language colorless and without expression. This is another irony: The parents who choose SEE II in order to learn a system quickly, so they can begin signing with their child, probably understand the importance of communicating expressively and creatively from the very beginning; yet their choice of SEE II yields a kind of rule-book communication that can be bland and lifeless.

Many deaf adults object strenuously to the SEE II system, because it is based on word-for-word communication rather than concepts. This means that a child can become proficient in vocabulary and structure without really comprehending or learning to convey the meat of the language—its meaning. The use of SEE II in schools and programs tends to foment controversy on this point between Deaf parents who use ASL and hearing professionals and parents who use SEE II—just what *isn't* needed in a world already rife with divisions!

Another objection to SEE II arises when we pull back and look at the wider society. Few would disagree that the major challenge facing the United States today is finding a way for all the groups in our multicultural "soup" to live together productively while maintaining their cultural identities and the languages and traditions that make them unique. Considered in this light, can SEE II work at all for parents whose native language is not English? Deciding which languages children should learn in our schools is important for many people, not just for the families of deaf children. It is an issue that everyone must confront as the nation's diverse groups struggle to live together while preserving their particular cultures.

SIGNED ENGLISH

In 1971, another group of educators set out to simplify the way deaf and hard of hearing children learn English. They developed a system called *Signed English* as an educational tool to be used with spoken English. The idea behind Signed English was to create a system that was simpler than SEE II but would function as a reasonable parallel of English.

Signed English uses two kinds of gestures—*sign words*, standing for English words, and *sign markers*, to show word-form changes, as in tense *(hide, hid, hidden)* or number *(apple, apples)*. The structure of Signed English is the structure of spoken English, and each sign word corresponds to an entry in an English dictionary. The basic signs come from ASL. Like SEE II, Signed English also has invented and initialized signs. Signed English has a one-word, one sign rule to simplify the number of signs needed. In this system, the word *run* has only one sign, no matter what its meaning. There are a few exceptions, of course, if the word has distinctly different meanings and distinct ASL signs. An example would be *fall* (the season and the verb). The fourteen sign markers make Signed English unique. These markers are used to indicate the most frequent word-form changes in English (see Figure 9.1 for illustrations). Together, sign words and sign markers are intended to give parents and children a simple and flexible way of communicating.

Two strong points of Signed English are that the child becomes acquainted with English as it is spoken, and the parents are able to communicate in their native language without learning a complex new system or language. The Signed English developers strongly encourage parents to sign in English to their children, even if they can't master all the sign markers. The developers also recognize that as children grow and their English improves, they will have less need for the markers.[10]

CODE MIXING

Modes of communication that have evolved naturally, combining the signs of the Deaf community and the speech of the hearing community, are known as *code mixing*. These vary with the language knowledge of the communicators, forming a continuum rather

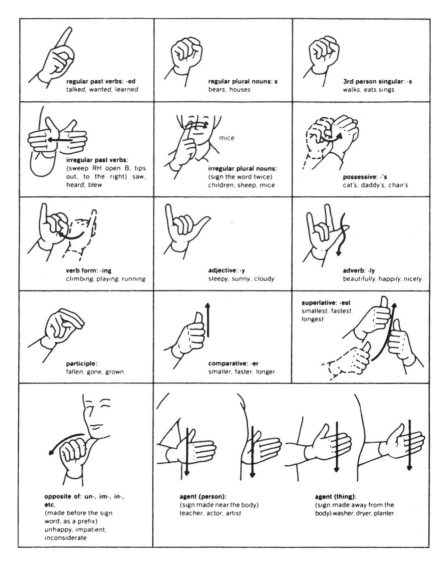

Figure 9.1. Signed English sign markers. Source: Bornstein, Saulnier, and Hamilton (1983). Reprinted by permission of the publisher.

than a single, strict system of signs. You may come across other terms for this, such as *English-based signing, Pidgin Signed English (PSE), Contact Signing,* or *Simultaneous Communication (Sim-Com),* and there is significant overlap between the two languages that can range from heavily English to more ASL. Some people may

Shannon and Ned's Story: Signed English within Total Communication

For Shannon and Ned, it was love at first sight. Both deaf, they met at a community college. "After years of dating deaf and hearing people," Shannon told the authors, "suddenly I could be myself, 100 percent. We could discuss anything, from the most ridiculous to the most intellectual topics. It was heaven."

Both were oralists who had learned Signed English in school—they didn't learn ASL until much later in life—and they felt as if they had had the best of both worlds. "We could sign and talk simultaneously. Then we could stop signing and continue talking. Or we could sign without speaking. All those choices!"

Their sons, Ben and Jerry, were born three years apart, and both are deaf. When the time came to enroll the first boy in school, Shannon and Ned searched hard for the right program. In the end, although both had been harshly punished in their own schools for "talking with their hands," they chose Shannon's alma mater. "Things had changed, we saw when we visited, and the teachers seemed to find more creative ways to discourage signing. And we decided that what was important was the high academic level and the continuity in teaching. We could sign with the boys at home. At school, we wanted them to *learn*."

This is an unusual decision. In the authors' experience, most hearing families that choose a spoken language program keep strictly to the "no signing" rule at home. It is unusual for deaf parents to enroll their deaf children in spoken language programs at all, especially if their own experiences with spoken language have been harsh. Shannon and Ned took a lot of criticism from their signing deaf friends for enrolling their boys in a spoken language school. But for them, the goal was to give their sons the best academic education they could find. Everything else, they believed, could be taken care of at home.

"We volunteered a lot at the school, and it was obvious even to me—and I have no background as a teacher or any credentials as a deafness professional—that some kids just didn't belong there. I hated seeing that the children were suffering through an education that didn't work for them, because their parents refused to see the truth. We were fortunate that our boys made clear progress. All four of us, not just Ned and I, agree that our decision was the right one."❑

Donald's Story: English-Based Signing

Donald is a biologist, aged forty-five. He explained to the authors how his parents chose not to pursue the oral method at a time when only two choices existed: options within oralism and what was then known as *English-based signing.* "They wanted to help me read and write well," he said. "That was their chief concern, not whether or not I could talk. I did have speech lessons, but my academic skills developed much more quickly than my speech skills."

Donald did very well in school. He graduated as salutatorian from Gallaudet University and went on to earn a Ph.D. in biology at the University of Minnesota. Today, he has a rich and full life, both professionally and socially.

"My parents supported me in everything I did, and they never expressed negative attitudes about deafness. I think this had to do with my grandfather, who had known some deaf people himself when my father was growing up. Actually *knowing* some of these mysterious people who read lips and speak with their hands—that made all the difference.

"My mother took my deafness hard, and it was my father who took the lead in tracking down information on school programs—not an easy thing to do in the 1950s. Since my parents agreed that the top priority was reading and writing, common sense told them to go with a program they found that used English-based signing along with some oral training. They learned to sign a little, but helped me most with reading and especially writing.

"The turning point for me, and the luckiest thing about my life, was the federal laws mandating that all universities be made accessible to deaf and hard of hearing students. This meant I could go to graduate school anywhere I qualified—that I couldn't be disqualified because of my deafness and that I would be eligible for any support services I needed to complete my education. The strong foundation my parents had insisted on made it possible for me to breeze through graduate school. I realized I could do anything I wanted."

In Donald's opinion, reading and writing were much more important than studying speech skills in order to function in the hearing world. "Not too many people *can* master speech skills," he pointed out. "And many deaf people I grew up with who can sign beautifully and are wonderful communicators—people who can socialize easily within the Deaf community—lose out despite their 'normality,' because they can't read and write well. For me, reading and writing opened every door."

For Donald, literacy in English was the critical factor in determining his quality of life, increasing his range of career options and social experiences, and reinforcing his self-esteem. The most efficient route to literacy for a deaf person is gaining mastery over English, and Donald's parents sensed correctly that a program that taught English through signing was a good route to that end. ❏

even code switch from one end of the continuum to the other, depending on the skills of the speakers.[11]

Code mixing is a sort of middle ground: a means of communication that evolves between people who have different native languages yet must communicate. Like any other makeshift language, code mixing is not set in stone. The basic vocabulary comes from both English and ASL, and the grammar shifts along an ASL-English continuum, depending on who uses it. If English is the native language of one of the communicators, then that person's English-based signing will reflect more English-like structures; if the other communicator's language is ASL, that person's signing will contain more evidence of ASL. Of course, as people communicate over long periods, they tend to learn each other's styles. For this reason, and because ASL is the first language of many Deaf Americans, the more experience hearing people have in signing and interacting with deaf people, the more their English-based signing resembles ASL.

It is difficult to generalize about the ASL-English balance of code mixing in various areas of society. However, it seems safe to say that the English-based signing used by hearing professionals in deaf education is often more heavily weighted toward English. Professionals who work in social service agencies and in religious settings seem to incorporate more ASL structures in their signing.

Although code-mixed signing is a good communication *tool*, it is not a true language in its own right. Because it is a shifting mixture of ASL and English, it does not teach children English grammar or ASL structure. Usually, the adults (whether Deaf or hearing) who use English-based signing already have knowledge of ASL and English; however, a child needs exposure to a *genuine* language, not only to gain information, but also to absorb and internalize the language itself. Code mixing cannot be used to teach reading, writing, or grammar; nor can it transmit the sense of belonging, the glue that binds individuals into a true culture, whether hearing or deaf.

For these reasons, English-based signing is not widely encouraged within the Deaf community, except as a means for communicating with less-fluent non-native signers.

Philosophical Approaches

This and the preceding chapter introduce the various modes of communication, the systems within those modes, and the strengths and weaknesses of each. The way a given educational program actually implements the systems at its disposal is often decided by philosophical, rather than scientific, debate. Philosophies come and go. In the early twenty-first century, four still predominate: Listening and Spoken Language (LSL), the ASL bilingual approach, TC, and full inclusion. To complete this overview of the modes of communication, we'll briefly review the first two approaches and introduce the other two.

Spoken Language

As you will recall, spoken language programs of education combine spoken English with or without speechreading and the development of auditory skills. They do not include signing and often discourage it. Success in these programs depends on the following several factors:

1. the age at which hearing loss occurred (before or after exposure to spoken language),
2. the amount of accessible hearing either via amplification or implantation,
3. individual learning style and skills,
4. individual temperament, and
5. parental support and involvement with fully accessible communication for their children.

To review the arguments for and against spoken language, please return to Chapter 8.

The ASL Bilingual Approach

When bilingual programs work, they work well. A number of such programs have been highly successful in teaching deaf and hard of hearing children to use and understand the languages of two cultures. A recently published and highly awarded Harvard dissertation replicated prior research that found ASL proficiency *and* academic English proficiency to be a statistically significant predictor of reading comprehension among Deaf students.[12] On the social side, ASL links the children to a vital, evolving culture, which gives them a sense of belonging and reinforces positive self-esteem; this, proponents say, allows the children to take up the difficult task of learning English in their own time, with greater success.[13]

For the reasons discussed earlier, there aren't many ASL-English bilingual programs in existence; however, a good number can usually be found near most major metropolitan areas. The success of these programs appears to depend on the following several shared ingredients, all related to a philosophy of respect for Deaf culture and language:

1. A clearly defined belief statement and guiding policies that promote early access to and acquisition of linguistic proficiency in *both* ASL and English as fundamental to a deaf child's academic achievement and sociocultural development. This includes ongoing development and training of the staff.

2. Strong deaf leadership among the faculty. In successful bilingual programs, deaf and hearing teachers work together, and the hearing teachers, who must be fluent in ASL, understand their role as one of bringing good and effective teaching into the Deaf world, not bringing their students into the hearing world.

3. Deaf administrators at the school. For most of the twentieth century, deaf and hard of hearing people did not occupy administrative positions in deaf education. This discriminatory situation is now relatively rare. In the most successful schools, deaf and hard of hearing people occupy decision-making positions—otherwise such schools would be only masquerading as part of Deaf culture.

4. Many deaf and hard of hearing teachers. The best programs hire as many qualified deaf and hard of hearing teachers as possible in order to give children constant exposure to ASL and to provide strong role models.

TOTAL COMMUNICATION

The educational philosophy known as *total communication,* or TC, which combines oral and manual methods, is the one most widely implemented in the United States today. In the TC classroom,

Diversity: The Challenge of Total Communication

Critics of TC ask whether it can meet the needs of many deaf children with widely varied skills and limitations, all in one classroom. Consider, for example, the following four six-year-old children who might easily wind up in the same TC classroom:

- Aaron, profoundly deaf, has almost no communicative skills. He is sullen, withdrawn, restless, and inattentive.
- Laurie, who has strong residual hearing and excellent oral skills, has been made self-conscious by hearing children about using her speech.
- Ben, whose deafness is severe, has been slow in learning to speak and speechread and even slower to sign. His frustration is growing, and he's almost ready to give up.
- Colin, whose parents are Deaf, is fluent in ASL and is anxious and restless. He can't speechread at all

Basic to a TC approach is the consistent and simultaneous speaking and signing of everything that is communicated in the classroom. TC teachers speak and sign every message, no matter which child they are attending to, thus simultaneously addressing and, it is hoped, reinforcing manual, oral, and auditory skills. The rest is a matter of individual emphasis. Imagine the following scenario:

- For Aaron, the teacher strives primarily to engage his interest and helps him focus on these strange movements of the lips and hands. Or the teacher draws him into the circle of activity by means of a pet rabbit, puzzle, or book.
- To Laurie, the teacher directs hard questions, helping the girl lose her self-consciousness in the process of forming answers.
- For Ben, the teacher offers patient encouragement and brings to bear any relevant techniques of psychology while acquainting the boy with the tools of communication at his own pace.

- For Colin, the teacher has to use ASL exclusively at first, but she attempts to expose him to English gradually.

So goes this teacher's dance: juggling the separate needs of each child while drawing the whole class together in a network of communication and, above all, language.

Sound possible?

The answer depends on the skills of the teacher, the size of the class, the learning and hearing levels of the children, and their ages at the onset of deafness. The task is demanding in any case. As you can see, much depends on the particular mix of people in the classroom. Because the incidence of deafness in the general population is low, the number of deaf students in a given school is generally too small to allow the grouping together of children with similar needs. This is the most common problem for teachers of TC classes. ❏

teachers use speech and manual communication (signs and finger-spelling) simultaneously, so that children can learn both modes. Fundamental to this approach is the recognition that children have different styles of learning. Providing alternative modes to choose from helps to ensure that each child will find ways to meet his or her own communication needs.

The combination of speech and signing determines the language to be used. All TC programs are English programs, because it would be impossible to speak English and sign in ASL simultaneously. TC was created to bridge the gap between strictly oral and strictly manual approaches to education. Manually Coded English was developed as a means of implementing the TC philosophy. Today, SEE II and Signed English are the most widely used sign systems in the United States.

TC may appear to be the ideal method, because it is designed to meet all students' needs. However, that something-for-everyone approach is one of the main objections of critics. Many professionals express this objection very directly. "It is physiologically impossible for one to obtain the same amount of information with all his senses at a single point in time," says George R. Karlan. "To presume that the deaf child will utilize his hearing, lip-read, speak and sign all at the same time is foolish." In other words, in the attempt to reach the child by a number of routes, the result is not total communication but total confusion.[14]

A more comprehensive criticism of TC programs is that many of them offer a less-than-optimum educational environment, focusing on the lowest common denominator and failing to encourage all children to realize their potential. When you begin looking into individual programs for your child, it will be important to assess each one not simply for its approach to communication but for its ability to challenge your child academically.

MAINSTREAMING AND INCLUSION

Mainstreaming, or what is now more commonly called *inclusion*, is a particularly American approach to deaf education, one that has evolved as society has become more aware of the need to provide equal services to all. It has been a mandate of the Individuals with Disabilities Education Act (IDEA) to educate students in the least-restrictive environment, with the general education classroom considered the least restrictive choice. In a nutshell, to mainstream deaf and hard of hearing children is to send them not to a special school or program but into regular public school classes, providing interpreters and other support services as necessary. This means placing the child in a purely English environment. If you think about it, when it comes to communication, this may not be the ideal or "least restrictive" for your child. Inclusion is the subject of a detailed section in Chapter 11, entitled "The Inclusive Classroom."

Notes

1. Colin Baker, *Foundations of Bilingual Education and Bilingualism*, 5th ed. (Bristol, UK: Multilingual Matters, 2011): 221–52.

2. Amy R. Lederberg, Brenda Schick, and Patricia E. Spencer, "Language and Literacy Development of Deaf and Hard-of-Hearing Children: Successes and Challenges," *Developmental Psychology* 49, no. 1 (2013): 15–30.

3. David Goldberg, Dennis Looney, and Natalia Lusin, "Enrollments in Languages Other than English in United States Institutions of Higher Education, Fall 2013," (New York: Modern Language Association, 2015). Available online at www.mla.org/pdf/2013_enrollment_survey.pdf.

4. Debra Nussbaum, Susanne Scott, and Laurene E. Simms, "The 'Why' and 'How' of an ASL/English Bimodal Bilingual Program," *Odyssey: New Directions in Deaf Education* 13 (2012): 14–19.

5. Gerilee Gustason, "Signing Exact English," in *Manual Communication: Implications for Education,* ed. Harry Bornstein (Washington, DC: Gallaudet University Press, 1990): 116.

6. Diane Nielsen, Barbara Luetke, and Deborah S. Stryker. "The Importance of Morphemic Awareness to Reading Achievement and the Potential of Signing Morphemes to Supporting Reading Development." *Journal of Deaf Studies and Deaf Education* 16, no. 3 (2011): 275–88.

7. Gerilee Gustason, "Signing Exact English," in *Manual Communication: Implications for Education,* ed. Harry Bornstein (Washington, DC: Gallaudet University Press, 1990): 112–15.

8. Nielsen, Luetke, and Stryker, "The Importance of Morphemic Awareness."

9. Marc Marschark, "Do DHH Students Succeed Better in Academic and Other Assessments by Using ASL or SEE?" *Educating Deaf Children* website, (2015). Available online at www.rit.edu/ntid/educatingdeafchildren/?cat=11#.

10. Harry Bornstein, "Signed English," in *Manual Communication: Implications for Education,* ed. Harry Bornstein (Washington, DC: Gallaudet University Press, 1990): 131.

11. Gerald P. Berent, "Sign Language-Spoken Language Bilingualism: Code Mixing and Mode Mixing by ASL-English Bilinguals," in *The Handbook of Bilingualism,* ed. Tej K. Bahtia and William C. Ritchie (Oxford, UK: Blackwell, 2008): 312–35.

12. Jessica A. Scott, "Beyond the Fourth Grade Glass Ceiling: Understanding Reading Comprehension among Bilingual/Bimodal Deaf and Hard of Hearing Students" (Ph.D. dissertation, Harvard University, 2015): 97–99.

13. Robert J. Hoffmeister, "ASL and Its Implications for Education," in *Manual Communication: Implications for Education,* ed. Harry Bornstein (Washington, DC: Gallaudet University Press, 1990): 99.

14. George R. Karlan, "Manual Communication with Those Who Can Hear," in *Manual Communication: Implications for Education,* ed. Harry Bornstein (Washington, DC: Gallaudet University Press, 1990): 171.

10 *Reading the World*

By the time a hearing child in the United States enters the first grade, he or she probably has been constantly exposed to the English language for six years. We say "probably," because many children in our increasingly multicultural society live in homes where English is a second language or is not used at all. Those children who have been immersed in language since birth are like sponges in the ocean, regardless of culture and type of language. Almost magically, without working at it or realizing it, in their early years, children absorb both the complex structure of their home language and an extensive vocabulary. In a transition that often occurs naturally, with a minimum of difficulty, the hearing child draws from his or her familiarity with English, at least in most American homes, to learn to read. This is known as *language acquisition.*

Deaf children, by contrast, may have had very little exposure to spoken or printed English language by the time they enter school. They face the challenge of learning to read it without that years-long familiarity. (In this, the deaf child and the hearing child raised in a non-English-speaking family are roughly analogous.) Not surprisingly, deaf children can be far slower to master the task. And some, like some children for whom English is a second language, may never master it at all. Although the average hearing American high school graduate leaves with an eighth-grade English reading level, the average deaf high school graduate leaves with a third- to

187

fourth-grade level. Not surprisingly, few things have been more highly researched and debated in deaf education than the topic of literacy. Some things we can agree upon are that historically, the results have been less than stellar, and that early accessible language learning *and* parental expectations and involvement can make a huge difference. This last part is where you come in.

An important variable here is not whether the child is deaf or hearing, but whether or not the child has been acquiring English for five or six years from their parents or caretakers before starting school. Those who have not acquired an internal base of language are at a disadvantage in becoming literate in English print. Note that we used the word *acquire* to describe this absorption process instead of *learn*. The difference is that language acquisition is subconscious and driven by the need to communicate. Learning language on the other hand, is not communicative in nature. It is the result of direct instruction on the rules of language. However, just knowing the rules of language does not necessarily result in good literacy skills.

The Significance of Reading

Literacy—traditionally described as the ability to use printed and written information—is necessary for learning and achieving academic independence. And literate thought (i.e., the ability not only to read but also to think critically and reflectively about complex topics) is necessary to participate in a society based on constantly changing, evolving ideas and information. The full extent of what happens to people without these abilities falls outside the range of this book, but it is possible to generalize by saying that unless we can read and bring to bear logic and reasoning on what we learn from our reading (i.e., unless we are literate and have the capacity for literate thought) what we know will be pretty much limited to what we can observe firsthand and how well we can interpret our observations. For the rest, we will be dependent on others to tell or teach us. With the power to read and think critically, we have the potential to learn everything that is known. Books, and now computer screens as well, are windows to the universe. And, to stretch the metaphor, for us in the United States, the glass in those windows is the English language.

How can you help your deaf child gain the ability to read and eventually to write? These two skills feed and reinforce each other, and much research has been dedicated to this question. The data make the following two important points clear:

1. Deaf children can acquire English in the same way hearing children do: *through meaningful exposure to as much real-life language as possible.* The only basic difference is that the hearing child typically receives the English language through the ears unimpeded. The deaf child will learn more readily through the eyes and possibly through the auditory pathway, depending on the amplification of residual hearing or cochlear implants.

2. The key to a deaf child's successful reading development is the family's effort to make language accessible to the child from the very beginning, immediately after the diagnosis that the child is deaf. This should extend eventually into a partnership with the child's school. The aim is to find alternative ways to bathe the child in English—through both the eyes and also ears when possible.

A Note of Reassurance

Before turning to concrete ways of making English visible, let's anticipate the following several responses—or outright objections—that may come to mind as you read:

"But I'm not a teacher. I'm just a regular person. I'm not even much of a reader. Shouldn't I leave the teaching of reading to the experts, the specialists, the teachers?"

"I don't have time to work with my child, to teach an English language course."

"I don't know grammar *at all.* I nearly flunked English in high school. What business do I have trying to train my child in the structure and vocabulary of English?"

These objections all are completely understandable. They touch on the exasperation parents are bound to feel as they face the extra responsibility of finding unconventional routes to learning. In a crowded classroom, however skillful the teacher, your child's access to English will be limited by the teacher's need to manage, organize, and discipline all of the students; deal with recess, meals, illness, and field trips; cover a range of academic subjects; *and* (in the best of circumstances) interact individually with every student in the room.

Expecting teachers of deaf students to give more of themselves than do teachers of hearing children strikes the authors as unrealistic. Teachers qualified by training and experience to work with deaf children may be more sensitive to their students' communication needs, more creative in accommodating them, and more expert at fine-tuning their students' education with regard to English and other language issues. They are trained to be specialists in monitoring children's progress and in identifying and explaining particular educational and communication issues. But like any other teacher, they will have less time than you do to spend with your child and have far fewer opportunities for one-on-one interaction.

The goal of this chapter is to suggest a range of concrete things you can do to bring the English language to your child, to pave the road to literacy. You don't need to be a language specialist or teacher or grammarian; you don't even need to be a terrifically great reader or writer yourself. You want your child to *acquire* the language, not just learn it. To do this, you do have to be willing to constantly interact with your child with language and print. Parents of young children are remarkably attuned—perhaps biologically programmed—to give their children access to their own language at appropriate age levels so they can soak it up.[1]

As the children mature, they may outstrip the parents in language complexity; then the parents and teachers can work together to help the child continue analyzing and learning the finer details.

To accomplish this, you will need the following:

- common sense,
- inventiveness,

- confidence in your intuitions,
- an interest in developing your own language skills to help meet your child's need for increasingly complex language experience,
- heightened awareness of opportunities for making language available—and visual, and
- a commitment, once your child enters school, to work in partnership with your child's educators to continue to expand and intensify the child's language experience.

As you begin to experiment, keep in mind these broad guidelines: First, whatever the mode you use to convey English, whether spoken or manual, communicate naturally with your child, not in one-word questions or commands. Especially avoid "yes-no" questions, as deaf children are notorious for nodding their heads and saying "yes" when, in fact, they have no clue as to what you just said. Additionally, yes-no questions do not tell you exactly what a person knows, only whether s/he can agree or not agree, which is a very superficial response.

Second, constantly explain things, especially aspects of language itself, such as the meanings of figurative language, like idioms and colloquialisms. Your deaf child will have a hard time picking up the many uses of certain expressions—for instance, of the word *cool* to mean "lacking in warmth," "hip," "terrific," or "unenthusiastic"— unless you explain these definitions and distinctions *explicitly* (after giving your child the opportunity to show what he or she knows and then to guess and experiment). This is the kind of subtle language lesson a classroom teacher is unlikely to have time for. One great book series both authors loved as children that assisted in learning figurative language are the hilarious Amelia Bedelia books, in which the main character literally does what people ask. Other children's books that feature figurative language include *My Dog Is Smelly as Dirty Socks* and *Crazy Like a Fox*, but don't limit it to these; there are many others.

Third, be gentle in your expectations. Give it a little time, and give your child access to the structure of English sentences (full statements, questions, commands, expressions of emotion) and as large a vocabulary as you can *without worrying about whether he or she can absorb everything*. Remember, English is a highly evolved, complex language. Everybody—whether hearing or deaf—acquires it in stages and runs into trouble spots along the way. The acquisition of language goes at its own natural pace, perhaps dictated by the physiology of the human brain. Remember that the goal is not to make children into schoolyard Shakespeares, but to immerse those little sponges in the medium they will need in order to read. Over time, you *will* be surprised at what your child says and wonder where they picked it up.

Fourth, avoid the tendency that many people have to keep language very simple for deaf children. For example, if your child knows one easy word (e.g., *dog*), don't just use it without teaching other words that mean the same thing (*canine, man's best friend*). Basic, one-meaning words, such as *dog*, that have different synonyms are known as *Tier 1 words*. Don't get stuck there with your deaf child; move on to the next level as she or he matures. Tier 2 words are the high-frequency words used in adult conversations that can have multiple meanings, such as *masterpiece, fortunate, measure, benevolent,* and so forth. Tier 3 words are the ones that are used in technical or academic situations that we don't often use in daily adult conversations. Those are often taught in subject areas at school, but don't be afraid to use them at home as appropriate.

Fifth, think out loud when you are doing things: Talk or sign everything you are thinking. What does it look like? Let's say you are going to make a bowl of cereal. In your mind, you are having a conversation with yourself: "I'm going to get the cereal. I wonder what I have in the cupboard. Ohhh, I have Cheerios and Corn Flakes; I think I'll have Cheerios today." Your deaf child needs to be shown how to use internal language to think through everyday problems.

You may find it reassuring to know that your child is likely to continue developing his or her reading skills even after high school. It often happens that deaf graduates become more enthusiastic about reading when they are released from the overwhelming academic pressures of school. Deaf adults, as a group, are highly motivated to learn all they can, and because print is their strongest information source, their reading skills may continue to improve gradually after high school. Leaving school and becoming more involved with the Deaf community gives many Deaf people a wider range of opportunities to learn English—not from a school curriculum, but from other Deaf people who know intimately the obstacles they face in mastering the language. Still, for deaf and hearing people alike, the ability to achieve a high reading level in adulthood is closely tied to early, meaningful exposure to English, in conversation and in print.

Language Development: An Overview

Let's begin with a once-over-lightly primer in human language acquisition, as it is generally experienced by hearing and deaf children in the first few years of life.

Before the age of one year, hearing children—who have been babbling and experimenting with the sounds they can make—begin to understand utterances from their parents, siblings, the television, and the radio. English language has been pouring into their brains since the day they were born, and at this age, their accumulated processing of information allows comprehension to dawn. At the same time, they begin to parrot back utterances in a way that is more than merely "sounding off"; their imitations are meaningful to them and to those who influence their world. Parents naturally respond to their one-to-two-year-olds' baby talk in the dialect known as *motherese:* vocalizations that mirror back and expand upon the baby's utterances, guiding the child toward comprehension and more refined expression.

Hearing children pick up words literally out of the air to increase their growing vocabularies with little effort. From every incidental source, whether directed to them or not, they absorb new words and new constructions—questions, commands, statements, and expostulations. This can happen thousands of times in an hour. All combine to increase their comprehension of syntax (i.e., how words fit together to convey meaning).

By the age of four, hearing children have unconsciously acquired approximately 40 percent of the English skills they will need in their lifetime. During the next two years, their language skills increase more quickly. By age six, they have acquired—almost effortlessly—80 percent of their future English skills.

When hearing children enter the first grade, they are experienced, one might even say sophisticated, in understanding and using English. Although most can't yet read or write, they have a working vocabulary of 3,000 to 6,000 words and will have been exposed to as many as *45 million words* by the age of four. Yes, that's right; they may see or hear words, mostly the same ones, up to 45 million times. That number is dependent on the parents' and caretakers' level of involvement with the child.[2] Through active involvement in their world—in play with friends, conversation with adults and other children, and exposure to Internet, television, radio, and movies—they increase their own internal vocabulary by about ten words a day. Experts tell us that as a goal in a structured, formal educational setting, this rate would be impossible to achieve.

Without communication access, children who are deaf are deprived of the meaningful exposure to language that hearing children achieve without effort. Yet their intelligence and cognitive development are unaffected by deafness: Their brains are fully equipped for language acquisition and development to occur.[3] The difference is simply in meaningful exposure.

As you know very well, coming to grips with the diagnosis that a child is deaf can be a time- and attention-consuming process. A period of gradual adjustment, during which parents make the many necessary emotional and intellectual adaptations, is natural and impossible to force to a conclusion. As we hope Chapter 2 makes clear, your child's health and well-being depend on your willingness to navigate this stormy sea for as long as it takes to achieve relative stability. Yet there is no denying that during this process, precious time could pass—often several years. And although now relatively rare in the current age of newborn hearing screenings, the loss of time may be compounded by a late diagnosis.

Over the past century, mostly due to late diagnoses, the majority of deaf children grew through the prime language-acquisition years (from birth through age five) without much comprehensible contact with the English language. When, in the course of things, these deaf children entered school, their vocabularies were much smaller than those of the hearing children in typical kindergarten classes. On average, deaf children of five knew only a few dozen words in English. With the current focus on newborn hearing screening, early intervention, cochlear implants and digital hearing aids, and acceptance of ASL as a language, deaf children have already seen modest gains. But the bottom line is still *what you as parents actively do to ensure language access.* In every case of success the authors know of, including our own as two successful college professors, it was clearly the parents that made the difference.

Making English Visible

In the rest of this chapter, we offer as much concrete advice as possible on making the English language visible to your deaf or hard of hearing child. Many of these suggestions are generalizations that are meant to be realized differently at different stages of the child's development. Remember that language acquisition is a natural process that unfolds in its own time. Your child will respond to whatever English language experiences he or she is "programmed" to respond to at a particular stage of development. It is not something you can rush. (See "Reading Skills: A Developmental Timetable" on page 196.) Questions, statements, instructions, and exclamations may be simple or complicated, and the child may or may not understand. But no effort is lost. Whether or not a specific message is grasped, language is pouring into the child's eyes. Keep in mind, too, that hearing children are exposed to the same language patterns and the same words thousands and even millions of times before they can and will use these units of expression themselves. These numbers might seem overwhelming, but children are exposed to words every minute and every hour, and they add up quickly without any superhuman effort. (Remember, up to 45 million words by age four.) Try to give your deaf child the same exposure, and when he or she makes a mistake, don't become excited or anxious. Simply repeat what you have said or pointed out in a correct form and then drop it and move on. Do not constantly correct your deaf child, as children are naturally resistant to instruction. But they *will* start doing it right when the time comes. You child has a natural, inborn desire to communicate and learn language. You will be feeding that need.

Reading Skills: A Developmental Timetable

By ages three to five, most children are able to do the following:
- see likenesses and differences in words set in type,
- recognize some words in type,
- understand the meanings of different words,
- comprehend short sentences,
- understand the sequence of events in stories,
- answer questions in detail, and
- follow directions.

By ages six to ten, most children are able to do the following:
- express themselves effectively (in other words, they can say and/or sign a lot of words),
- use picture and word dictionaries,
- see relationships among written concepts,
- read and follow complicated instructions,
- analyze and infer meaning from what they read,
- summarize stories and other reading material,
- understand more and read a bit faster than before,
- visualize situations in written form,
- form mental images from descriptions in type, and
- identify the central thought of a story.

GENERAL GUIDELINES

Children learn language from interacting with their parents and caretakers. *How* they learn it is a matter of great speculation by scholars, linguists, and researchers, but the fact that social interaction triggers the process is a given. Scientific research dovetails with common sense to confirm a high correlation between extensive early language experiences in the family and strong reading skills later on.[4] So how, on a concrete level, can you assist in this development of language?

House rule number one will sound familiar: From day one, communicate in every way possible. Use body language, gestures,

By ages eleven to thirteen, most children are able to do the following:

- retrieve facts easily from the page,
- select key words and sentences,
- summarize their own thoughts and feelings,
- grasp the overall thoughts in a paragraph,
- predict the outcomes of a story, and
- show increased sophistication in vocabulary and description.

By ages fourteen to eighteen, most children are able to do the following:

- retrieve information quickly and easily from maps, graphs, charts, pictures, tables, and the like,
- use any general reference books,
- formally outline a story,
- use critical-thinking skills to identify relationships among elements in reading material,
- skim a book and know what the story is about,
- select passages of special interest or that are related to certain topics,
- distinguish between author's evidence and truth,
- organize material to serve a particular purpose, and
- recognize writing excellence. ❑

speech, signs of any variety—including spontaneously invented ones if necessary—in your baby's line of sight. Remember, however, that reading in English is related to *using* English, so although you exercise your creativity and imagination in communicating with your deaf or hard of hearing child, make sure to *keep using English*. Make it visually available through ASL translation, Signed English, speech, or cued speech, and find ways to help even your very young deaf child gain access to written English. Books and print materials are essential in your home. If you watch television or videos, turn the captions on and leave them on permanently. Some parents place printed labels on common items around the house and make sure their child not only recognizes the print but also is able to associate it with signs or spoken words.

Once you choose a mode of communication, begin learning and using it yourself and involve all the members of your family, including all hearing siblings and close extended family. It is important to establish the new mode of communication with everyone in your family, not only for communication's sake but also to lay the groundwork for your child's learning to read.

Again, *get books!* If yours hasn't been a reading family, those days should be over now. We have visited many homes of deaf and hard of hearing children and are always saddened when we find a scarcity of books and periodicals. There is a high correlation between the number of books in a home and the reading ability of the children living there.[5] Books are windows to the world, but children need to be shown how they work. So, the minute you understand that your child is deaf or hard of hearing, books, magazines, newspapers, and computer resources should be all over the house. Simple books, complex books, comic books, cookbooks, picture books, serious books, fun books, e-books, tactile books: Keep them in every room and make them an important part of your home environment. Remember, a long-term familiarity with language is the first step on the road to literacy.

For convenient lists of general guidelines, see "Ten Things Parents Can Do" and "Ten Things Teachers Can Do" on pages 198–201. These lists were compiled and written by Jason Gillespie, a graduate of the deaf education program at California State University, Fresno. These guidelines are based on interviews he conducted with parents of deaf and hard of hearing children.

BRINGING BOOKS ALIVE

The invention of movable type, which spurred the creation of the printed book, took place in the fifteenth century—pretty recently in the long stretch of human history. A lot of thinking, evolving, and creative insight had to take place before the power of books was recognized; and on a small scale, for every individual child, this is still the case. All of us, whether deaf or hearing, have to be taught what a book is, what print is, what reading is, and what the

Ten Things Parents Can Do

1. Begin communicating with your child as early as possible, in any way possible. If you don't know signs, speak to your child and use clear gestures and facial expressions. Find a way to communicate about everything that is happening in the child's world.

2. Establish a fluent and consistent system of communication with your child. Whatever your modality, make sure that the child's siblings and extended family members have access to communication with the child as well. This language input is essential to the child's development.

3. Play language games with your child. Try to make language a fun part of everything you do. You needn't worry about teaching structures explicitly; if exposed to them consistently, the child will internalize them.

4. Make sure you understand everything your child is communicating to you and respond to it appropriately. Likewise, make sure the child understands everything you communicate to him or her. If you don't succeed the first time, try an alternative method.

5. Let the child do things and explore the world independently! There is no reason to shelter your deaf child from the world; you can deprive the child of much valuable experience by steering him or her away from new situations.

6. Don't correct your child's language. Instead, model the correct forms. Gradually, the child will internalize them.

7. Encourage any and all attempts at vocalization. Engage in vocal play with your child. It is fun for both of you, and it can enhance later speech development.

8. Stimulate your child's imagination with silly questions and word games. Encourage the child to respond and be creative. Build on his or her responses and encourage further responses.

9. Ask your child lots of wh-questions (who, what, where, how). Many deaf children have problems with these concepts, and they can be internalized naturally at an early age. If your child does not respond immediately, model an appropriate response. Gradually, the child will get the hang of it.

10. Select an academic program for your child that is consistent with your communication method.

Ten Things Teachers Can Do

1. Be fluent in all the most common communication methods used with deaf children, including ASL and spoken language, and if necessary, Signed English, SEE II, or cued speech. Your students will be coming from a variety of home situations; it is up to you to be able to communicate clearly with all of them.

2. Don't try to make modality decisions for parents. Although we all have strong opinions as to which communication systems are best, the parent is ultimately responsible for the decision.

3. Always view the parent as a partner in providing the child's education. Take advantage of this valuable resource.

4. Take advantage of available technology. There are many language-related software programs and applications on the market that can be incorporated into effective, natural language lessons.

5. Praise your students not only for their achievements but also for their efforts. Some tasks are simply much harder for children who are deaf, and this can be frustrating for them.

6. Take your students on field trips whenever possible. Apply for a small grant if you must. Language is best learned out in the world, where children can see and experience things firsthand.

7. Have your students keep a personal daily journal that you promise not to read. This gives them an opportunity to play with language freely without fear of the teacher's opinion.

8. Laugh a lot and use humor with your students. Be as visually expressive as you can.

9. Set detailed objectives for the students in your classes, and decide on the best activities to meet your objectives in as natural a way as possible. Keep careful track of your results; in this way, you can see what works and what doesn't.

10. Don't be too easy on your students. They are cognitively capable of everything that hearing children can do; be sure to challenge them constantly. High expectations are paramount. ❏

rewards of reading are (pleasure, entertainment, learning, and so on). And all of us have to learn how to read print, and how to see and comprehend pictures.

Familiarize your baby with the *feel* of a book. Involve him or her in helping you position it in the right way (topside up, open to the left) and eventually in turning the pages. Young children love tactile books, such as *The Touch-Me Book* and *Pat the Bunny*. Familiarity with these books will automatically lend familiarity with the way a book "works," such as holding them and turning pages.

Beginning to Read

BEFORE FORMAL INSTRUCTION BEGINS

You can do several things to prepare your preschooler for reading.

1. Read or tell stories to your child regularly and inter-actively—this appears to be the single most important activity fostering the knowledge and skills required for reading.
2. Try to have meaningful interactions with your child about books and other print media in order to convey the function of print.
3. Use language activities and big books to establish print awareness.
4. Work on letter recognition, both in books and in the environment, before expecting your child to respond to print. Letter recognition should be well established by the time the child reaches kindergarten.
5. When working on letters, work on their names first, then their shapes.
6. Children need to be helped to conceive of language as consisting of individual words or units, such as signs. Expose your child to written words, including onomato-poeias (sounds things make, such as animal sounds or mechanical sounds) to help convey this concept.
7. In activities and games, draw attention to words. With a young child who knows the names and shapes of let-ters, work on the association between individual letters and words.
8. Encourage your young child to begin printing as early as possible as a way of reinforcing letter recognition skills and preparing for writing.

STARTING TO READ

As you monitor your child's reading program, consider the following points:

1. According to research, all children seem to learn reading best when they are given systematic instruction in the "code" of language as well as practice in reading meaningful text.
2. Matching children to different programs based on different perceptual styles does not appear to have an effect on reading success.
3. Writing and spelling activities help to develop and reinforce the knowledge of spelling.
4. Independent writing activities develop a child's deeper appreciation of the nature of written text as well as the child's comprehension.
5. Children's reading abilities are influenced by the texts they read. The more words in the text that are decodable at their level, the greater their word-recognition skills and their success in both writing and reading.

ON THE PARTICULARS OF CLASSROOM INSTRUCTION

Find out whether your child's teacher uses the following approaches to teaching pre-reading skills:

1. Phonics instruction for deaf and hard of hearing children should focus on attention to spelling (plus sound if the child has access to auditory input).
2. Letter recognition is basic to word recognition.
3. Children who enter school without letter-recognition skills should not be taught upper- and lowercase letters right away. Start with uppercase letters.
4. To promote the growth of word-recognition skills, the reading texts children use should be carefully coordinated with the content of their other lessons.
5. The text should be repetitive and patterned with visual representation in the pictures to help figure out the words. For example, "I see a blue boat"; "I see a red flower"; "I see a yellow bus."

BEYOND THE BASICS

When your child has learned to read, you can provide help and encouragement in a number of ways.

1. Give your child as much opportunity and encouragement as possible to practice reading. Reading facility depends strongly on how much text children are required to read.

2. Comprehension depends on quick, effortless word recognition and on the conviction that the reader is meant to think about the text in order to understand it. If your child is having difficulty with reading, consider urging the teacher to return to the basics of word recognition. Also, make it clear to your child that *thinking* and *trying to understand* are part of the reading process. Model how you think about what you're reading. For example, "Oh, that reminds me of my dog. He likes to sleep on the bed."

3. Make sure your child is not being encouraged or allowed to skip difficult words. Part of the process is taking the time to study a word, recognize and comprehend it, and then reread the entire sentence or phrase in which it appears.

4. Repeated readings produce a marked improvement in children's word recognition, fluency, and comprehension.

5. Spelling, too, affects reading ability. Make sure the school is focusing on spelling skills as well as reading training. ❏

The information in this box is adapted from the classic text by Marilyn Jager Adams, *Beginning to Read: Thinking and Learning about Print* (Cambridge, MA: MIT Press, 1994).

Conveying the function of type is a more complex and long-term process—and one that should not be restricted to the world of books alone. Pointing out and discussing "environmental type"—road signs, restaurant and store names, the writing on cereal boxes—teaches a child what print is for and shows him or her that type comes in all shapes, sizes, and colors. The ways of learning from environmental type vary with a child's age. It would be appropriate to draw a three-year-old, for example, into a letter-recognition game, whereas an older child might have great fun and gain a sense of pride from helping to make a shopping list and finding the items on the market shelves. All activities of this sort will contribute to your child's awareness that we live in a world awash in type and depend on it for nearly everything we do.

Conveying the pleasure and usefulness of books is less a matter of games and activities than of a lifetime commitment to reading. As early as you can, start reading stories to your child, conveying the meaning in any way you can. Make print and books a familiar world to your child—one that he or she looks forward to entering, not only for the story but also for what follows: a conversation with you about the story you shared together. Through storybooks, your child will partake in a treasure trove of English-language experiences, including the following:

- the joy of the story itself,
- the rhythms, structure, vocabulary, idioms, usages, and figures of speech of English, many of them unlike what the child encounters at home,
- the impetus and grounding to inspire the child to learn to read independently,
- more ideas than any one family or educational program could encompass, and
- a range of experiences and activities that could spark the child's interest and become a path to his or her eventual profession and personal identity.

THE WRITTEN WORD

How can you introduce written English into your household? Begin by using the mode of communication you have chosen in order to *name* objects, as you would with a hearing child. The idea is to weld words to things and actions right away, creating links in the child's mind between words and real-life experiences. By speaking or signing English words, you'll feed your child's growing vocabulary.

If your family is using sign language, you can alternate between fingerspelling and signing words as a way to foster good spelling skills. It is never too soon to fingerspell with your child. They may not understand at first, but they *will* pick it up. It is distressing to visit classrooms where students are fluent in signs but are unable to spell. By the way, fingerspelling games are popular and fun, and easy to devise on your own. One family the authors know plays a fingerspelling version of Ping-Pong: A player fingerspells a word to another player, who signs back a synonym (same meaning) or antonym (opposite meaning). Children love even the simplest fingerspelling games, and these little entertainments are a great way to slip some spelling practice into a long car ride or an after-dinner hour.

To build on the effort to introduce written English early, consider physically labeling objects around the house. The slight concession in home decorating will be more than outweighed by the association your child will eventually make between the written words and familiar objects. An important footnote to the labeling suggestion: Several teachers of deaf children have strongly suggested that you add the article with the noun in labeling household objects—"*the* stove," "*a* chair," "*an* ottoman." Many deaf people have had a lifelong struggle using articles correctly. These same teachers encourage you to change noun labels to simple sentences ("This is our stove") as the child grows older, at about age four or five.

Some families who start off labeling get into the habit of leaving little notes around the house. Post-its, that wonderful invention, can turn the family refrigerator into an ever-changing bulletin board.

Here's a hint to parents of young children ages two and up: Mail-order catalogues and magazines can provide a source of endless games that stimulate a child's use of symbols. Cut out and paste pictures of animals on cardboard and get the child to group them—birds in one pile, dogs in another, cows in a third—to build up experience with word meanings and categories. Branch out from just nouns to using adjectives, verbs, adverbs, prepositions, and the like. If you stick just to nouns, that's all children will learn.

THE ART OF CONVERSATION

Conversation may seem natural to you, a thing that just "happens." But the fact is, conversation is a complex and subtle dance that everyone who knows it has to learn. Rules govern it. Good conversation partners know how to do the following:

- take turns,
- refrain from interrupting each other,
- make it clear that they are paying attention when the other person takes a turn,
- respond to the other's message, and
- ask politely for a repeat if they don't understand.

And so on. These rules may seem like second nature to us as adults, but children must learn them over and over, and practice to get them right.

Similar to teaching dancing, where you walk the learners through their steps and then guide them in practice, the best way to teach your children to converse is to constantly engage them in conversation. In other words, discuss, discuss, discuss—talk with your child about everything that comes up. Your child will learn conversation style by your example, just as hearing children do. One warning: Make sure *you* play by the rules as well. Sometimes parents are so anxious to teach language skills that they practically bury their child in a barrage of talk, signs, and gestures, forgetting to allow the child equal time. This effusiveness may result from parents' fear of failing to understand their child—they simply dominate the conversation rather than face the challenge. Sometimes you have to force yourself to wait for a response. Remember to give your children time to interject or answer, as they are still learning language and organizing their thoughts. They are not as quick in responding as you may be. Interrupting is not only rude but inhibits their chance to express themselves.

Listening to your child, interpreting what they are saying, and asking questions won't always be easy. However, conversation is a two-way street.

READING ALOUD

In the past, many teachers of deaf children read aloud or encouraged their students to read aloud for hours and hours, with no assurance that the students had a solid understanding of what they were reading. Just because someone can decode words does not mean that he understands what is being read. When you establish the ritual of reading aloud to your child, we urge you, remember to discuss the details of the story. Conversing about a story is a chance not only to practice conversation and abstract reasoning but also to make sure that the child comprehends these excursions into the English language. (See "Storytelling" on page 210.)

> Isaac's father, John, began reading to Isaac when he was ten months old. At sixteen months, Isaac was diagnosed as profoundly deaf, and the news seemed to deepen John's resolve to make story time a nightly ritual. John had used nonverbal communication techniques from the beginning, and he continued to do so—in a sad story, using his fingers to show tears on his cheeks; in a happy one, showing excitement. John was completely uninhibited about miming stories to Isaac, and as a result, Isaac was exposed for years to stories made visible— through mime, pictures, print, and finally signs. At the age of eleven, Isaac was reading at an eighth-grade level.

Here's a suggestion for parents with children ages seven and up: Comic books and graphic novels, with their mixture of action-oriented pictures and fast-paced dialogue, are great for children who are just beginning to read on their own for pleasure. They have come a long way from the days when they were considered "trashy" reading. They have a very high interest level and have been shown to help improve children's reading skills. The mature content of some comics may leave a lot to be desired, so you'll need to keep close tabs on what comes into the house; but age-appropriate classic comics and graphic novels offer valuable learning opportunities. There are graphic novels that have been adapted from classic novels and some that are classics themselves. Be sure to monitor their reading to make sure your child actually is reading, not just skimming along looking at the drawings.

RADIO DAYS: LETTING KIDS IN

The authors have heard the following story or something similar many times from their deaf friends when talking about their long-ago childhoods: They are riding in a car with their family or sitting around the dinner table, and suddenly everyone goes still.

Child: "What's going on?" asks the deaf child.

Family: "Oh, nothing. We're just listening to the radio."

Child: "What's it about?"

Family: "Nothing. Just the shootings in Chicago."

Child: "What shootings? Where is Chicago?"

Family: "We'll tell you later."

Result? The child feels left out and frustrated, and may get the impression that events in the news are too boring, or too complicated, to explain. Worse yet, perhaps without realizing it at the time, the child misses out on a lot of the richness and diversity in life. Also missing is that all-important practice in discussing abstract concepts and mastering the not-so-automatic art of conversation.

So, how, ideally, might the conversation have gone, between parents and a teenager, for example?

"Mom, what's on the radio?"

"We're listening to a special report on the shootings in Chicago. It seems a worker at the post office got fired, and he flipped out. The next day, he came back with a rifle and shot his boss and two other employees. It is very tragic."

"Did the police catch him?"

"Yes, but it wasn't easy. They had to call in the SWAT team. The man refused to come out of the building. Finally he did, though, after three hours of negotiating."

Storytelling

Storytelling—that is, telling rather than simply reading stories to your child—exercises and stretches your child's comprehension skills and helps prepare the child for independent reading. Two well-known deaf parents, Dr. Thomas Holcomb and Sandra Ammons Rasmus, offer parents the following advice on how best to tell stories to young deaf children:

1. When your baby is too young to sit on his or her own, sit on a chair with your feet elevated on a stool or ottoman, and set the baby on your lap, so he or she can see your face while you tell the story.
2. When your child can sit, make sure you sit directly across from each other, so that you can see each other's faces, and you can make sure your child is watching and following the story. If your child needs to watch you and not the book, allow this to happen; however, do not forget to give him or her an opportunity to look at the picture after you read it aloud.

"Why is it called a SWAT team?"

"I don't know what SWAT stands for. It is an acronym, one of those words made from the first letters of several words. It means a group of police officers specially trained to go into dangerous places."

"How did they get him out?"

"We don't know, but it seems he had a lot of troubles and getting fired was the straw that broke the camel's back."

"Camel?"

"It is an expression that means things keep piling up and then one thing triggers anger. . . ."

And so forth. The second example conversation included concepts, idioms, new word uses, scenes that set the imagination

3. Tell and retell familiar stories again and again, and use the chance to observe the following:
   a. how well the child understands your mode of communication,
   b. how much the child remembers from stories you've told before,
   c. how much vocabulary and language structure the child has mastered, and
   d. whether the child has comprehended the ideas.

   In other words, use storytelling sessions not only to entertain and educate the child, but also to monitor the child's progress in developing language skills.

4. Encourage your child to make up stories with you. This is one way to counteract the often rigid sentence patterns learned in school. Home is a place to break out of formal study and push back limits on the imaginative use of language. Simply asking your child for a response here and there in a familiar story—"What color was Goldilocks's hair?" "YELLOW!" "Why couldn't the bears eat the porridge at first?" "It was TOO HOT!"—makes storytelling interactive and allows your child to use his or her language comprehension to enhance the fun. ❑

running, practice in reciprocal conversing, and a reminder that human beings all over the world are connected.

Radio, and other forms of audio, can push back the horizons of our lives—and not necessarily through words alone. You will be surprised how many deaf folks are highly interested in music and enjoy it. A deaf friend described how his family often passed the time on long car trips describing the music they heard on the car radio. These discussions took the whole family into realms where they might never have gone, as they tried to convey the qualities of ordered sounds and explain how wind, percussion, and stringed instruments work. Music can be, among other mysterious things, a shared experience of feeling. Attempting to convey that experience in language can be challenging and exciting for the hearing explainer as well as the deaf receiver.

CALENDARS

Playing with calendars gives parents a chance to discuss time. Future, past, present—although we take them for granted, these concepts are anything but self-evident. Calendars offer visible demonstrations of the way time breaks down into units that follow one another with regularity.

> "Today is Wednesday; tomorrow is Thursday. On Friday, we're going to the zoo. On Saturday at ten o'clock, Dad is going to take you to your brother's Little League game. Last Saturday was the game where your brother got hit with a bat."

Time is difficult to understand, and too many deaf children are routinely left out of discussions of family plans, because no one has taken the trouble to work through these concepts with them. Find a big calendar that marks out the time units clearly, and you'll be amazed at how useful it will be with even the youngest children.

PHOTOS

In conversations with deaf people about their early childhood, photos and their importance come up with amazing regularity. Each photo can be a little treasure chest of family and personal information, and with even the barest details written on the back—who's in the picture, where and when it was taken—it becomes a record that makes the shared family life clearer.

Photos serve more than just informative functions. One deaf friend, Barbara, described that the only time she felt comfortable with her father was when they sorted through printed photographs together. Her father had a passion for photography; his nostalgia and humor were liberated by the pictures, and the barriers between father and daughter melted momentarily. In Barbara's very early years, her father hit upon photographs as a way of explaining complicated family relationships to her and identifying all the various aunts, uncles, and cousins. At first, he'd merely write names on the back. Later, when Barbara could read, he wrote descriptive sentences, then funny sentences and comments. By the time she was in high school, he was drawing crazy cartoon bubbles in the pictures. The photos served as a record of family jokes, puns, and her father's personal take on certain events.

From very early on, sort through your pictures, either printed or on your phone and computer, with your deaf child, and we think you'll find that you're sharing not only valuable family information but also a rich layer of family history and feeling. Use a phone or computer to add captions to pictures and make a file for your child to use again. Find one of the many apps on iPads, smartphones, and tablets that allow you to upload our own photos or make our own stories. The possibilities are endless.

FROSTING ON THE CONVERSATIONAL CAKE: IDIOM, HUMOR, AND WORDPLAY

One of the well-intended but tragic adjustments parents often make in response to dealing with a deaf child is to water conversations down to the barest minimum. The parents do it to help the child understand everything; however, if the conversation level remains low and unembellished, the child will never get a handle on complex, grownup, *living* English. (Remember to use Tier 2 "adult" language.) So, as your child develops, keep the conversation peppered with new words and expressions, slang, idioms, and figures of speech, as you would with a hearing child of the same age. Learning to use figurative language like this is just as critical for deaf children as any other component of language. Figurative language makes up a huge portion of our English language. It is, therefore, extremely important that you teach your child what these phrases really mean. As a source, children's storybooks often have figurative language.

A deaf person, Jeff, offered a recollection of a family discussion about his Uncle Ernie. Jeff's parents were wondering if Uncle Ernie was planning to visit next summer. The phone rang, and it was Uncle Ernie himself. "His ears must have been burning," said Mom, returning to the table.

Jeff had no idea what this meant and asked his sister. She explained, "Uncle Ernie phoned just when we were talking about him. He must have felt us discussing him." A week later, Jeff's friend, Jerome, showed up just when Jeff was thinking of calling him. "Jerome's ears must have been burning," he told his family. "No, I mean his *eyes* must have been burning." The family loved the play on words and often repeated it, reinforcing Jeff's natural inclination to experiment with words and expressions. One of the authors' favorite plays on words is to say "Let's play it by eye" instead of the more common expression "Play it by ear." We are deaf after all.

You don't need natural talent to enjoy language games. Remember Simon Says, the old command game? Players are supposed to do what the leader tells them to, but only if the leader repeats "Simon says" before each command: "Simon says wiggle your foot; Simon says bend your arm; Simon says run around the room. Nod your head." In this case, head nodders would be out. The great value of this game for deaf children is that it requires the players to attend to all parts of a message, not just the subject and object.

As anyone knows who has taken a long car trip with children, the possibilities for word games are endless. As long as you have the patience, it is an almost sure bet that your child will play them with enthusiasm. What a painless way to encourage language practice— and a fabulous way to share an empty hour as the miles roll by.

WRITING ACTIVITIES

Being literate means writing as well as reading, and skill in one builds skill in the other. You don't have to wait for a child to begin reading; you can start activities associated with the telling and, eventually, the writing of stories long before your child can read. Start with scrapbooks. Working with preschoolers to make scrapbooks yields a wealth of benefits, such as the following:

1. It teaches the parts of a book.
2. It teaches the symbolic nature of pictures.
3. If you introduce labeling, it can be a way to begin to name objects in written form.
4. If you use photographs of trips and other activities the child has been involved in, it can help the child begin to link memories with language.
5. The scrapbook can grow in complexity with the child's English language skills. One-word labels can grow into sentences, and simple descriptions can turn into journal entries.
6. The scrapbook can link written names with friends and family members.

All of this helps your child relate written English to his or her own realm of experience. After your child has begun to read and write, the real-life opportunities to practice and gain mastery are endless: writing letters, keeping a diary, reading and copying recipes, writing stories, playing computer games, word processing—the world is full of ways to exercise English language skills enjoyably, creatively, and productively.

In recent years, technology has opened up the world for deaf people, making communication and information sharing possible through literacy. Captioned television and movies offer deaf children and adults the chance to enjoy dramatic stories and informative shows while exercising their reading skills. Nearly all televisions today have captioning available and can easily be turned on from the menu. Some parents think they need to wait until the child can read before they begin using captions, but to the authors, this is a missed opportunity. We recommend exposing your child to the captions as early as he or she shows an interest in television, even if he or she can't read yet. At the very least, your child will start associating pictures with words, and words with language and communication! If you make the captions a part of the natural home environment, the child won't feel that special arrangements are being made. Plus it will benefit siblings as well. So again, turn the captions on and leave them on.

Internet, emails, and texting put deaf people, like hearing people, in touch with all the information in the world and on an equal footing too. No communication barrier there. As never before, a child's curiosity on any subject can result almost instantaneously in a search that yields an answer. Old obstacles to specialized information are crumbling.

If you haven't noticed yet, using communication and information technologies depends on one skill above all: keyboarding. To take full advantage of computers, it is imperative that every deaf child—and every child for that matter—learn to type. If you have a computer, look into keyboarding software designed for children. Aside from learning activities, you should be able to find a program to teach typing skills. Also, if they do not already do so, urge your school to include typing in its curriculum. And make sure your child has access to the school's computer resources from the first day of school—and we *do* mean nursery school. Of course, we are not suggesting that penmanship is no longer important. Handwriting is still a useful skill in today's world.

Knowledge of English and the ability to type are the keys to the electronic universe, where the only barriers to communication and information gathering are inexperience and intimidation. Today, the concepts of literacy and literate thinking embrace three, not two, arenas: reading, writing, and computers. English is the gateway to all of them.

Notes

1. Jeanne Machado, *Early Childhood Experiences in Language Arts: Early Literacy* (Boston: Cengage Learning, 2015): 4.

2. Betty Hart and Todd R. Risley, "The Early Catastrophe: The 30 Million Word Gap by Age 3," *American Educator* 27, no. 1 (2003): 4–9.

3. Peter Paul, *Language and Deafness*, 4th ed. (Sudbury, MA: Jones & Bartlett Publishers, 2009): 65–144.

4. Connie Mayer and Beverly J. Trezek, *Early Literacy Development in Deaf Children* (New York: Oxford University Press, 2015): 27–52.

5. Mariah Evans, Jonathan Kelley, and Joanna Sikora, "Scholarly Culture and Academic Performance in 42 Nations," *Social Forces* 92, no. 4 (2014): 1573–605.

4 Outside the Garden

11 *The School Environment*

IT IS TIME to move out of the home and into an environment that sometimes looks alien and mysterious, and sometimes hopeful: school. Many, if not most, parents feel ambivalent about this home away from home, the first place where their child spends a substantial amount of time away from them, in an atmosphere determined and controlled by others. On the one hand, parents want to exercise some influence on the school, and particularly on the classroom environment, on the other, they often feel inhibited about putting forward their opinions and desires on behalf of their children. Most are at least a little relieved to share with other adults the demanding work of setting their children on the path to a productive, independent future. However, the first day of school is not the time to breathe a sigh of relief and turn the job over to the professionals. It is true that the teachers and other educators your child will meet in school should know more about their field than you do, but they can't take over your very special role as your child's ambassador to the world. The idea is for you to play that role with the full, enthusiastic, and informed support of the education professionals.

Your role of ambassador is never more crucial to your child's healthy maturing than when the child goes to school. You'll find that it requires skills and qualities you never knew you had. Perhaps the most important skills you'll need are diplomacy on behalf of your child and a cool, analytical eye attuned to the effectiveness of the classroom program and your child's progress within it.

This role isn't very different from the one many parents of hearing children assume in monitoring their child's education. It is not unusual for parents to visit each new classroom, meet the teachers, get a grasp of the curriculum, and learn how they can help the child on the home front. The special needs of your deaf or hard of hearing child make your continued evaluation and participation particularly important. To be blunt, a lot more can go wrong in a school program for deaf children, particularly in a public school where deaf children are included, or "mainstreamed," in regular classrooms with hearing children. And, by the way, if your child *is* mainstreamed, you'll need to be something of a legal eagle as well, making sure that your child's educational needs, however special, are being met. It is the law!

In Chapter 12, we'll look at the specific kinds of school programs available for your child, in both public schools and deaf schools. Here, our purpose is to show you how to walk into *any* classroom where deaf children are being taught and assess the *feel* of the place, the atmosphere for learning, and the subtle aspects of communication in the room. This chapter should help you plan the questions you want to ask, whether you are looking for a school or visiting one where your child is already a student. Before you visit, you may want to use this chapter to make a list of your questions and concerns.

Does all this mean we're urging you to become an aggressive, unpleasant "helicopter parent" whose very presence on the school grounds causes teachers and administrators to scatter and lock their doors? Not at all. Good educators see themselves as part of a team effort in your child's education and should welcome your participation. In fact, most classroom teachers wish for more parental involvement and feel abandoned without it. Make it a golden rule to schedule a visit to your child's classroom at the very beginning of every semester, keeping in mind the following broad guidelines.

1. Notify the teacher when you would like to come and visit, make sure that class will be in session and that it is a good

time to visit. Valid reasons for saying no might include days when there is a test or when the teacher is being evaluated by his or her supervisor. Treat it as a red flag if the teacher refuses to allow you to observe during classroom hours without telling you why.

2. As you prepare a list of questions to carry with you, ask yourself what *you* really need to know, about both the teacher's personal approach and your child's progress in the class. Write these down as you observe the classroom.

3. When you are dissatisfied, confused, or concerned about something, arrange a time to discuss your problem as thoroughly as possible with the teacher in private. If you find that things cannot be resolved that way, move up the chain of command. Contact the program administrators or principals, all the way to the superintendent's office. If necessary, broach the subject publicly in the school's parent–teacher organization or the school board. In this way, you'll open to public discussion an issue that could yield new perspectives and information useful to everyone—teachers, administrators, other families, and yourself.

The Classroom

Let's begin with some basic considerations about the physical setup of the classroom in a residential school or a special class for deaf students. Surprisingly, even trained teachers of deaf children sometimes overlook these factors.

NOISE LEVEL

Auditory training is a significant feature of many deaf education programs, regardless of mode of communication, so a room that inhibits sound discrimination in any way is a serious problem. Besides that, a lot of noise can simply be a distraction, because hearing aids and cochlear implants (depending on their settings) are capable of amplifying *all* sounds, not just the sounds associated with speech. A noisy, echoing classroom can nullify all your child's efforts at discerning distinct sounds. Think of this when you visit, and *listen* to the nature and level of the classroom noise. Remember, an effective ambassador is, in large part, a great empathizer. Make sure that during your visit, you spend a lot of time looking at (and listening to) the classroom from your child's point of view.

The ideal classroom for deaf students is designed and arranged to mute all extraneous sounds. Floors should be carpeted to reduce internal noise and eliminate the scraping noises made by chairs and desks (tennis balls on the feet of furniture are a cheap and effective way to do this if there is no carpet). Walls and ceilings are lined with acoustic tile. All equipment, including computers and projectors are insulated to minimize any clicks and hums. If outside noise is a problem, a quiet air circulation system permits windows to be closed.

Most classrooms for deaf students today use an FM system, where the teacher wears a microphone, and a tiny receiver is attached to the child's hearing aid or cochlear implant processor or worn by the child as a neck loop. The advantage of this system is that it filters out a lot of the room noise and enables the child direct access to the teacher's voice by making the teacher's voice louder than the background noise. One disadvantage is not being able to hear classmates' responses or overhear incidental conversations among them unless there is a microphone near them.

Glazed tiles and high-gloss paints, which are not sound absorbent, should be nowhere in sight. If you find that your child's classroom is too noisy, remind the program director that insulating blankets and acoustic plasters can improve the acoustics of a room without retiling.

The five minutes it takes to determine that a classroom has poor acoustics could save your child months of effort at auditory training made useless and frustrating by uncontrolled environmental noise. Teachers tend to get used to classroom conditions that they feel they can't change—and you'd be surprised how many teachers are unaware of or forget the importance of reducing noise levels for deaf students. Just by walking in and seeing whether a teacher has tried to reduce ambient sound, you'll get a sense of this teacher's sensitivity to your child's educational needs.

LIGHTING

It bears repeating here that for deaf children, the eyes are usually the main door for information. No matter what mode of communication your child uses, having a clear view of the teacher, the teacher's aide, and other students is absolutely crucial. The child using listening skills must be able to see the lips of everyone in the room; the child using sign language, whether in a school for deaf children or a public school with an interpreter, must be able to see everyone's hands, bodies, and faces. Without a clear view of all potential communicators in the room, your child will miss critical bits of information and may lose the whole sense of some exchanges.

What is the ideal lighting setup in a classroom with one or more deaf students? Consider the following lighting wish list:

1. Ideally, windows should be located on both sides of the room to provide even, natural lighting. You'll need to watch the way the light plays on all the communicators, just as if you were a stage director. Is some corner of the action lost in shadow? Is someone's face blurred for some reason, so that lipreading becomes impossible? Do you find that the children are squinting up at the teacher because light is glaring from behind him or her, practically rendering the teacher a dark silhouette? Look for clues in people's behavior that suggest the lighting may be wrong.

2. The paint color on the walls instead of white or off-white should be a quiet pastel color to provide good contrast and a soothing effect.

3. The best location for ceiling lights is not the center of the ceiling, where they tend to cast shadows on people's faces, but around the sides of the room.

4. If ideal lighting can't be arranged, the teacher should be aware of the problem and do whatever is possible to minimize glare and shadows and maximize the visibility of everyone in the room.

5. The quality of the light should be soothing, not harsh. Full-spectrum fluorescent lights are preferred over the standard institutional "cool-white" version, as they can actually improve student performance and make them calmer. If the

light in the classroom is unpleasant, bring it to the attention of the teacher or principal.

SEATING ARRANGEMENT

The conventional row-by-row seating arrangement is terrible for a class containing deaf students. Again, students need maximum visibility of teachers and each other, and this means visibility not only of the face but also of the hands and the rest of the body as well. The best arrangement is a semicircle of students facing the teacher, but this may not be possible with a larger class. If traditional row seating must be used, then having the child sit to the side of the front row and turned slightly inward will allow him or her to follow the teacher and the rest of the classroom. This arrangement will also reduce the vision range needed to watch the teacher, the board, their desktop, and the interpreter (if used). Deaf students are often scanning these three or four things simultaneously, so reducing the line of vision is helpful. Teachers and children should be encouraged to work together to find a setup that works for them. And seating can be changed to fit various activities: reading sessions, small-group discussions, conventional lectures, and so on.

The light source is an important consideration in seating arrangements. If the semicircle of students faces into a window or other light source, the glare will make it hard for the students to see the teacher. Communicators all should have their backs to a wall. Check for blind spots in the lines of sight between all participants.

THE "PERSONALITY" OF THE ROOM

Step inside the classroom and check its social climate. Is it welcoming? Intimidating? Cheerful? Depressing? How would *you* feel about entering this room every morning, knowing you would spend the next six hours there with just a few breaks? The climate of the classroom is quite important for an optimal learning environment.

Several administrators of elementary school programs for deaf students shared with us what they looked for when they entered a classroom—how the atmosphere of the room figured into their evaluation of the teacher's effectiveness with deaf and hard of hearing children. Here they speak for themselves:

I want the room to reflect the person who put it together. After all, that teacher is going to spend most of his or her working hours in the room and ought to want to feel comfortable there. I get worried if the classroom is "just right" but sterile. I wonder, how much does this teacher care about bringing things in to make themselves happy in this environment? There are rooms like that. You walk in and see nothing of the teacher. Anyone could walk in and be the teacher. It makes you wonder how much they care, how much they're prepared to give.

I want to see visuals galore, done well and cheerfully—but not overbusy and wild looking. The whole thrust in deaf education is to make language and information visible. One of the things I'm assessing is the ability of the teacher to give information in a clear, visual way. We want the children to be able to glance up and receive incidental learning (like the stuff hearing children overhear without necessarily focusing on it). We want the material that's on the walls to reflect specific information or lessons that are being taught. When the children look up from their work and gaze around the room, they should be able to review something familiar to them or to have a lesson reinforced. They should be able to pick up information from the environment on their own. But we don't want them drowning in it. There has to be a balance.

I'm looking particularly for *language* made visible in the classroom, and language at the appropriate level for the students there. Parents undoubtedly will have trouble discerning the appropriateness of the level of language presented, but they should be wary if they see little or no language posted on the boards.

Another thing I want to know is whether the teacher uses instructional media effectively. Is the classroom projector covered with dust, or is it clear that the teacher uses it daily to present information? The idea is to determine whether the teacher knows how to present information quickly and visually in a number of different ways. Although language is a chief concern, especially in the early years, we don't want the teacher depending on speech and speechreading, or sign language, or reading and writing alone. Rather, we want the teacher to present the materials in a variety of ways.

The worst room I was ever in had an intense glare with nothing to soften it. There was not one living thing in the room except people—no plants, no animals, no fish; and this was a first-grade classroom. Worse, there were no comfortable places in the room, no places where you could sit down and hang out and not worry about working. There was one worktable, but nothing to indicate that creative work went on there—no puzzles or paints or anything like that. Basically the kids just sat in that room with their hands folded. I wasn't surprised to discover that the teacher relied almost solely on rote as a teaching technique—the teacher spoke and signed, the children responded as a group. The whole environment, the whole approach, was boring.

I look for activity and learning centers in the classrooms. Is the room just posted with displays for incidental learning, or are there areas in the room where kids can go off and work independently, privately? Maybe it is just a study carrel, or maybe a place where the child does arts and crafts. You'll see a list of directions over it: "Would you like to make something today? Follow these steps. . . ." Or maybe there's a nature corner with plants, animals, or a microscope. But most important of all for deaf children is the library corner—a place where they can sit down and read during free time, a place jammed with lots of books at all different levels. Library corners—I don't see them all the time, but I wish I did.

I always want to see a schedule when I go into a room. If I don't see one, I get worried. Somewhere in the room, I want to see a schedule, and big, so it is not just the teacher's schedule but there for everybody in the room—visitors, aides, students—anyone who comes in can see the schedule. But I like to see a schedule that you can tell has been changed a lot to show it is adaptable, not too rigid. I don't like to come in and see that the only schedule is on the teacher's desk, a private thing for the teacher alone to refer to. All children need practice in scheduling and time management, and deaf children often don't receive enough of it. That's why I want to see them in the classroom, saying, "Oh, it is 9:30, and I'm supposed to. . . ." I also want to see the teacher saying, "Stay where you are, let's finish this, don't worry about the time." But still, the schedule is very important.

Along the same lines and equally important is a job chart of some sort. There should be jobs in the room that the kids like to do or need to do, even if they don't enjoy them. This means that everybody's sharing the work—it is not all falling onto the teacher or the aide—and the children are learning and practicing appropriate behavior. The responsibility should be divided up on a chart visibly, with the names shiftable from job to job.

The Teacher

Here's where your intuition will go into high gear. When you observe a trained teacher of deaf children, you don't have much hope of accurately assessing that teacher's every talent and capability on the basis of a one- to two-hour classroom visit; however, you can learn a lot in that time, especially about the teacher's sensitivity to the needs and capabilities of deaf children. And there's a lot more that you can conclude later in sorting through your observations. You needn't stop with intuition; try research. If you are worried about your child's progress and doubt the teacher's reassurances, request the official guidelines from the principal or program administrator. With a little legwork you may even find the materials to compare the norms of progress for deaf and hearing children. Too often, teachers adopt a wait-and-see attitude instead of making accurate, up-to-the-minute assessments. The authors' bias is for the latter: It is better to know right away that your child is slipping behind than to come up short at the end of the school year.

Don't pass over one of the most valuable sources of information on teacher effectiveness: your child. Ask your child about school every single day and listen carefully to the response. Don't dismiss or underestimate any of the child's reports, and if you get a consistent negative theme—"I *hate* school" or "I don't feel well; I can't go to school"—resist the temptation to pooh-pooh it. Negativity is a red flag that may indicate a serious adjustment problem. Think back over the various signals that have come your way. Do you get positive reports of the teacher, or does the relationship seem troubled? Does the teacher communicate with you easily, and in those communications, do you recognize your child? Or do you feel the teacher is misinterpreting your child and his or her educational situation? Pay attention to comments, remarks, and written messages that don't quite ring true, and follow up on them *immediately* by discussing them with the teacher. Remember, evaluating your child's teachers is not a science, and you don't have to be a lab psychologist. Your personal impressions, observations, and intuitions can coalesce to form a pretty informative picture.

The following questions may help you to focus your observations. If you decide to make a checklist to take along on your classroom visit, consider putting some of these questions on it.

WHAT ARE THE TEACHER'S EXPECTATIONS OF THE CHILDREN IN THE CLASS?

This question comes first because, as has been well documented, if you expect children to fail, that expectation will be communicated to them by body language and actions. Sure enough, they will fail.[1] This is not to say that if you expect children to succeed, they will, just by thoughts and actions alone. But most children—for that matter, most people of any age—will pick up on expectations and stretch their capacities and try harder for a caring, involved teacher than for one who considers their efforts useless. Deaf children are quite sensitive and perceptive to their teacher's expectations of them and often want to be given more challenging work to do in the classroom.[2]

Teachers should set high standards for our children. The criterion is simple: Teachers should expect the same achievements of deaf students as they do from hearing students. Any statement or implication of academic limitation based on being deaf is utterly unacceptable. Ask what hearing students of the same age are doing, and then compare your child's assignments and performance levels to that. And make sure that the results aren't isolated among the deaf group—achievement should be ranked within the whole class, with the same criteria applied to all. If you sense discouragement or resignation in the teacher's attitude ("The child is hopeless in language—I wouldn't expect significant gains," or "This group has never had a strong grasp of math—I guess it never will"), take those impressions seriously. This may be a teacher who is undermining your child's best efforts.

On the other hand, it is important to recognize an honest and constructive opinion when it is given. There's a difference between the negativism of a burned-out teacher with no faith in deaf children's abilities and the measured observation of an astute professional observer. The latter is too valuable to dismiss lightly. It's one thing to hear, "Your child can't learn word order. If I were you, I'd stop pushing her." It is another to hear, "Your child seems to have difficulty in grasping English word order, perhaps due to late detection and a relative lack of exposure. I think she needs extra tutoring." Note the difference: The first teacher simply wants you to give up, the second one made a constructive suggestion.

You may spend a lot of time trying to understand the real meaning of what a teacher tells you. For the benefit of an extra pair of eyes and a different perspective, it is a good idea for both parents to make the visit. Alternatively, bring a friend or relative. Or even better, discuss your questions with the parent of another deaf child; such parents undoubtedly will find a way of asking you to reciprocate—another productive and useful form of networking that guards against isolation and errors of judgment. Remember to pay forward the help you got from other parents of a deaf child.

DOES THE TEACHER CONCENTRATE HEAVILY ON LANGUAGE?

As a layperson, you won't necessarily be able to evaluate a teacher's competence in the chosen mode of communication, particularly if that mode is American Sign Language (ASL) or Manually Coded English. However, you can get a sense of the emphasis the teacher places on good language use. The clue lies in how carefully the teacher monitors the children's use of language and corrects their mistakes. If a child uses the wrong verb form, does the teacher correct the child gently, in a way that doesn't frustrate the communication effort? This sort of monitoring—listening hard and deciding whether or not the child's language needs fine tuning—is difficult to maintain. You'll be able to tell, to some degree, whether the teacher pays attention and keeps standards high, or is letting them slip.

As in all things, seek a balance. Some teachers—like some parents—can go overboard in correcting every tiny error. Children often retreat from such a barrage of criticism, sometimes from using language altogether. This is known in academic circles as an *affective filter*: the child will simply tune out when they get what they perceive as negative criticism. So look for a balance in the teacher's approach between correcting and letting communication flow—all based on a healthy, robust teacher-child relationship. If the children know that the teacher really cares about them and their ability to use language correctly, they'll accept correction more easily than if they experience it as a personal criticism.

Another sort of balance you want to look for is how much control the teacher has over the dialogue in the classroom. You certainly do not want a teacher who controls every word and completely dominates their class. Instead, look for teachers who actively engage their students in a dialogue and allows them to freely contribute to the discussion while giving appropriate and positive feedback. Also watch their line of questioning; a good teacher is quite persistent and patient in getting answers from a student rather than giving up and "spoon feeding" them the answers.[3] Remember that, above all, in teaching language, the goal is to teach *comprehension*. Skill in manipulating empty language forms—constructions without meaning for the child who is working so hard—is not the goal. Remember our "parrot" analogy we mentioned previously. A living language that deepens and grows in meaning will be your child's highway to independence. The chief goal of your child's education should be providing access to that highway via literacy.

How Much Time Goes into General Education?

Children who are deaf need to learn more than language. We must expect and require that they are taught math, science, history, problem solving, library skills, computer literacy—the full range of subjects that make up a well-rounded education and adequate preparation for the next stage of learning. True, all these subjects bring with them particular vocabularies, spelling and grammatical challenges, and so forth, but this applies to hearing as well as deaf children. Make sure your child's curriculum is identical to that of hearing children of the same age.

How Strongly Does the Teacher Emphasize Listening Skills?

This section will apply more to children with cochlear implants and hearing aids. Try to determine how seriously the teacher takes your child's potential in learning listening skills. To break the subject down further, you can ask yourself the following questions when you make your classroom visit:

- How do the teacher and audiologist work together with the deaf students?
- What happens when assistive listening devices break down? Is this treated as important, or are the devices allowed to sit around without being repaired while the children who need them go without?
- Are children helped to become responsible for their own listening needs, making independent decisions about their cochlear implants and hearing aids—when to wear them, how to use them—and keeping them maintained?
- Does the teacher understand that not all deaf children need amplification and that the need for assistive devices is related to parental choices and the child's level of hearing, mode of communication, and type of educational program?

A teacher who seems resigned—"Well, they're all deaf, so why teach them to listen?"—does not understand residual hearing or the wide range of hearing levels, from hard of hearing to profoundly deaf. Such a teacher is ignoring a significant potential route to communication and learning. Whatever the mode of communication your child uses, look for activities in the classroom designed to encourage the development of listening skills. Does the teacher ask the children to respond to specific sounds—to discriminate, for example, between an unseen drum and bell? Does the teacher speak distinctly when using spoken English? Determine to your satisfaction that the teacher understands and respects children's hearing potential, whether or not it has been measured. Note: Keep in mind that if your child's teacher is deaf, this should not be construed as meaning they do not value listening skills. Some do, and some do not. Their primary concern will still be *literacy* for your child. Your child will only spend 10 to 15% of their time in a classroom compared to more than 50% at home and in the community. So teaching your child to be responsible and independently wear and maintain their amplification device is a good idea.

How Careful Is the Teacher about Making Sure Your Child Has Amplification Every Day?

Scan the classroom to see how many children are wearing a hearing aid or cochlear implant. If you see a child without one, ask the teacher for an explanation. The teacher's answer may vary, depending on the child's situation. Let's look at some sample answers to the question "Why isn't that child wearing an aid?"

"Her parents have chosen not to use a cochlear implant or hearing aids for their child."

This indicates that the teacher respects the choices and decisions made by parents.

"He has one, but it broke yesterday, and it is being repaired."

This answer indicates that the teacher is aware that the aid is missing and knows the reason why.

"Hmmm. Oh, thanks for mentioning it. Well, they forget sometimes, you know, or try to sneak out of wearing the aids."

This can be interpreted two ways; sometimes a child is avoiding wearing aids and purposely trying to deceive the teacher. But you can be sure that the teacher who seems lackadaisical about the idea that a student's aid is missing won't be stressing listening skills to their fullest.

"That child just simply refuses to wear his hearing aid or cochlear implant. I have discussed this with the parents already."

This is most likely to happen as a child gets older and becomes more self-conscious about his or her appearance and trying to "fit in" with their peers. The authors saw this many times as adolescents. Children will wear their aids at home and then hide them at school. Whether the child eventually goes back to wearing it or rejects it from then on depends on if he or she feels it is beneficial. Teachers need to keep parents abreast of such developments, so that a discussion can take place with the child about this issue. Be sure the child is making this choice for valid reasons and not merely out of social consciousness. A teacher's awareness of this issue shows a commitment to deliver information in a variety of ways and to make strong use of whatever hearing each child possesses. Teachers need to take initiative on behalf of children's education and social awareness, and not step back and let things slide simply without telling the family.

A good teacher who takes a hands-off attitude while a child sits in the classroom cut off from all potential sources of information is missing an opportunity to play his or her professional role: finding ways, all possible ways, of conveying information and ideas to every student in the classroom. The authors are not saying the teacher should make decisions about a child's amplification; however, he or she should ensure the family is aware of what the child is doing.

IS THE TEACHER SENSITIVE ABOUT USING APPROPRIATE COMMUNICATION IN YOUR CHILD'S PRESENCE?

Probably all of us remember from childhood what it is like to be discussed as if we weren't present. Many deaf adults report this irritating, often humiliating, experience as one that occurred frequently throughout their school careers. Watch out for insensitive teachers who make remarks about deaf students in front of them— remarks they'd never dream of making in front of hearing pupils. "Oh, Carol's never going to progress much further. Her parents started her too late." Or "Nobody understands James. His speech is completely unintelligible." Or even, "You'd never know Alison was deaf if she didn't open her mouth."

A teacher who ignores or forgets the possibility that students may be speechreading such remarks or picking up their significance in other ways betrays a lack of faith in the effectiveness of the communication skills being taught in the classroom. Use the criterion of what would be acceptable in a completely hearing classroom to judge the appropriateness of the teacher's remarks about deaf students.

Another big pet peeve of deaf adults and students are teachers who either do not use sign language in front of them or talk as if they were not there. This is just rude behavior, plain and simple. Also, most learning is incidental, and picking up on adult conversations is a crucial means of learning and gaining cultural knowledge of the world around us. Why should it be any different for your child? If the conversation is meant to be private, then they should leave the room, not just merely cover up their mouths. Again you'd be surprised what children can actually pick up sometimes.

DOES THE COMMUNICATION BETWEEN THE TEACHER AND DEAF STUDENTS FLOW FREELY IN BOTH DIRECTIONS?

Here are some points to consider in assessing the reciprocity of teacher-student communication:

1. Does the teacher understand (or at least try hard to understand) everything the children say?
2. Does the teacher seem to dominate the dialogue as one way to avoid listening to the children?
3. Does the teacher give appropriate feedback to the children?
4. Do the children enjoy being in the classroom and interacting with the teacher, or are many exchanges anxiety-producing "lessons" that are painful for both parties?
5. Does the teacher give all the students a chance to express themselves and participate?
6. If the children have differing levels of communicative ability, does the teacher attempt to help all other people in the room understand those who have difficulty expressing themselves?
7. As mentioned before, does the teacher *absolutely refrain* from covering his or her mouth to keep children from speechreading private comments to another adult? (This sounds like a cruel practice, but many of the people interviewed for this book reported being cut out of conversations in just this way.)
8. Does the teacher have the bad habit of comparing deaf children among themselves, turning their communication strengths and weaknesses into an uncomfortable competition?

Some teachers are inclined to lump all deaf and hard of hearing children together and draw attention to those with the "best" speech in the group, the "highest" intelligence, and so on. Hope for—*clamor* for—the finely trained teacher who understands that individual students learn at their own pace. Fanning the flames of competition only creates anxiety and self-consciousness that can actually interfere with the education process.

DOES THE TEACHER ENCOURAGE FREE-FLOWING COMMUNICATION AMONG STUDENTS?

If communication among students is discouraged, you're going to need to find out why. A classroom where the only communication is between student and teacher deprives students of an important aspect of education. Remember, your child is in school to learn social interaction with his or her peers as well as to study academics.

IS THE TEACHER'S APPROACH CONSISTENT WITH THAT OF OTHER TEACHERS IN THE SCHOOL?

Continuity is a crucial factor in education. Going from grade to grade can be a bumpy trip if each teacher has distinct and conflicting ideas about communication and language learning. In this area, you're going to need to do a little interviewing to see how much attention the school has paid to ensuring continuity in terms of classroom services and practices that affect language learning and communication.

The Inclusive Classroom

If you are looking into an inclusive program for your child, you will need to consider not only the general attributes of the program (discussed in detail in Chapter 12) but also aspects of the particular classroom where your child will be assigned. The following are some specific questions to consider:

1. Is someone in the school responsible for helping the deaf and hard of hearing children make the transition comfortably?
2. Are procedures in place for drawing your child into social interaction with hearing peers?
3. Has the teacher considered instituting a buddy system, so that hearing students alert deaf students to when directions are being given or a change is taking place in classroom activity?

4. If your child uses sign language, are there hearing peers in the classroom who know sign language or are willing to learn it, so that the child will not be isolated? In the ideal classroom, you will find a teacher who includes sign language training in the curriculum for all students. Hearing children usually are enthusiastic about learning sign, and they learn it much more quickly than adults. The two-pronged advantage of teaching sign language in an inclusive classroom is that it quickly demystifies the question of alternative modes of communication while enabling all the deaf and hearing children to communicate freely.

5. If hearing students are learning to sign, are they competent enough to communicate effectively? Hearing students may appear to be communicating with deaf students while actually engaging in a form of "baby sign" that limits access to social and educational dialogue. Unless you're a skilled signer yourself, you may be fooled by energetic signing between hearing and deaf students and assume that the level of communication is high. If necessary, bring in a professional interpreter or a skilled signing parent to observe and report to you on this and other sign-related matters.

6. Does your child have full access to the education being offered? Does every class have a qualified interpreter, including during extramural activities? If no interpreter is used, is a form of captioning, such as CART, available (see Chapter 12)? If your child uses amplification, does the teacher use an FM system or other sort of microphone?

7. Does the school hire qualified/certified interpreters? Consider the following criteria:
   a. Does the certification come by way of a local or state agency or a national certifying organization, such as RID (Registry of Interpreters for the Deaf) or the Educational Interpreting Performance Assessment (EIPA)? Often, certification from the larger, national organizations is more reliable; however, professionals with this level of certification are in great demand and may not be available at your school. Most states now have specific requirements for educational interpreters.

b. Are the interpreters skillful enough to enable deaf students to learn at the same level as their hearing peers? (This is the requirement under federal law.)

c. How do the interpreters interact with deaf students in the classroom? Are the students really watching them with enthusiasm—nodding to show they agree or get the message, revealing other signs of comprehension and engagement?

d. Do the interpreters enable the deaf students to participate fully, or is there a marginal quality to the deaf students' involvement?

e. Do you sense a good relationship between the teacher and the interpreters, or is there, perhaps, resentment at the presence of "extra" adults on the scene?

Summing Up

In ending this chapter, let's look again at the interviews with administrators of elementary school programs for deaf students. The administrators were asked to describe the worst and best classroom situations they had ever visited. Here are two of the most revealing responses. They can serve as reminders of what to look for when you visit your child's class.

The Worst Classroom

The worst classroom for the deaf I've ever visited? Oh, that's easy. It comes to mind in all its awful detail, because it was such a terrible class and such a delicate situation. The school was in a fairly rural area, about an hour's drive from the nearest city. The children were all in fourth or fifth grade and came from all over a two-county area. The really tragic part was that the kids had been in the same group with the same teacher for four years, and they had every prospect of remaining with her for several more years.

The heart of the problem was the teacher. The room looked okay at first—cheery and comfortable. There were lots of materials of various kinds on the walls. It wasn't until later that I started seeing—well, you'll understand.

I could sense a huge gap between students and teacher as soon as I sat down. The teacher just wasn't getting through to the kids, she wasn't *communicating* at all. She was talking—it was an oral program—at a level and in a vocabulary that I knew the children couldn't understand. The awful part was that the teacher didn't know she wasn't getting through. She had absolutely no self-knowledge regarding her effectiveness.

She wasn't trained as a teacher of deaf children. She was a regularly credentialed teacher and licensed speech pathologist. It seems that she was the closest to a teacher of the deaf that the district could find to fill the job—it wasn't the kind of place that was likely to attract a highly trained teacher.

This teacher seemed to feel comfortable and competent in her role, but she was clearly unqualified to teach language. She had taken a lot of classes, but she obviously couldn't put book learning into practice. She had plenty of good sources, all the right books—but for herself, not for the kids. There wasn't even a projector in the classroom.

I watched her teach a reading lesson to a little girl, and the reasons for her ineffectiveness became clear. The girl would pronounce every word in a sentence—the teacher had taught her how to say each word—but without a glimmer of comprehension. The teacher would repeat every word after her: "Bobby (Bobby) went (went) to (to). . . ." Then the teacher would ask a question: "Where did Bobby go?" The girl would have no idea, none at all—wouldn't even understand the question—but after a slight pause the teacher would say, "Yes, Bobby went to the store." And the girl, a good speechreader, would repeat, "Bobby went to the store."

For four years, the teacher had been answering her own questions or feeding the answers to the kids, and she had no idea she had been doing that. Those kids were four to six years behind where they should have been. (Authors' note: Remember our comment about "spoon-feeding".)

After I'd been in the classroom for a while, I started reading some of the things written on the bulletin board. I remember clearly a very long poem. This teacher liked poetry. This long poem was probably at a ninth-grade level. It was easy to see that it was inappropriate for every child in the class, as none were reading above a first-grade level. I found out later that the teacher was really working on that poem with the children. They'd been reading it aloud for weeks and weeks. She was just getting them to say the words, but there wasn't any comprehension. That's all she ever taught those kids to do.

The Best Classroom

The best classroom I've visited is one I'm quite familiar with. I think the key is that everything that goes on there fits together. The teacher teaches a science lesson and then uses the vocabulary from the lesson in the language lesson. The words also go onto the bulletin board with a picture of the principle being explained, and perhaps there's a living demonstration of the lesson in the science corner.

It would be obvious to any visitor that plenty of language is taught in this classroom. Everywhere there are things posted on the walls to reinforce language skills. Obviously, this teacher is above all a great language teacher with terrific communication skills. She's completely tuned in to the children's signing skills and studies their writing minutely—she doesn't let any errors slip by without mentioning them. If the child writes *sister* but really means the plural *sisters,* she points it out and asks for a repeat. Her corrections are gentle and patient, but her standards are very high. And her kids really want to perform for her.

Another wonderful thing about this classroom is the teacher's aide, a young deaf woman with some residual hearing and excellent communication skills. She is very popular with the students and a great role model. I remember one incident in which she made use of her own deafness to great effect. Two of the students in the room absolutely hated wearing their hearing aids—they'd leave them home, break them, or take them off and lose them at school. The teacher was at her wit is end about it, so one day, the aide took up the challenge. When she noticed that one of the students was missing a lot of important material that she could have heard with her hearing aid, the aide got angry: "How can you leave home without your aid? You have so much hearing! How can you give it up? I'd never *dream* of going anywhere without my hearing aid!" The day after this outburst both wayward hearing aids appeared. The image of the aide as a successful working person who made use of every route to communication seemed to have made a deep impression.

The teacher and aide in the second classroom worked *with* the deaf children's needs rather than in opposition to those needs. They acknowledged the specialness of the situation and found ways—great ways, new ways, customized and imaginative ways—to get the information flowing back and forth.

We hope these little sketches give you a springboard for making assessments on your own classroom visits. Let's turn now to the types of school programs you'll be choosing from.

Notes

1. Rhonda S. Weinstein, *Reaching Higher: The Power of Expectations in Schooling* (Cambridge MA: Harvard University Press, 2002).

2. David H. Smith, "Deaf Adults: Retrospective Narratives of School Experiences and Teacher Expectations," *Disability & Society* 28, no. 5 (2013): 674–86.

3. David H. Smith and Claire L. Ramsey. "Classroom Discourse Practices of a Deaf Teacher Using American Sign Language." *Sign Language Studies* 5, no. 1 (2004): 39–62.

12 Choosing a School

TIME TO get down to specifics and describe the kinds of schools available to your child. There's no need to point out that the type of school you choose will determine the course of your child's education, unless and until you decide to make a change somewhere down the line.

As you begin studying the range of available options, we would like to make three general suggestions. First, whatever your child's age, begin *early* to collect information: Make inquiries, visit schools, meet with teachers and principals, and get on every school mailing list you can. Talk, talk, and talk to other parents, to deaf adults who have children in the programs you are considering, to deaf alumni of the programs, and to deaf adults outside the school system in the world at large. Keep in mind that choices may be limited, depending on where you live. Obviously rural areas tend to have fewer options. It is not unusual for a family to move to a different geographical location to be closer to a specific type of program that better meets their child's needs.

Second, set aside everything you've ever heard about deaf education, especially about the various kinds of schools and schoolrooms where deaf children are enrolled. This subject is absolutely contaminated with buzzwords, stereotypes, distortions, and ridiculous beliefs. Allow us to offer you a fresh introduction. (A note on terminology: To avoid confusion in using a vocabulary that is often value- and emotion-laden, we'll try to define the terms in this chapter as clearly as possible, and in a manner that coincides with reality.)

Third, you will often hear the term *least-restrictive environment* (LRE) being bandied about during meetings and discussions with school administrators and teachers. This term came about after the passage of the original Education of All Handicapped Children Act (Public Law 94-142) passed in 1975, which we will discuss later in this chapter. This law is the basis of allowing children with special needs to be placed in public school systems with appropriate supports. The original idea behind LRE (and still being promoted as policy) was that, on a continuum, the regular education classrooms were the least restrictive for children with disabilities, whereas on the other end, the most restrictive were residential programs or specialized institutions.

LRE policy as applied to deaf children is actually quite a contradiction. Remember our mantra that being deaf is about communication access. Which setting, regular education or a school/program for deaf children, would you generally consider the least restrictive in terms of communication? Of course, a program that caters to the specific communication needs of deaf children is going to be far less restrictive and more accessible than a regular education classroom. This is what the authors like to call the *paradox of LRE*. So keep this in mind as you look at programs and ask questions.

This chapter covers the following various types of schooling available today for deaf and hard of hearing children:
- mainstreaming or inclusion within regular education schools,
- day classes within regular schools,
- co-teaching programs,
- day or charter schools for deaf children,
- state residential schools for deaf children, and
- private residential schools for deaf children.

Note that some of these settings listed above may or may not include early childhood intervention programs. If your school district doesn't offer an early childhood education program, then you will be more likely to find these in specialized deaf schools and programs than in regular education schools.

Inclusion

It is important to understand that although the terms *mainstreaming* and *inclusion* are typically used interchangeably, they are *not* the same thing. Both involve the process of sending children with special needs into regular classes—as opposed to special classes or special schools. The difference between the two is described in the following:[1]

- Mainstreaming came out of the original Education of All Handicapped Children Act (Public Law 94-142), which emphasized education in the LRE. The idea was that students with disabilities who were able to adapt and fit into regular classrooms would be able to *receive an equivalent education and the social experiences of their peers* with some accommodations, such as interpreters, note takers, and tutoring.

- Inclusion came out of the reauthorization of the original law, Individuals with Disabilities Education Act (IDEA) in 1997, with the added mandate that children with disabilities would be educated to the maximum extent appropriate with their nondisabled peers. Basically, the focus is on the classroom to be *adapted to meet the needs of the deaf child rather than the child fitting into the class.* In other words, the child is included as a full member of the classroom and school community.

For deaf and hard of hearing children, in both situations, this means attending classes with their hearing peers. Deaf students using any mode of communication can be mainstreamed or included into regular classrooms. The law requires that the school provide the support services required by the individual student, as determined by mode of communication, skill level, hearing level, and so on.

At the core of inclusion is the legal requirement by IDEA that your child will be provided the following services below. Who gives these services depends on the age of your child; birth to age three services are provided by early childhood intervention programs, and you can usually find them with an Internet search of "early intervention services" with the name of your state. After age three, the early interventionists will help you transition to an appropriate preschool in coordination with your local school district, which is responsible for the education of your child until the age of twenty-two or when your child graduates at eighteen, sometimes at seventeen, with a diploma. The latter is what you are expecting, right?

1. *A thorough, fair assessment of the child's situation and educational needs, free of discrimination and done in a child's native language.* Ideally, this is done by professionals with a strong background in deafness. The word *ideally* is a concession to reality; professionals with the necessary skills and expertise are a rarity and are unavailable in most communities. The risk is that your child will be assessed by professionals who *don't know that they don't know.* This is why it is important for you to be well informed.

2. *A free and appropriate education* (FAPE) that meets the child's needs, which should occur to the maximum extent appropriate with nondisabled children. For babies, the rule is that to the maximum extent appropriate to the needs of the child, early intervention services must be provided in natural environments, including the home and community settings in which children without disabilities participate.

3. *An individualized family services plan* (IFSP) for children up to age three. At three years of age, an *individualized education program* (IEP) must be developed that is unique to the child. The IFSP guides the early intervention process. It contains information about the services needed to foster a child's development and helps the family appropriately nurture the child's development. A service coordinator works with the family by coordinating the services outlined in the IFSP. An IEP, under law, *must* be aligned with your state's academic content standards for the grade in which the child is enrolled. Additionally, it specifies the child's unique educational needs, states present levels of performance, identifies measurable annual goals and short-term objectives, and describes the specific special education and related services that will be provided to help the child attain those goals and benefit from education.

4. Placement of the student in the *least restrictive environment (LRE)* possible—in your child's case, the one most accessible

to effective communication, as we said before. For early childhood, the natural environment is the preferred environment. We do recommend early childhood deaf programs outside the home to enhance the communication skills of both the child and parents. To ensure an LRE, service providers and school districts must provide a continuum of placement and service alternatives. (If a private deaf school is deemed appropriate, costs are sometimes, but not always, covered by the school district.)

5. *Due process safeguards* to protect the rights of children and their parents. Parental consent must be obtained for initial and all subsequent evaluations and placement decisions regarding special education. If you disagree with the results of an evaluation performed by the school or service providers, you can obtain an independent evaluation at your own expense. When the school and parents disagree with the components of an IFSP or IEP for the child, the parents may request mediation and a due process hearing. Parents may have the right to reimbursement for attorney's fees and other expenses if they prevail in due process proceedings.

6. *Parents and students must be involved* in the planning and implementation of their IFSPs and IEPs. Obviously, an infant will not be able to give input toward an IFSP. But the parents' and student's input (when mature enough) and desires related to their future goals need to be considered in all of the contents of an IEP. The authors *strongly* encourage the participation of your child in these meetings and deliberations when age appropriate, definitely by middle school age. After all, you will be discussing *their* future. One other thing: Parents can invite people who have special knowledge and expertise about your child to IEP meetings. It could be professionals, parent advocates, a friend, and other family members.

As you meet to discuss your child's IFSP or IEP, there are many factors to consider, and it can be quite intimidating at first. For this reason, we strongly suggest you find another parent who is familiar with the process to attend the meetings with you. Keep in mind that the IFSP/IEP reflects the resources of the state early intervention agency or public school—what it has to offer in terms of specialists, support, and expertise—as well as the needs of the individual child.

Inclusion isn't just one kind of arrangement, but an array of plans determined on the one hand by the available public resources and on the other by the student's individual needs. Here's a brief run-down of the most common types of mainstreaming or inclusion:

- *Total mainstreaming without special services.* The deaf student goes to his or her neighborhood school, attends regular classes with hearing peers, and receives no special services at all. *This kind of mainstreaming is illegal unless you agree to it, which we don't recommend.*

- *Total inclusion with support services.* The deaf student attends regular classes at the neighborhood school with accommodations provided in the classroom and during extracurricular activities. This is responsible inclusion under the law. (See "Support Services for Deaf Children in Inclusive Classrooms" on page 248.)

- *Partial inclusion or split placement.* The deaf student attends a local public school but is based in a special room with a trained teacher of deaf children. The student attends selected classes or activities with the hearing students. Conversely, the deaf student may be based in the regular classroom and attend special sessions with a visiting teacher, called an *itinerant teacher of deaf children,* at certain times during the week.

- *Co-teaching* (also called *co-enrollment*). Teachers of deaf children team up with general education teachers to teach a significant number of deaf children within the regular classroom environment.

The first type of inclusion defined here—total mainstreaming without special services—was basically the only choice before 1975 as an alternative to sending one's deaf child off to residential schools. It often accomplished the very *opposite* of true inclusion by setting a child down in the midst of hearing peers without the tools to enter into the educational process—a little like putting the child in a canoe in a fast-moving river and urging him or her to navigate without a paddle.

Parents still *can* choose this route by refusing special education services. In our experience, parents of hard of hearing children or those with "successful" cochlear implants sometimes do make this choice—an unfortunate one—because these children often seem enough like hearing children that their special needs within the classroom can be completely overlooked. Please, if you are a parent of a deaf or hard of hearing child and are considering total mainstreaming without special education services, put off your decision until you finish this book, and contact one or more of the professional organizations devoted to informing and supporting the public on deafness and deaf education. (See the Appendix: Resources for Parents on page 325 for a list of resources in the United States.)

RESPONSIBLE INCLUSION

Public Law 94-142, and its later version, IDEA, saved hundreds of thousands of families across the country, and will save millions more, from the anguish of finding their children shut out of the public school system and having to come up with their own way to secure an education for them. But there's more to the story than appears on the surface. Inclusion is an area of debate where feelings run very high.

We've called this section "Responsible Inclusion" to draw attention to the fact that not all legal inclusion or mainstreaming efforts *are* responsible. In this context, the word *responsible* has a precise and crucial meaning. Responsible inclusion is an arrangement that is *in the best interests of the children.* Except for a very small group with severe disabilities, deaf children are capable of successfully learning grade-level content and making significant academic progress when *appropriate instruction, services, and supports are provided.*

At the risk of appearing to be cynical, the authors feel it is necessary to warn you of the great danger that your child may be isolated in an *irresponsible* inclusion situation. You need to know that the public education system is vulnerable to the following two kinds of professional educators who have misplaced goals at cross-purposes with educating deaf children:

1. Overeager and zealous teachers and others who insist on "normalizing" all children with special needs, with the result that the particular educational issues related to deafness never get addressed; and

Support Services for Deaf Children in Inclusive Classrooms

The following are the support services a school district should supply in order to deliver a complete education to a deaf child in a regular classroom:

- *A trained teacher of deaf students.* A special resource teacher trained in the effects of deafness on communication and education is a necessary requirement not only for the benefit of deaf students but also to train the general education teachers in a school with deaf students. Schools and school districts have various ways of providing a special resource teacher, usually depending on how many deaf children are enrolled in the school or district. Some schools have a special resource room for deaf students; some districts establish a special program in one elementary, middle, and high school for all deaf and hard of hearing students in the district. In some districts, an itinerant teacher of deaf students "floats" from school to school.

- *Certified interpreters.* In most regular classrooms, the teacher does not know sign language and is difficult to understand, even for a child trained in oral skills. Interpreters, using the child's particular mode of communication, translate all communication that takes place in the classroom. Although you probably already know about sign language interpreters, it might surprise you that there are also oral interpreters who sit near the child and carefully mouth (or enunciate) at a normal rate of speed and will generally be a few words behind a speaker in the smooth repetition of statements. Any interpreter hired by the school should be qualified and have the proper certifications required by the state.

- *Note takers.* Imagine the difficulty of reading lips or watching signs and taking notes simultaneously. It can't be done. Deaf students need someone to take notes for them while they absorb the information visually. Sometimes note takers are friends who agree to take notes; sometimes they are fellow students paid by the school district. One interviewee offered an astute tip on note taking: Very often, the best students are not the best note takers. The ideal note taker may be an average student—one who has to work hard to keep up.

- *Speech-to-text services* are often used in place of sign language interpreters for students who do not use sign language or when the classroom content may contain specific vocabulary that is more easily presented in print. These can go by names, such as CART (Communication Access Realtime Translation), Typewell, or C-Print.

- *Tutors.* Deaf students may need tutors to help them stay on course, but an overreliance on tutors could mean it is time to reassess. The law guarantees an appropriate education in the LRE, but if the student is having to spend hours and hours in special tutoring to receive the information delivered in the classroom, might not these grueling extra hours be considered restrictive?

- *Other specialists.* In an inclusive environment, your child may require or benefit from the services of speech therapists, auditory therapists, audiologists, psychological counselors, occupational therapists, adaptive physical education specialists, and vocational counselors experienced in working with deaf children.

- *Special equipment.* To make information available visually, the mainstream classroom must provide visual aids, such as captioned videos and television monitors. ❏

2. Money-minded administrators who see inclusion as something to be done as cheaply as possible, (i.e., the fewer services, the better), because funding for their school or district is based on enrollment numbers. They, of course, will never admit that money is an issue.

The upshot is a tendency in some schools to include every deaf and other special-needs child *without regard to the appropriateness of the education provided for each individual case,* and often without the necessary and legally required support services.

This doesn't mean that inclusion may not be appropriate for your child, only that it is important to know the possible pitfalls. The decision is a weighty one. In a public school program, your child may be the only deaf student or one of only a few in the entire school. The professionals involved in such a program are unlikely to be highly trained and may be ignorant of the telltale signs that a deaf child is not functioning well. Despite the legalities, there is no guarantee that the school will offer the best possible services appropriate to your child's particular educational needs. Your child could well be isolated both socially and educationally, and this could lead to emotional problems and a debilitating sense of differentness. We articulate these possibilities bluntly in order to paint a complete picture. However, inclusion holds equally positive possibilities: an ease at being in both worlds, Deaf and hearing, and full access to the mainstream society.

Refer to the "Checklist for Evaluating Deaf Education Programs" on page 252 to ask yourself some important questions as you consider this option. You'll find that each question is related to one of two general questions:

1. Is the school equipped to provide the special support services your child requires in order to receive an education equivalent to that of the hearing students, as required by law?
2. Does your child have the particular characteristics that would allow him or her to thrive as the only deaf child in the school, or one of only a few?

Let's look at the first of these two questions. What are the components of responsible and responsive inclusion? The following list includes the minimum requirements a public school should provide to ensure a good education to a deaf student:

1. The school should have a large enough number of deaf students, so that they can be grouped by age, grade level, and skill level—not, as in some less-than-ideal settings, grouped all together.
2. The staff must include qualified teachers of deaf children and knowledgeable supervisors, all fully trained to communicate with deaf and hard of hearing students.
3. The curriculum must be appropriate to the abilities and needs of the children enrolled and aligned to the grade-level education standards of your state.
4. The school must provide supplemental services as needed to ensure that the students *receive* the education provided.
5. The school should offer extracurricular activities to which deaf students have full access and in which they can participate meaningfully. Yes, you can request interpreters for these activities.
6. Parental support and parent education should be built into the program.
7. The school should provide deaf students access to strong role models who use the students' particular communication modes.
8. Vocational counseling and transition training designed especially for deaf students should be provided in the higher grades.
9. The school must be equipped with the instructional equipment necessary to convey information to deaf students: amplification, captioned videos, overhead projectors, and so on.

The second question—whether your child is a good candidate for inclusion—is more difficult. To answer it, you need to know your child very well and be a bit of a fortune-teller. Let us save you a little networking and share some information from interviews with deaf adults and children. Those who have already gone through inclusion themselves used the following elements to achieve mainstream success in school:

1. strong social skills (one person said his sense of humor and passion for sports were key to his success in inclusion),
2. a strong desire to be part of a regular classroom, and

Checklist for Evaluating Deaf Education Programs

You may find it useful to study this checklist before a school visit or to carry it with you when you interview teachers and administrators. These questions are appropriate for any type of school program and for whatever mode of communication your child uses.

Questions about the School's General Philosophy and Attitudes
1. What is the school's point of view on deafness—does it approach deafness primarily from a clinical, educational, or cultural perspective?
2. What are the school's goals with respect to my child? How does the school expect me to participate?
3. What general expectations do the faculty and staff have for deaf students?
4. What is the school's philosophy regarding discipline?
5. In a deaf school, what opportunities are available for inclusion into hearing society? And in particular, what opportunities are there for gaining English language experience?
6. Whatever the program—whether in a deaf school or an inclusive public school—what is the philosophy regarding inclusion of deaf children in regular classes?

Questions about the Curriculum
1. What philosophy underlies the school's educational curriculum?
2. How does the curriculum integrate auditory training, English, reading, writing, science, and so on?
3. What is the program for developing the students' English skills?
4. In a spoken language program, does the classroom teacher develop and maintain the speaking skills of the students, or is this left to a speech and language specialist outside the classroom?
5. Is there a teacher's aide in the classroom?
6. What is the homework policy?

7. How heavily is writing emphasized as part of the English program?
8. What are some of the unique features of the curriculum?
9. What subjects are covered every single day?
10. In a spoken language program, are speech, speechreading, and auditory training part of the daily classroom work, or are they handled outside the regular classroom?
11. What sign system do the teachers use? What system does the school recommend for use at home?
12. How are social skills fostered in the classroom?
13. How does the curriculum address the students' emotional and psychological needs?

Questions about Student Evaluation
1. Are the evaluators trained to work with deaf children?
2. How are students tested to identify their academic strengths and weaknesses?
3. Are achievement tests given to show where each student fits in academically?
4. What is the school's grading system, and how is student progress reported to parents?

Questions about the Organization of the School
1. In a mainstream school, is a knowledgeable administrator in charge of the deaf education program? If not, does a specialist in deaf education visit at least once a week?
2. What is the program's main funding source?
3. In a high school program, what extracurricular activities are offered, and are deaf students encouraged to join and given communication support?
4. How large are the classes? What is their composition? What are the students' age ranges?
5. In a mainstream program, is there a mixture of deaf and hearing students in the class?
6. Who is the person ultimately responsible for the program? What is his or her email address and phone number?
7. Who is the on-site person responsible for the program? What is his or her email address and phone number?

Questions about Faculty and Staff Qualifications
1. What are the teachers' levels of expertise in Listening and Spoken Language, English development, and/or sign language?
2. Are the teachers fluent in ASL or English sign (depending on the language used in the classroom), and do their receptive skills match their expressive ones—that is, do they really understand what the students are saying?
3. Do all faculty members have state certification or licensure in deaf education, or master's degrees?

Questions about Support Services
1. What support service professionals are available, such as audiologists, speech and language specialists, psychologists, and counselors?
2. What interpreting services are available? Are they qualified and certified/licensed?
3. What note-taking services are available?
4. Are speech-to-text services available (CART, Typewell, or C-Print)?
5. Is the school equipped with specialized faculty, staff, and support personnel to work with students who have one or more conditions, in addition to deafness, that affect learning and communication?

Questions about Extracurricular Activities
1. What extracurricular activities are available?
2. Are interpreters provided for extracurricular activities?
3. Are teachers, administrators, and staff involved in extracurricular activities?

Questions about Parent Involvement
1. Does the school provide support services for parents? Is there a parent group? If not, is the school open to having one?

2. In an inclusive school program, how are parents involved in developing and implementing the individualized education plan (IEP)?

3. Are parents welcome to make classroom visits? May they visit classrooms other than the one where their child is a student?

4. How is communication assured between home and school? Is there a system of written notes or emails? Who is responsible for contacting the parents if there is a problem? The teacher? An administrator?

5. As the primary caregiver, you have full access to your child's IEP files. All you need to do is request a copy of it in writing from your child's teacher. How easy is the process?

Questions about Deaf Community Involvement

1. Are there deaf administrators, teachers, aides, and support professionals in the school serving as adult models for deaf students?

2. What is the school's perspective on the Deaf community and Deaf culture?

3. Do the hearing personnel have deaf friends, or is involvement in the Deaf community limited to the workday?

Questions about Amplification

1. Are the faculty and staff committed to making sure deaf students wear hearing aids or cochlear implants at all times?

2. Does the school assist families in maintaining the aids or implants by ensuring batteries are available, minor repairs or adjustments, and so on?

3. What amplification system is used in the classroom?

4. Is there an educational audiologist on staff or contracted for services? ❑

3. strong, enthusiastic, and continuous family support, including a willingness on the part of parents to enter into the curriculum with the student, helping with homework, making
sure assignments get done, monitoring progress, and so on.

The interviews provided a wealth of anecdotal detail, some of
which the authors present here to illustrate the range of possible
outcomes in total mainstreaming. Again, we risk the charge of accentuating the negative by beginning with the story of Nate, a sur-
vivor of a classic "mainstream disaster."

> You could have guessed there was trouble ahead: At Nate's house,
> it was dismaying to see him routinely shut out of the dinner-table
> conversation. Nate's parents believed he could pick up anything he
> wanted to know from family discussions; they hadn't a clue about
> the impact of deafness on communication. So Nate was completely
> isolated in his own family. When his parents decided he should be
> mainstreamed at the public high school, they did virtually no re-
> search on the program or its appropriateness for Nate. He was the
> only deaf student at the school.
>
> Going with him to a football game at the high school and seeing
> right away that *nobody*—not his hearing peers, not the teachers, not
> the school principal—felt comfortable with Nate was truly sadden-
> ing. He'd been at the school for several years, and one would have
> thought that Nate and his classmates would have found ways of com-
> municating comfortably, but it was obvious (and probably humiliat-
> ing for Nate), that, at best, both students and faculty perceived him
> as a sort of pet freak. They were polite enough and expressed a kind
> of nervous friendliness, but it was as clear as day that nobody knew
> how to begin to communicate with him. Nobody even tried—and
> this very much included the teachers and the other so-called inclu-
> sion experts.
>
> Nate graduated with a B average from that school, but he was
> emotionally ruined. He then attended Gallaudet University, a lib-
> eral arts university for deaf and hard of hearing students, where he
> felt completely at home and received a wonderful education. But to
> this day, he has deep emotional scars from being totally isolated in
> high school. In the authors' opinion, Nate was "dumped" into the
> public school system—by his parents, his teachers, his principal—
> by all the people who should have known better, who should at

least have seen that there was a problem and stepped in to make a change.

It should be clear why we've begun a series of anecdotes with this particular story. We want you to know that this kind of thing *can* happen. Without an ambassadorial parent constantly monitoring the situation, an included student can be stranded and emotionally traumatized—even while bringing home acceptable grades. Let's go into this with our eyes open.

MAKING THE DECISION CASE BY CASE

The main criterion in assessing the inclusion question is *your child*—his or her cognitive, social, and emotional characteristics plus that inexpressible *something* that is perceivable only through a parent's intuition (of course, intuition can turn out to be wrong, too). Also, remember to keep talking to people.

The idea in describing several more case histories here is to duplicate the networking we urge you to pursue in all decision making on behalf of your deaf child. Find deaf adults who've been through it and parents of deaf children who are ahead of you on the path. Consider the stories of Laura, Jason, Alice, and Pablo as part of your growing collection of real-life stories.

Laura

Laura had always been a straight-A student. She spent the first eight years of her education in a private oral school for deaf students and began mainstreaming in the ninth grade. Her grades remained high after the change, but by the tenth grade, Laura was a nervous wreck—she was even diagnosed at her young age with ulcers! She *seemed* well-adjusted in the high school, but she missed her deaf friends terribly. Every day she spent there, she wanted to go back to her old school.

Laura's parents were violently opposed to her going to a deaf school. They were afraid she'd become trapped in the Deaf world and lose her drive to go to college. Laura argued that she wouldn't—she wanted to be an architect and nothing was going to change her mind about that.

But her parents were adamant. Luckily, when Laura entered the eleventh grade, another deaf girl enrolled in the public school. The two became friends, and that made all the difference. Suddenly, Laura had a life of her own within the school, and she spent her last two years of high school happy and feeling a part of her class. The two girls graduated together, and when Laura enrolled in the National Technical Institute for the Deaf, which is part of the Rochester Institute of Technology in New York, she joined many of her old deaf school friends there.

It is worth noting, however, that Laura's eventual happiness in high school resulted quite accidently. If the other deaf student hadn't enrolled, Laura could have ended up as lonely and humiliated as Nate.

Jason's story is very different from Laura's, although both end well.

Jason

Jason's parents were easygoing, always assuming that "things would work out." Miraculously, they did—probably because Jason's older sister was a tremendous reader and a great academic role model. Jason went to a regular nursery school and then on to his neighborhood public school, which had one trained teacher for deaf students and some very enthusiastic general education teachers. Jason read incessantly. In the first grade, he took classes in sign language in the afternoon, and in the third grade, the school began providing the services of a sign language interpreter in class. Jason went on to the public junior high and high school, always with his nose in a book, and never felt the slightest urge to be elsewhere. He was a mainstream success if there ever was one—a fabulous student and a low-key but completely comfortable socializer.

Now comes a story of distortion and misunderstanding.

Alice

Alice was hard of hearing, and her parents and teachers considered this to be a minor inconvenience, reduced to insignificance by the hearing aids she wore. Her parents enrolled her in her local school; the possibility that she might go to a deaf school was never discussed. However, Alice's hearing loss was centered in the upper frequencies of sound, causing her to miss all "s" sounds. Although she was a good guesser, her language skills developed slowly, and she began to do poorly in her schoolwork. Her sinking grades were ascribed to a lack of aptitude rather than to the fact that she was hard of hearing.

Alice's story underscores inclusion's greatest weakness: the lack of constant monitoring. Alice's parents, her teachers, her principal, her aides—all should have been evaluating her progress with a clear understanding of the impact of deafness on communication and learning. Unfortunately, all the adults involved were lulled by Alice's performance into thinking she was just not very bright.

Let's end not with Alice's sad story but with the story of Pablo, which illustrates the best possibilities of the inclusion experience.

Pablo

Pablo mainstreamed as a freshman into a public high school from a state residential school for deaf students. Always bright, curious, and sociable, he had had plenty of exposure to the hearing world by way of his older brothers, who drew him into their activities whenever he came home from school. When he moved home for good and entered the public high school, his brothers threw themselves into helping him with his schoolwork. The whole family had a lively communicative life, and everybody in it took a great interest in Pablo's progress.

Still, Pablo had problems. He was the only deaf student in the school; and most of his teachers, although willing to help, were not sure how to do it. Slowly, with his brothers' help, Pablo found his own way: He asked other students to be his note takers, showed teachers where he needed to sit to see them clearly, and talked freely with students and teachers about deafness. His biggest boost came from being appointed photographer for the school yearbook. From that job, Pablo gained recognition and respect from the whole student body—not as "that deaf kid" but as a talented photographer. That's how he was remembered at the school after he graduated.

Pablo chose to enroll in a large university that offered a full range of services for deaf students. He plunged right in but met with difficulties that he hadn't faced before—the work was hard, harder than he had expected. Still, he pushed through and graduated, largely on the strength of his positive attitude.

In planning your child's educational future, you'll spend some time gazing into a crystal ball—or at least relying on your intuition to a great degree—to determine whether your child is a good candidate for inclusion. If you *do* decide to enroll your child in a regular school, you'll need to pay attention constantly. You should monitor your child's work and his or her feelings toward the teacher, the school, and other students in the class. You should also pay attention to test scores in order to keep tabs on your child's learning.

Watch! Ask! Monitor! This will be the constant refrain as you continue through this book. It is all a part of being your child's best advocate and ambassador to the world.

PARTIAL INCLUSION

The next option, partial inclusion, combines regular classes and special classes for deaf and hard of hearing students within regular school programs. In many cases, the special offerings for deaf students are limited to physical education, art, and other elective courses. In assessing a partial inclusion program, it is important to ask yourself: How useful are these offerings? Have they been made simply to pacify parents, school administrators, and federal monitors to ensure the federal mandate of participation to the fullest extent possible? Again, the criterion is access. Does the program give deaf students access to a full education equal to that available to hearing students?

Partial inclusion usually is implemented in schools with enough deaf and hard of hearing students to justify the hiring of highly qualified, full-time teachers of deaf students. (Ordinarily, the resources are centered at one school in the district, and this can mean significant commuting time for some students.) The system works differently in different schools. In addition to teaching special classes, the teachers of deaf students frequently serve as resources in case their students need help. Their classes often become social centers for deaf students—places where they can withdraw to build up confidence and to work out whatever social and educational difficulties come up in the regular classroom.

Katimara is a teacher of deaf students who works as a specialist in a school where a number of deaf and hard of hearing children are partially included. These students take most of their classes with the regular student body but return to Katimara's resource room for English and reading. One of Katimara's most valuable talents as a teacher is her ability to work well with administrators and other teachers in her school. Law or no law, many general education professionals can be unenthusiastic about working with deaf and hard of hearing students. Often, they feel overwhelmed by the need to establish support services and ensure deaf students' access to information. Katimara quietly and efficiently takes it upon herself to check out the interpreters, see that students are matched effectively with tutors and note takers, and order special equipment that will convey information visually to her deaf and hard of hearing students.

In other words, Katimara does what needs to be done. The law and the school district can only create the skeleton of an effective program. The heart and soul of that program depend on the teacher.

TEAM TEACHING

Another variation on the inclusion concept is a mixed classroom—one that includes deaf, hard of hearing, and hearing students, with two teachers working as a team. One teacher, qualified and certified to teach deaf students, is fluent in sign language; the other is a general education teacher with at least beginning sign language skills. The class follows the regular school curriculum. The teachers plan lessons jointly, and each teaches all the students. Several times a week, the deaf and hard of hearing students leave the classroom for auditory and speech training.

This is the team-teaching method, also known as *co-enrollment*. It has met with encouraging success but unfortunately is not as widely used as the authors would like it to be. Its creators, Carl Kirchner and Cynthia Murphy, explained the success of their team-teaching program in terms of the two following factors:

1. The deaf and hard of hearing children have prolonged inter-action with both signers and English users; they are isolated from neither.

2. Because the signing teacher and English-speaking teacher are equals in the classroom, neither language dominates. In typical deaf education classrooms, teachers find it diffi-cult to sign and talk simultaneously, and they tend to favor one mode over the other. The results are notorious. If the teacher does more signing than speaking, students who rely on speech, speechreading, and listening are left out; if the teacher speaks more and signs less, the students who use sign language exclusively are left out. Here, with the team in place, two language role models are always functioning, and deaf children can rely on either or both.

When the team-teaching model functions well and is used in rooms with both hearing and deaf students, it clearly exemplifies the chief advantage of inclusion, which is the equalizing of expectations. Historically, deaf students have been dragged down by low expecta-tions; their performance scores in successful inclusion programs demonstrate the benefit of competing on an equal footing with hearing students, working through the same curriculum side by side.

Well-matched teachers experience advantages in team teaching, too. Sharing the load is beneficial, and the children like the rela-tive informality—it is easier for two teachers to keep a loose grip on the class. Also, team teaching lends itself to more small-group activity and less lecturing, which permits more interaction among deaf and hearing peers. Small groups can be designed to deal with special linguistic needs that deaf and hearing children share—and the result is the opposite of isolation. There are real opportunities with the team-teaching model to wipe out the distinctions between deaf and hearing children and simply get on with education.

At its best, team teaching involves deaf adults as teachers and aides at every educational level, providing the students with role models throughout their schooling. During the heyday of oralism in the early to mid-20th century, deaf teachers were excluded from teaching academic subjects and relegated to shop classes or gym. Team teaching, with its "different-but-equal" philosophy, has the potential to educate both hearing and deaf students—and their parents—to the talents and potential that have been hidden for so long.

Schools for Deaf Students

Let's leave the inclusion concept and turn to programs designed exclusively for deaf and hard of hearing students. Day schools, state residential schools, and private residential schools for deaf students share many similarities. All currently provide curricula based on state standards that are adapted specifically for deaf students, and all employ teachers who are trained, certified, and qualified to work with this population.

Special school programs for deaf students offer exceptionally hospitable educational environments that are fully accessible. Their advantages can be summed up in four categories: the teaching environment, the communication environment, the learning environment, and the social and emotional environment.

THE TEACHING ENVIRONMENT

Classes in schools and programs for deaf students tend to be small, usually less than ten students per teacher, with children grouped according to age, ability, intelligence, learning style, and so on. This means that the specialized teachers of deaf students can work closely with each child instead of running interference between the hearing and deaf students, as in a mixed, mainstream classroom. The teaching therefore tends to be more focused—and the teachers are more likely to have a chance to scrutinize students' progress. Because the teachers are specialists, they are better able to identify the effects of a child's deafness on communication and learning.

THE COMMUNICATION ENVIRONMENT

Usually, in special programs for deaf students, there are no communication barriers. Many Deaf adults are on site, serving as role models in the child's mode of communication. This makes the environment a fertile one for language development, whether the language is English or American Sign Language (ASL). (By contrast, in inclusion and partial inclusion classrooms, only a few people use a given child's mode of communication freely and easily.) In a school for deaf students, where all staff and students use the same mode of communication, the children take great pride in their particular mode; you can feel a sense of group self-esteem when you enter the school.

THE LEARNING ENVIRONMENT

Deaf and hard of hearing students aren't constrained in their communication efforts in these special schools. Understandably, they participate more freely in discussions both in class and in social interactions with peers. Furthermore, the teachers usually have experience in getting deaf children involved in learning. They are (or should be) well aware of deaf children's need for visual communication and incidental learning opportunities. And ideally, they take the opportunity, as general education teachers may not, to teach time management, independent living skills, critical thinking, and real-life lessons (how a bank check works, what a family tree looks like) that often fall by the wayside in deaf students' education, leaving the students bewildered about things that others assume they know.

THE SOCIAL AND EMOTIONAL ENVIRONMENT

Deaf students who are in inclusive settings often have to deal with prejudice, stereotypes, misunderstandings, and other communication barriers before they break through into friendship with hearing peers. In a deaf school, because communication is not an issue, friendships have the potential to grow more easily. There may be other constraints on friendships, but not the obstacles that inevitably lie between the two groups.

Deaf and hard of hearing children have more opportunities to assume leadership roles in a school for deaf students. In a regular school, there are always communication barriers to overcome before the deaf child can compete on an equal footing; however, in a deaf school, communication doesn't interfere with opportunities to try out for school teams or student government offices.

The environment in a school for deaf students offers many opportunities for practice in social situations. Interacting with peers and adults in a comfortable, informal environment stimulates emotional growth.

A repeated theme brought up during the interviews for this book was the nurturing sense of social and emotional ease, the feeling of "safe harbor," that many interviewees experienced upon entering deaf schools. There, they found respite from difficult family lives, where they had felt isolated, left out, and discounted. Time after time, people conveyed this kind of message: "I would *never* have survived if I hadn't gone to a deaf school. My family never learned to communicate with me. They never even tried. They didn't want to know what my life was like—I really think they didn't want to take the trouble. I felt the same way around any hearing people—isolated, left out, lonely, self-conscious. But when I finally got to a school where everybody was like me, it was heaven. I really mean it. If I hadn't wound up at that school, I never would have made it."

Although such a comment points out one advantage of deaf schools, it reflects less on the choice of school than on the home environment and the family's understanding of the impact of deafness on communication and learning. We hope that the information in this book will save many deaf children from the terrible fate of needing respite from their own families. When parents are in tune with their children and aware of the issues, they can weigh the pros and cons of a deaf school program in a spirit of calm deliberation rather than a state of emergency.

CHOOSING AMONG THE SCHOOLS

There are three kinds of schools dedicated exclusively to deaf education: *day and charter schools, state residential schools,* and *private residential schools.* Day and charter schools are for students who live at home and commute; most of these schools are located in large cities and serve a large population of deaf and hard of hearing children. State residential schools are boarding schools, but most offer day programs for commuting students from nearby communities. Private residential schools are typically oral programs; as a rule, they are small and expensive.

Since the passage of Public Law 94-142 in 1975, the number of schools or programs for deaf students has dropped sharply. In response to the law, more and more school districts mainstream deaf children, and parents are drawn to the public school program, because it allows them to keep their children at home. So the choice of a school often rests on the parents' emotional pangs over separation. We urge you to resist the temptation to make your decision on that basis alone and to carefully consider the available options and the needs of your particular child. If your inclusion choices fall into the "irresponsible" category and choosing one of them may result in painful confusion and isolation for your child, then working a commute into your life or spending weekends with your happy, well-adjusted child may not seem like such a terrible hardship.

During extensive interviews, Deaf parents of Deaf children were asked to describe the ideal school setting. Most of their answers, broken down here point by point, led to day or residential programs specifically for deaf and hard of hearing children. Most of the Deaf parents asserted that it was close to impossible to find a school program conforming to these standards in any but a dedicated program for deaf students. Based on their criteria, here is a sketch of an ideal school.

1. There are a good number of Deaf teachers on the staff who function as role models not only for the students but also for the hearing educators involved in the school. These specialists inform hearing staff about the day-to-day effects of deafness on living, learning, and communicating, describing the experience of deafness from the inside.

2. The deaf faculty and staff members have significant roles in shaping school policy. They are not "token deaf" but are equal partners in determining the direction of the school.

3. Communication is 100 percent free-flowing, and there is no possibility that a deaf child will ever be left out or misunderstood due to being deaf. All teachers, Deaf and hearing, are absolutely expert in their expressive signing.

4. The school recognizes ASL as the official language of the Deaf community and affords all students the opportunity to learn and use ASL in a supportive environment.

5. The school curriculum embraces the history, culture, and literature of Deaf people. To form a positive self-concept and healthy self-esteem, Deaf children need exposure to the experiences of Deaf adults who have made valuable contributions to society and dealt with their own deafness in constructive ways. So biographies of Deaf political leaders, authors, inventors, scientists, actors and actresses, artists, and so on are all integrated into the school program.

6. In its teaching methods and cultural orientation, the school gives priority to "the world of vision" over "the world of audition." Right down to its philosophical foundation, the school is committed to providing creative and constructive visual ways of conveying information and experience to students.

7. The school provides a full range of extracurricular activities, and students have completely free choice in deciding where and how to participate.

8. Students are grouped by age, grade level, skill level, work performance, and so on, rather than by their place on the deafness spectrum.

Conclusion

We've given you quite a potpourri of information here. How to process it all? Psychologist McKay Vernon wrote an article full of pertinent advice called "Parent Strategies! How to Get What Your Child Needs from the Education System." He generously gave permission to adapt that article here.

Vernon begins where we begin: Parents have no choice but to be eagle-eyed monitors of their children's educational progress. With that in mind, he urges parents of deaf children to do the following:

1. *Learn your child's educational achievement test and IQ test scores.* These measurements may not be perfect, but they are more detailed and pointed than the general assessment that winds up on a report card. Make sure your child is tested regularly. This will give you a solid basis for assessing his or her progress through school.

2. *Visit your child's classes and go over homework assignments.* In particular, pay attention to how much writing the child is assigned. Deaf children need practice in writing English, but too often, for a variety of reasons (many involving laziness) teachers are reluctant to assign compositions and to grade them carefully. If reading and writing are well taught in your child's program, they could signal a fundamental strength in the program as a whole. On the other hand, a noticeable lack of writing assignments could be a real danger signal.

3. *Continually evaluate your school choice.* Each year, meet the teacher, visit the classroom, analyze the curriculum and extracurricular activities, and talk to your child. Is the child sleeping well? Eager to go to school? Or is every morning full of complaints of "tummy aches" and "hate my teacher, hate my school, have no friends"? Don't depend solely on professional advice in your continual evaluation. When it comes to the complicated world of children, there's nothing more powerful or significant than a parent's gut feeling.

4. *Make sure your child is sufficiently challenged academically.* Many deaf adults complain bitterly of having spent all their school days doing "baby work." As your child's ambassador, you need to insist that your child has the opportunity to learn and progress.

5. *In an inclusion program, insist on a knowledgeable administrator.* Most inclusion situations are administered by a school principal who knows nothing at all about deafness and its impact on communication and education. This is the first major obstacle to your child's rightful education. You have the legal right to demand that the inclusion program be designed and guided by a *knowledgeable* specialist in deaf education. If necessary, consider going so far as to establish a special board composed of parents, Deaf adults, and other informed people who can create and maintain a program that truly keeps deaf students in the educational mainstream. Like it or not, you are the self-made expert on your child's needs, and to a greater or lesser extent, it will be up to you to secure what your child needs from the school.

6. *Make sure vocational education is available.* Not everyone, deaf or hearing, is college bound. When your child reaches around

thirteen to fifteen years of age, you and the child will face another important life choice: whether to stay on the academic route to college or acquire practical vocational training. Too often, school programs ignore the vocational alternative, leaving many children burdened unnecessarily with feelings of failure. Be careful not to reinforce this bias by insisting on college as the only realistic goal. Know your child's scores, know his or her performance, know his or her strengths, and try—using all your powers of empathy, imagination, and intuition—to see into your child's heart and mind.[2] You may find that you can give no more loving gift to your child than the support he or she needs in withdrawing from an academic track and pursuing another dream.

In summary, to get the best educational outcomes, parents of deaf children need to pay attention to following three factors:

- placement in the least-restrictive environment (LRE) with full communication access,
- fair assessment procedures that the child understands, and
- parental involvement and consent in educational decisions.

Notes

1. Nanci A. Scheetz, *Deaf Education in the 21st Century: Topics and Trends* (Upper Saddle River, NY: Pearson Education, 2012): 155–56.

2. Jerry Bigner and Clara Newhardt, *Parent–Child Relations: An Introduction to Parenting*, 9th ed. (Upper Saddle River, NJ: Pearson Education, 2014).

13 Moving toward Independence

HISTORY HAS BEEN unkind to deaf people. Discrimination has intensified the difficulties hearing parents often have in accepting and working effectively with their children's deafness. This, in turn, can slow the children's growth toward independent, productive lives that refute the stereotypes.

Today, thank goodness, many of the old prejudices are giving way. The hearing world's increased interest in and understanding of deafness since the writing of the first edition of this book are really quite remarkable. These changes are due, in great part, to a number of popular books and movies on the subject of being deaf, and to a new generation of deaf teachers, activists, writers, actors, and professionals in various fields who have felt a personal responsibility to break the stereotypes.

Still, the old prejudices have amazing staying power. Their influence extends even into households where deaf children are raised with sensitivity and love. Our own prejudices are the hardest to recognize. To help your deaf child develop a strong sense of identity and grow toward full independence, it will be necessary to combat prejudices both from without and from within.

Traditionally, hearing and even deaf people have accepted and internalized the false beliefs that undermine the confidence of deaf children. Even in our relatively enlightened time, in a thousand subtle ways inside and outside the home, deaf people are exposed to the view that they are less capable, less intelligent, less serious, less emotionally controlled, less independent, and even less important than hearing people. As a result, far too many subliminal signals—flickers of the eyes, down-turnings of the mouth, avertings of the head—have sent far too many deaf people off the path toward full self-reliance and on to underemployment or even worse, unemployment and reliance on government welfare. As is the case whenever life decisions are based on low expectations of self, deaf people who take those byways automatically exclude themselves from jobs and professions that involve more thought and creativity.

Enough is enough! No more settling for less! Anyway, not if the new generation of deaf writers, educators, scholars, doctors, lawyers, students, artists, activists, policy makers, administrators (and so on) has anything to say about it. Today, deaf people are found working in every field—and not because they were invited in! They are strong self-advocates, and they're there because they visualized themselves there—usually with the support of their parents and a great education—and then found the means to reach their goals.

Don't Hold Your Child Back

In a sense, this chapter is an extended pep talk with the following core message: "Above all else, keep a positive attitude." Is this simplistic? Not really. It is another way of saying, "Don't let your attitudes, ambitions, or decisions be shaped by negativity." Scour and unpack your own beliefs to make sure you're not being influenced by inaccuracies and the long history of low expectations for deaf people. Try to identify *in yourself* and your family any beliefs that may hold your child back on the path he or she is traveling by nature—the path toward independence.

How can you root out those destructive inaccuracies from your family life? To begin, it is important to look them straight in the eye. Let's consider two major negativities that are likely to come up in households where hearing parents are raising deaf children: overprotectiveness and underexposure to other deaf children and adults.

OVERPROTECTIVENESS

At every stage of child rearing, parents typically find themselves nudging their children on to new experiences and responsibilities. When you discover that your child is deaf, the temptation may be great to keep him or her nearby and act as an anxious buffer against all discouragement and failure; to protect your child. Far too many hearing parents wind up becoming "helicopter parents," hovering nervously and constantly stepping in to help. What any child, deaf or hearing, learns in such an environment is the very opposite of self-reliance and self-advocacy: learned helplessness. The child learns to rely on you to do everything and to advocate for them.

The urge to intercept and protect may keep parents from recognizing ways in which their children can function independently. A typical example is the mother who dresses her four-year-old deaf son every morning, even though her hearing daughter has been choosing her own clothes and putting them on since she turned three. With a bit of reflection, this mother would realize that deafness has nothing to do with the ability to get dressed in the morning. The habit of overseeing and helping has become ingrained.

When children venture outside the home, their parents' urge to protect may become even stronger—this is natural, with hearing as with deaf children. Safety considerations breed caution, and with good reason. When parents are outside with their deaf children, how do they alert them to approaching cars, warning shouts, and other unheard auditory cues? What precautions do parents teach their children for self-protection when unsupervised? Research shows that hearing mothers of deaf children have a tendency to be more stressed, intrusive, and controlling in their relationships with their children than are mothers of hearing children or deaf mothers of deaf children.[1] (Fathers' interactions with their children are not as well researched and documented—much to the authors' annoyance and that of the fathers we know, who are all deeply involved in their children's upbringing.)

There's no denying that parents of deaf children will naturally feel the urge to overprotect and even overcompensate for their child's deafness. To a great extent, a solution to this problem can be found in the preceding chapters. *Communication,* in whatever mode you have chosen, can be the equalizer. A parent who is uneasy with a deaf child's explorations on the playground is usually afraid of failing to convey necessary information to the child. This indicates lack of confidence in the chosen mode of communication. If you feel this way, take a fresh look at the communication option you have chosen and your own mastery of it. The trouble may lie in *your* level of skill in communicating with your child.

Let us sum up the point of this potentially painful self-examination by reminding you of the dangers of setting your sights too low. Like hearing children, deaf children deserve the opportunity to succeed and fail to make mistakes, even to embarrass themselves. Without chances to experiment independently, how can they gain real-world experience in solving real-world problems? Sports, cultural activities, community events, parties, family gatherings, just "hanging out" with friends—all these are opportunities for children to try their wings. Not all hearing children will succeed in these arenas, but parents seldom discourage them from trying. Deaf children deserve the very same opportunities as their hearing peers to fall on their faces, pick themselves up, wipe away their own tears, and find another route to their goals. Life takes practice!

"UNDEREXPOSURE"

Another kind of overprotectiveness that hearing parents frequently indulge in is shielding their deaf children from exposure to other deaf people. The effect of this, whether intentional or not, is usually to deprive the children of much-needed perspective and camaraderie. Generally, the parents who do this view being deaf as a devastating disability. Many see themselves not as shields but as educators, carefully exposing their children to *hearing* role models while overlooking the critical importance to their children of meeting successful *deaf* people.

The authors have known young deaf children who believed that they would grow out of being deaf and become hearing adults, because they never met older Deaf people. In their home life and in school—particularly in public schools, where until the last decade, deaf teachers were as rare as California condors—these children had never seen a deaf adult. So deafness must be a trait limited to children, right? It makes perfect sense to them.

If the only deaf adults children are exposed to are people their parents pity or who pity themselves, the children may well identify with the deaf adults but develop self-deprecating tendencies and negative self-images. Let's say it again: *Enough is enough!* From an early age, let's get deaf children out in the world, where they can work and play with other deaf children and with proud, productive, well-adjusted Deaf adults.

One parent, Marilyn, told a story about her son, John, who didn't learn to sign until he was eight years old. The family learned together, but John was absolutely paralyzed with embarrassment when Marilyn or other family members tried to sign to him in public. However, on a trip to Washington, DC, the family saw people signing fast and furiously everywhere in the city. On the last day of the visit, John walked up to a police officer and signed: "Hi, my name is John. I am deaf." Marilyn and her husband were stunned by this seeming turnabout. "Then we realized that for the first time in his life, John had seen deaf adults who felt free to sign anywhere they went," Marilyn told us. "Nobody pointed these people out to him—we hardly noticed them ourselves. But he saw, and that made all the difference."

Many Deaf adults have shared similar stories. Frequently, those who were children before the 1970s were brought up to be ashamed to be seen with other deaf people in public. Consequently, *they themselves* looked down on deaf people, *including* themselves. By adulthood, most overcame these negative feelings about being deaf. "I would never have survived without my deaf friends. Never!" They say this time after time. Whatever their communication mode, they describe the same feelings of gratitude for the company of deaf people. As one friend of the authors puts it, "I wasn't alone! I wasn't the only one. In my family, I was the only deaf person, even in my huge extended family. I'll never forget seeing a deaf couple in a restaurant signing and speaking all evening long. I couldn't keep my eyes off of them. My parents kept urging me to finish my meal, but all I could think of, watching those two, was, 'I'm not the only one!'"

The Value of Deaf Friends

Generally, the experience of deaf adults in their forties or younger has been different. They have grown up with visible deaf role models in the popular culture—movies, plays, the children's television program *Sesame Street*, and other recent programs, like *F.B. Eye* and *Switched at Birth*. Recently, a deaf male model, Nyle Dimarco, won two intense competitions against his hearing male and female peers on the television shows *America's Next Top Model* and *Dancing with the Stars*. This generation of deaf people is far more familiar with the concept of role models than prior generations. Today's young deaf people shared detailed insights into the value of their exposure to other deaf people. Nowadays, some of them even read a magazine called *Deaf Life*.

Four basic advantages of having deaf friends surfaced again and again in conversations with the authors. They are illustrated in the following accounts of four interviews.

BEING DEAF AS INCONVENIENCE

Wayne was eloquent in describing how he met and got to know several deaf adults during his teenage years. These interactions fired up his enthusiasm for life and fueled his drive and determination to excel in school and, later, at work. "If I hadn't met them, I would have led a very mediocre life, with no goals or big dreams. Just seeing how these deaf people led normal lives and went about their business as if being deaf was just not a big issue—it was amazing to me. Everybody else seemed to imply that deafness was such a huge obstacle, but these people made me feel as if being deaf was a simple inconvenience that could be handled easily." This realization was liberating, a turning point for Wayne. He began to focus on the means to independence and not on his supposed limitation of deafness, as his parents had always done.

For you, as hearing parents of a deaf child, Wayne's story is good news. You don't have to be the one to single-handedly convince your child that he or she can succeed in life. Rely on members of the outside world, and particularly on deaf people, to demonstrate that truth by example. Trust us; they'll be more than happy to oblige.

COMMUNICATION AS KEY

Joni explained that becoming friends with deaf adults showed her the way to a normal life. Through her friends, she found what had been lacking in her life. Joni had always had great difficulty in communicating freely and easily with her family and hearing friends. Joni and those she interacted with were always unsure whether they were getting their points across and understanding each other. After a frustrating childhood and preadolescence, Joni met several deaf adults, and when she found she could communicate effortlessly with them, the relief was so overwhelming it pervaded every aspect of her life.

When Joni was asked, "What does it mean to you that you can't communicate with everyone? Are you troubled that you have difficulty interacting with hearing people?"

"Well, no," she answered. "Not really. I just made the choice that I wanted to spend my time with people whose life was like mine. I can visit with deaf friends for hours and hours, do things with them or just sit around, simply because they're deaf and I'm deaf. We're sensitive to each other's communication needs. I never had that 100 percent comfort with hearing people, and my friendships with them were always strained. We can be close up to a point, but it's a lot more work and can become tiring on both sides. It is just like we belong in different categories of friendships, that's all. My hearing friends find it difficult to communicate with my deaf friends, and the same is true the other way. So I don't invite them all to the same parties or social gatherings. But the great thing is I have a life where I can feel comfortable, and that wasn't always true for me at all."

EXPOSURE TO DEAF CULTURE

Clyde's parents exposed him at an early age to the Deaf community, and he feels very strongly that all deaf children should have similar advantages of early and frequent exposure. "The Deaf community and Deaf people are culturally different from the people and culture of the hearing," he says. "Their native language is American Sign Language. I don't think it is fair to keep deaf children apart from this native language. I think they should all be encouraged to become fluent in it and to take a lot of pride in Deaf history and heritage and not be forced to become 'hearing person' clones."

Clyde was fortunate in that his parents never felt threatened by his interest in the Deaf community. Almost as soon as they learned he was deaf, they learned ASL and practiced hard in order to communicate effectively with their son. Some families find it difficult to be this open-minded, fearing that if they risk exposing their children to the Deaf world, they may lose them. This defensive attitude is understandable, but it is naive as well: All children, hearing or deaf, eventually make choices that take them away from home. Parents need to see the benefit of exposing children to the experiences in life that can yield them comfort, excitement, stimulation, and satisfaction. Restricting their options because of your fears is to hold them back in life. And that's where you could really lose your child.

BATTERY RECHARGE

Morris is delighted with his life. He feels that he fits completely into the hearing world and functions smoothly there. "It is because I was exposed to both hearing and deaf role models as a child that I can do as well as I do," he told the authors. Among the deaf people in his early life were deaf adults who functioned particularly well in the hearing world. They shared many tips with him on how to adapt despite hearing loss. "My deaf friends asked me to spend time with them and visit them in their workplace, and this was really important to me. It was like finding out how to beat the odds. I picked up a bag of simple tricks from them—ways to understand what was happening, how to follow what was going on in a group of hearing people, language tips I would never have understood without their help. Seeing them and spending time with them now is a little like getting my batteries recharged. I get along great in the hearing world, but I need to spend time with my deaf adult friends.

"I know a lot of deaf people who go through life in the hearing world on very low batteries. I wish they could do what I do: go back to my deaf friends and discuss everything that happens 'out there,' get a recharge, and then go back out again."

WHAT YOU CAN DO

We hope you are convinced that exposure to other deaf people and deaf adult role models is worth a thousand classroom lessons on how to succeed in the larger society. Again, children are sponges, learning and adapting by imitation. Without knowing it, your child may desperately need a lesson or demonstration that you, as a hearing person, would never think of. So let us be specific in suggesting how to increase your child's exposure to other deaf children and adults.

If your child is very young, arrange for deaf playmates on a regular basis. Follow leads, track down clues, follow up on casual remarks—*find* those families who might be on the same search you are for deaf playmates for their children. Many early intervention programs are a good resource for these contacts, so ask your early intervention provider, if they did not already offer you this option, for play dates and other social activities.

As your child gets older, it is important that you keep up the effort. Most first-time parents are a bit irritated to find themselves playing the part of social secretary, setting up play dates for their pint-sized offspring; however, children are dependent, both physically and emotionally, for help in making social arrangements and getting here and there. The authors advise that you stay on the lookout for other families with young deaf children. You may locate them through educators, support agencies, school meetings, social gatherings, and the gossip tree in your community. Prepare yourself to cheerfully become part social director, part front-office screener. All parents play these roles for their children early in life.

There's another advantage to bringing Deaf people into your child's life. Not only your child but also you and all the other members of your family will benefit from the exposure as well. A teacher one of the authors once knew spoke of a strategy she adopted on discovering that her deaf junior high students, mainstreamed into a public school, were forming a clique.

> They refused to associate with hearing students during snack and lunch breaks, and refused to sign among themselves, because they

felt self-conscious in front of the hearing students. So I started our "Sign-and-Song" program. It was deaf kids signing and dancing to music, and pretty soon we were being invited all over the place. The group got so popular, it was performing two nights every weekend, and the self-esteem of those kids just soared.

But it wasn't just because the Kiwanis Club folks liked them that they began to feel good about themselves. It was because their parents and brothers and sisters went to the performances and were really proud of what they saw the kids do. The parents started thinking of their kids as artists. They'd sit in the back and listen to the other parents around them, parents of hearing kids, whispering, "That's a beautiful thing those kids do. I wish my child could do something like that." And these parents just puffed out with pride for their children. That was a case of teaching, "You're deaf, you'll always be deaf. Take pride in what you are and what you can do."

This teacher's beautiful idea yielded bonuses galore, such as the following:

- for the parents, confidence in their children and their children's future,
- for the community, an antidote to the lack of understanding that can build a wall between the hearing and deaf populations, and
- for the children, a source of self-esteem that no amount of special training, special books and supplies, special in-service programs, special tutors, and professionals could top.

Self-esteem—the capacity to value and like yourself—and self-advocacy—the capacity to stand up for your needs—is the well from which confidence, courage, and creativity are drawn. Self-esteem and self-advocacy are the source of independence.

TRANSITIONING: NOT JUST FOR OLDER KIDS

Preparing your child for life after high school and on their own is often something parents don't think much about or bother with until their children reach adolescence. Then all of a sudden, your child is entering high school, and the realization sinks in that graduation is just a few short years away. In fact, individual education programs (IEPs) do not even mandate until age fourteen the inclusion of a component called the *individual transition program*. This is the part of the IEP where you, your child, and the IEP team discuss future career and life goals, and then design objectives to meet those goals. The authors think age fourteen is *far too late* to begin planning for your child's future.

So when should you start planning for your deaf child's transition? Our answer is: *When your child enters kindergarten.* You may wonder: How in the world will I do this and where do I start? This chapter's recent discussion of self-advocacy is a good place to begin with simple things, like learning to help your child select toys and foods from the available options, learning the wants and needs of your deaf child, and learning to work with interpreters or other support services. The Laurent Clerc National Deaf Education Center at Gallaudet University has transition skills guidelines that you can use for your child's IEP, starting in kindergarten all the way through to their senior year in high school. You can easily find the guidelines and a wealth of other useful information on a variety of topics at www.gallaudet.edu/clerc-center/info-to-go/transition.html.

One other important thing you can do for your child's self-esteem and self-advocacy skills is to let them start leading the IEP meetings as they get older. Remember, this meeting is about your child, their own vision of their future, and what they need to get to that point. Your child will learn how to make appropriate decisions for him- or herself with proper guidance from you and the rest of the IEP team. It is certainly *not* about what the school administrators think your child needs. Few things can be better for your child than being able to speak up for him- or herself in this sort of situation. This practice of student-led IEPs is becoming widespread, and your child's teacher should know when and how to facilitate the process. The earlier you start transitioning, the easier it will become, and you'll stress a lot less when the time comes to send your child out of the nest and into the world.

Technologies for Independence

Today, deaf people have access to technological communication access devices that prior generations could only dream of. As much as possible, make use of helpful technologies in your efforts to foster independence in your deaf child. Give special consideration to the following communication devices.

TELECOMMUNICATION DEVICES

The advances in telecommunications since the last edition of this book have been tremendous. How many of you can even remember what it actually felt like not to have a phone with you at all times? We used to have to be at home, in the office, or a building, or find a phone booth, in order to make calls. Now many of us do not even have landlines anymore. One device for deaf people that has quickly become almost obsolete over the past decade is the TTY or TDD, a teletypewriter for deaf people. It was a marvelous invention only fifty years ago. There was even a whole section about TTYs in the previous editions of this book. A few folks still use them, but that form of typed communication has pretty much been replaced by e-mails and texting.

What is currently prevalent is the use of video technology. Videophones have been around for more than half a century, but they were not practical or reliable until the advent of high-speed Internet and mobile networks. There are now various forms of video communication available as stand-alone devices, like dedicated videophones, or more increasingly incorporated into desktop and laptop computers, tablets, and smartphones, with software or apps that make use of the videocams built into these devices.

When it comes to your child, think about the central role telecommunication plays in the lives of preadolescents and teenagers. You'll need to use your common sense in judging when your child is old enough to make calls independently—but when the impulse hits, it is best to be prepared. Of course, you need to give your child the standard "safe and appropriate use" lecture, just like all other kids should be getting. It's a good idea to explain to them about not using up too much data, if you are on a limited data plan. (Note: Many providers have an unlimited data/no-voice plan available for deaf customers for a very reasonable price. Be sure to ask about it.) If your child already knows ASL and how to work with an interpreter, then it is usually just a matter of showing them how to use the technology, although chances are they probably know more than us adults. The important point here is, in teaching a child to make video calls, *do* help, but *don't* take over. Let the child make his or her own calls.

Several nationwide video relay services (VRS) now exist that allow deaf people to communicate with hearing people via third-party interpreters. Many of these VRS companies will provide either free videophone equipment or the software for their service for laptops and smartphones. Using a VRS instead of relying on parents or siblings—for example, to find out when a movie starts, whether a store sells a particular brand of bicycle, or what the assignment was in history class today—is a great way for a child to become familiar with the world outside the home. We urge you to let your child do some exploring by way of the relay service.

For children who do have some hearing, look into accessibility options on their phones, like amplification; but don't take away the video option. It is important to give these children a choice between talking and signing or simply using text messages. Many hard of hearing interviewees mentioned that when they come home from work after listening all day to an amplified telephone, they prefer to use the videophone for their personal calls. Needless to say, this is just one more reason for you and your child to learn ASL, so you can communicate directly via video instead of using a VRS.

TELEVISION CAPTION DECODERS

All television sets built since 1993 with screens thirteen inches or larger must contain internal caption decoders. So, figure out the menu option for closed captioning on your television as soon as your child is diagnosed—and then keep the captions on whenever the set is in use. Even if he or she is not yet reading, this is a terrific way to immerse your child in written language and motivate him or her to read and appreciate English.

Some parents want to wait until their children show commitment to their schoolwork before allowing the use of televisions, but we argue that the value of exposure to the printed word *and* the opportunity for family members to enjoy television shows and movies together far outweigh the possibility that TV will become a distraction from education. All parents struggle with the problem of how to monitor and limit their children's television viewing. One effective strategy is a "No TV before Homework" rule. It keeps your children free of distractions from homework but allows for recreational viewing as a reward if they get it done.

SIGNALING DEVICES

Devices that flash lights or set off tactile vibrators can be attached to doorbells, smoke and fire alarms, and alarm clocks. With these signaling devices, you can give your deaf child the responsibility of waking up on time, answering the door, and even rescuing other family members in case of emergency. Signaling devices are marvelous fosterers of self-reliance. Many of the current devices can connect wirelessly to phones and signal their owners as well as providing control options.

"Living signalers"—professionally trained, licensed signal dogs— fall into this category. However, signal dog owners feel strongly that the responsibility and time required for taking care of a highly trained dog is too great for a school-age child. We always advise children interested in signal dogs to wait until they complete their education, begin working, and live on their own before taking on this responsibility. One more thing: *Please avoid the temptation of falsely claiming your family pet is a signal dog* or even going so far as to get a fake signal dog vest, just so you can bring it along in public places. Fake signal dogs do a big disservice to the real ones when they don't behave appropriately in public and just generally give a negative impression. We thank you for this. But don't hesitate to check out the real service dogs when your child finishes their schooling. Such a dog would be a really neat accessibility option as well as a good companion.

A Checklist

You've probably noticed by now that what deaf children need in order to learn self-respect, competence, and self-reliance is not so very different from what hearing children need. Your deaf child will have a few special requirements, and these can be summed up as follows:

1. A mode of communication that enables you to communicate freely with your child and your child to communicate freely with others.

2. A familiarity with written English fostered through daily reading. You can begin to read to your child *every night,* starting right from birth.

3. Early and constant exposure to other deaf people. Your child should meet other deaf children for friendship and as a way to normalize being deaf; he or she should also meet deaf adults, who can function as role models, fine-tuners, and "battery rechargers."

4. A sense of humor about being deaf—and everything else. Families can become overwhelmed by the decisions they must make. Remind yourself: Life is difficult, but it is also fun, and sometimes hilariously funny. You have the choice of focusing on the difficulties to the exclusion of the humor— or keeping your eyes open for the unexpected funny moments that brighten everything. Which do *you* choose? And which do you think your child would choose? (Trust us; we have *plenty* of funny stories of our own.)

5. Unconditional love for your child. With so much to learn, think about, and monitor, it is possible to fall into the bad habit of treating love as a reward for achievement. The authors urge you very strenuously to avoid this common pitfall. It is a problem that comes with the territory in parenting—all parenting, not just the raising of deaf children. We must remind each other that we love children for their uniqueness and the gift of life they bring to *our* lives, not because they do well in school or manage to finish a project. Celebrating children simply for who they are adds to the pleasure of life. Parents don't need to read a book to find this out, but it doesn't hurt for us to remind each other of the fundamental truths of life. In that way, they can become shared touchstones for us all at our different places on the path toward maturity and independence.

Notes

1. Marc Marschark, *Raising and Educating a Deaf Child* (New York: Oxford University Press, 1997).

14 *Cochlear Implants*

THE BORDER between the Deaf and hearing worlds is a very lively place where debates, arguments, misunderstandings, and burning controversies break out with alarming regularity. These skirmishes do not always cross the border—sometimes all the arguers are hearing people, each with their own point of view; sometimes they are all Deaf. Every issue that arises on this border takes on several realities, all dependent on the particular arguer's perspective. This volatility should not be surprising: Reality is as variegated and pieced together as the most detailed mosaic. The separate tiles that make up this beautiful and diverse picture of the world and our place in it are nothing but the separate perspectives that each of us brings to everything. Reality is diversity—no wonder we disagree.

However, some debates are more significant than others. A major controversy, tied to the very nature of deafness, took place in the 1970s surrounding the recognition of American Sign Language (ASL) as the authentic language of the Deaf community. Another serious disagreement, one that also goes to the core of the meaning of being Deaf, is that surrounding cochlear implants. This is no mere technological issue; the controversy over cochlear implants goes right to the heart of the difference between the Deaf and hearing worlds' perspectives on deafness.

Proponents of the implants assert: "We must do all we can do to cure deafness." Critics respond vociferously: "To attempt to 'cure' deafness is to suggest, wrongly, that being deaf is an illness, whereas it is really a state of being different from but equal to the hearing state."

How do we get so quickly from a seemingly benign technological issue to a raging battle on the morality and ethics of altering deafness (or attempting to)? Let's try to account for the heat of this debate as neutrally as possible, moving step by step from *what*, precisely, cochlear implants are to *when* they might be considered, and then on to the criteria for deciding when, if ever, they are appropriate.

What Is a Cochlear Implant?

A cochlear implant is an electronic device that provides sound information to profoundly deaf individuals who do not benefit from, or choose not to use, regular hearing aids. Whereas conventional hearing aids work by amplifying sounds—that is, making them louder—cochlear implants use digital technology to convert sounds into electronic impulses and to feed those impulses into the nerves that take them to the brain, where they are transformed into perceptions of sound.

The "delivery systems" of the two devices also differ significantly. Whereas a regular hearing aid is externally fitted and delivers amplified sound through the outer ear and middle ear to the inner ear, the cochlear implant's delivery component must be implanted surgically under general anesthesia, in the inner ear, deep within the skull. People who undergo this surgery get the implant in one ear, or they may get the implant in both ears (called *bilateral cochlear implants*).

As you can well imagine, the cochlear implant is extremely expensive. At the time of this writing, the cost of the surgical procedure plus all the evaluations, programming (digital adjustments), follow-up, and rehabilitation generally costs more than $100,000. For implantation in children, the cost is generally at the high end of the range, because they tend to need extensive and frequent follow-ups, programming, and auditory training. Medical insurance can cover most of the cost, but varies with regard to the amount covered, depending on your health insurance company.

How Cochlear Implants Work

To help explain how cochlear implants work, here is a quick and simple refresher in how the ear transmits sound to the brain.

1. Sound waves move from the environment into the outer ear and down the ear canal to the eardrum.
2. The sound waves cause the eardrum and the three small bones of the middle ear to vibrate.
3. The three middle-ear bones are linked to a membrane called the *oval window*, which vibrates when the bones vibrate.
4. The vibrations in the oval window are passed on to the fluids in the snail-shaped cochlea, which is part of the inner ear, and the motion of the fluid, in turn, moves thousands of microscopic hair cells there The hair cells stimulate the hearing nerve, and the nerve sends electrical impulses to the brain, which interprets the signals as sound.

As was pointed out early in this book, deafness has many forms and causes. Some kinds of hearing loss result from damage to the inner ear. In people with sensorineural hearing loss, or nerve deafness, some hair cells or nerve fibers are undeveloped or damaged. A cochlear implant can be positioned to bypass the damaged area and stimulate the intact nerve fibers, thereby transmitting auditory signals to the brain (see Figure 14.1).

What the Cochlear Implant Looks Like

A cochlear implant consists of the following five distinct parts:

1. A sound processor.
2. A microphone, positioned near the ear (very much like a hearing aid), receives sound information from the environment and translates into electronic signals the elements of that information that are most important for sound discrimination and understanding speech.
3. An external transmitter, held in place against the skull by a magnet, conveys the electronic signals from the sound processor.
4. An internal receiver, implanted just under the skin above and slightly behind the ear, accepts the signals from the transmitter.
5. An implanted wire with electrodes on it extends into the cochlea itself. The electrodes stimulate nerve cells, which

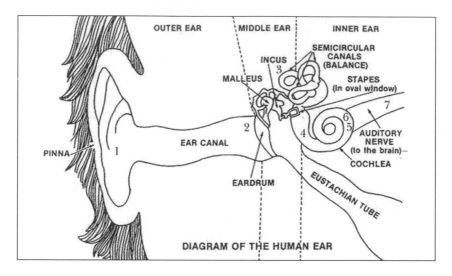

Figure 14.1.

1. Sound waves come through the outer ear into the ear canal.
2. The sound waves hit the eardrum and make it vibrate.
3. The vibration is passed on to the three tiny bones in the middle ear.
4. The bones pass on the vibration to the fluids in the cochlea (part of the inner ear shaped like a snail shell).
5. The fluids move the tiny hairs on the sensory cells (the hair cells) inside the cochlea.
6. The movements of the hairs on the cells, which are attached to the hearing nerve, send electrical impulses along the nerve.
7. The hearing nerve carries the message to the brain.
8. The brain interprets the message as sound.

Source: Text—Cochlear Corporation; diagram—National Information Center on Deafness, used by permission. Illustration by Angeline V. Culfogienis.

send the messages to the brain, where they are interpreted. Each electrode is programmed to deliver signals that represent variations in loudness and pitch (see Figure 14.2).

WHAT COCHLEAR IMPLANTS MAY ACCOMPLISH

Cochlear implants provide many deaf people with an opportunity to perceive the presence of sound, specifically the sounds

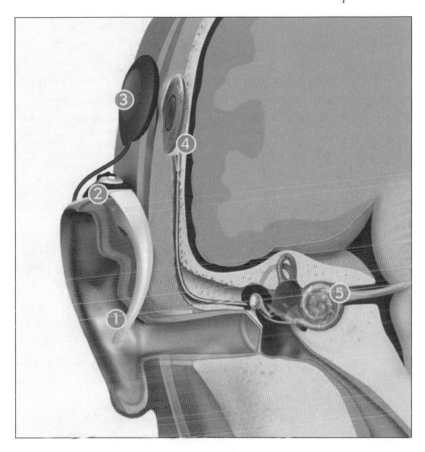

Figure 14.2. Cochlear Implant Diagram (courtesy of Advanced Bionics).

A cochlear implant works in the following way:

1. The microphone picks up sounds on the sound processor.
2. The sound processor breaks down the sounds and converts them to digital information.
3. The information is sent to the magnetic external transmitter coil, which, in turn, transmits the digital signal to the implanted receiver under the skin.
4. The implant converts the digital information and sends the appropriate electrical signals to the electrodes in the cochlea.
5. The electrodes then stimulate the nerve tissue there. The auditory nerve carries the impulses to the brain, which interprets them as sounds. This entire process happens almost instantaneously, just as it does for a hearing person.

associated with speech. However, predicting the success of an implant in any individual is a tremendously uncertain endeavor. At this point, all we or anyone can tell you about the outcome of a cochlear implant for your child is what it *might* do to improve sound perception. A cochlear implant may do the following:

- improve the hearing of and discrimination among sounds in the environment,
- improve speech recognition and particularly lipreading,
- improve speech, and
- reduce the dependence on context for understanding others' speech.

Let us repeat that these benefits are possible for some who receive a cochlear implant. Furthermore, among those who are deemed by reputable cochlear implant programs to be appropriate candidates for the device, each and every individual will experience different results, depending on all the related variables: rate of language development, previous exposure to sound, age of implantation, and benefit from sounds perceived.[1, 2]

A common misperception is that all children who can recognize sound will understand spoken language automatically and speak fluently.[3, 4] Early intervention contributes to greater language development and exposure to sound with a cochlear implant, which can increase access to spoken language. However, a cochlear implant, by itself, does not translate into speech that is easily understood; nor does it automatically give the recipient age-appropriate language and vocabulary development, and the reading skills needed for academic success.[5, 6, 7, 8]

In no sense do cochlear implants "cure" deafness; rather, with extensive, long-term training, they can change the recipient's position on the spectrum of hearing loss—for example, from profoundly deaf to moderately deaf or severely hard of hearing. It is important to mention, too, that the benefits of cochlear implants are particularly uncertain for young children, because they need more training than older children or adults to learn to interpret the sounds perceived as a result of the implant. Everyone who receives an implant needs extensive training for this purpose, so if you go this route, be prepared to commit the time and effort yourself as well as to seek out professional assistance.

Although most children with a cochlear implant will learn to respond to sound in some manner, a small percentage of children receive no perceivable benefit from the device. Approximately one-fourth of children with a cochlear implant learn to communicate primarily with spoken language, and about two-thirds use some combination of visual language and spoken language.[9, 10] Many young adults who received implants as young children and who grew up using only spoken language, choose to use ASL or a combination of sign language and spoken language as young adults.[11]

Advances in cognitive neuroscience research have made it possible to track the development of brain tissue, commonly referred to as *auditory tissue*, which has been identified as important for developing spoken language. Researchers at Gallaudet University's Brain and Language Laboratory used advanced brain imaging to observe auditory tissue development in deaf children.[12] This area of the brain was stimulated by patterns of language, *regardless if the language was spoken or signed*. A young brain is capable of learning sign language and spoken language without one language impeding development of auditory brain tissue for the other language.[13]

In addressing the cochlear implant issue, the authors' commitment is, as usual, to air all sides of the question; however, here this commitment weighs particularly heavily on our shoulders. We urge you to learn *everything* you can about cochlear implants, if you are considering this option for your child. It is particularly important that you seek out and talk freely with deaf people who have first-hand experience with the implant. Read, yes. Consult knowledgeable *unbiased* professionals, certainly. But please do not fail to make contact with people who have a cochlear implant themselves and have been trained to make use of them. You may have a variety of responses from very positive to extremely negative, but we think the more relevant comments will be from young deaf adults or adolescents who were implanted before the age of two.

PREPARING FOR A COCHLEAR IMPLANT

Simply listing the steps involved in receiving and learning to use a cochlear implant will make it clear that the process will be a complex, life-changing one for both you and your child. There's more to it than simply having an operation and recovering. Of course, like any surgery, it carries the potential of adverse reactions.

Before continuing, we would like to discuss an issue that both authors find bothersome and highly unethical among some medical practitioners who provide cochlear implants. There is still an old relic of clinical training going around that sign language is to be avoided at all costs or the child will not learn to talk. No research has ever proven this. Remember also that many of these surgeons come in with the medical viewpoint that deafness is a disease to be cured. No surprise there. Some will still tell you not to use ASL or sign language with your child after implantation. Worse yet are those who may actually demand that you sign an agreement that you will not do so as a condition of surgery and follow-up treatment. This is blackmail. Our advice for you, if faced with such negativity, is to head for the door as soon as possible and find a different medical provider who is more supportive and sensitive to the needs of a deaf child.

Let's take the case of Kevin, the son of a friend of the authors, who had a cochlear implant installed as a toddler. He's done very well and even learned to speak Spanish successfully as a bilingual. Initially, he was never exposed to ASL, at the insistence of his surgeon and other professionals. As Kevin got older, his parents became aware that he struggled while trying to follow the conversation when in classroom group discussions with several hearing peers. At that moment, Kevin's parents were open-minded enough to request an interpreter, to make group discussions more accessible for him. Although it may seem absurd to provide an interpreter to a deaf student who doesn't know more than a few signs, Kevin was able to hear enough of the conversation combined with the interpreters' Signed English to learn it. Over time, he became more fluent. We can see here that his surgeon was not sensitive to the possible challenges of every child he implants; Kevin needed all the communication tools to which he had access to succeed. So Kevin got "stuck" for a while. So with that example, we urge you to find an open-minded medical professional.

Here is a list of what is entailed in the cochlear implant process:
1. Before surgery, the child goes through a series of assessments

to determine if he or she is eligible for the surgery. At this stage, a professional team—ideally consisting of the child's parents plus an ear, nose, and throat (ENT) doctor, a pediatric audiologist, a speech pathologist, a teacher, a psychologist, a deaf adult, and any other professionals who will be involved in the follow-up training—attempts to determine whether the child meets the criteria for receiving an implant or might better benefit from conventional hearing aids.

2. If surgery is indicated, the device is implanted under general anesthesia.
3. Approximately two to four weeks after surgery, the device is electrically stimulated and "mapped" for sound—meaning that the child goes through intensive programming sessions with an audiologist, who matches the electronic input with the child's particular "listening thresholds." This mapping needs to be frequent, and an ongoing regularly scheduled process to ensure optimal results begins.
4. With the device calibrated to the child's particular needs, he or she embarks on an extensive training program that includes short-term listening-skills training, and long-term speech and listening training of which you are an integral part. You will need to commit a significant amount of time to working one-on-one with your child to help him or her develop listening skills.
5. Once in school, the child's speech and language development are monitored on an ongoing basis.
6. Throughout the child's life, the implant site is monitored for possible medical complications.

As you can see, getting a cochlear implant for your child is a major life decision involving a substantial commitment of time, money, and energy. Making the choice is a delicate matter of imagining what the child will want *as an older person*. As you well know, virtually any decision on behalf of a child is based, in large part, on a wing and a prayer. In this case, the prayer is that the continuing effort and expense will bear fruit in an improved quality of life for your child. But in this, as in so many decisions we make for our children, there are no guarantees.

Who Can Benefit from Cochlear Implants?

Not every deaf child is a candidate for a cochlear implant. The determination is made through a complex selection process involving otological, radiological, audiological, psychological, speech, and language considerations, as well as family and educational assessments. Without attempting to explain in detail, it is possible to sketch in a general way the *preferred* conditions and the contraindications for cochlear implants.

Preferred Conditions for Cochlear Implants

- The deafness is recent (caused perhaps by bacterial meningitis) or congenital, and the child has no significant gain from well-fitted, consistently worn conventional hearing aids, even after extensive training.
- No other special conditions, such as intellectual and developmental disabilities, learning disabilities, or autism, and no major emotional or educational difficulties are present.
- The child and the family have realistic expectations for the outcome of the implant.
- The child is highly motivated to learn to use the implant (of course, there is no way to determine this in an infant or toddler).
- The parents are highly motivated to assist their child in developing listening skills and to ensure the implant equipment is always functioning appropriately.
- School personnel and other professionals who embrace the challenges of pre- and post-surgical training are available to you and your child.

Contraindications for Cochlear Implants

- The ear is physiologically unsuitable for the implant.
- Existing medical problems, such as damage beyond the cochlea to the acoustic nerve or to the central auditory pathways, would render the implant ineffective.
- The child or the family have unrealistic expectations of a "miracle cure."
- Active middle ear infections or other relevant disease conditions are present.

- There is no cochlea or no functioning auditory nerve.
- The child benefits significantly from conventional acoustic amplification.
- The educational environment is not conducive to the development of Listening and Spoken Language skills (speech, speechreading, and listening).

These sketches are intentionally vague, because the process of professional assessment is too complex to cover here, and the candidacy criteria has evolved since the devices were first approved.[14] The rest of this chapter is better spent outlining some issues that bear on your part of the decision process. The following sections summarize the current cochlear implant debate and present some real-life stories to help you begin to form your own conclusions.

Why the Controversy?

Again, how does a technological development as seemingly benign as the cochlear implant engender such deep antagonisms? Let's sort it out.

Proponents of cochlear implants argue the following:

- To some measurable extent, cochlear implants can "cure" deafness by transmitting sound to the brain; in a limited way, in many cases, deaf people can be helped to hear and develop spoken language skills.
- Many people whose implant does not enable them to carry on "normal" conversations use the electronically transmitted sounds to improve their speechreading.
- An implant enables many deaf people to avoid isolation from hearing society. Some people with an implant become bilingual, mastering English and ASL, and participate successfully both in hearing society and in the Deaf community.

Opponents of cochlear implants argue the following:

- Implanting the device involves major surgery, with attendant risks of infections, like meningitis, permanent facial paralysis, dizziness, headaches, ringing in the ears, and facial pain. Those who have implants may not be able to have MRIs (magnetic resonance imaging) due to the metal present in the device. Whether or not the implant works, the recipient will be committed to a lifelong program of medical monitoring.

- Even if no physical risks or hardships were involved, cochlear implants would be unnecessary. Being deaf is not a disease that must be cured; it is a state of being, different from, but equal to, the state of being a hearing person. To suggest that deaf children should be altered physically to make them more like hearing people is to threaten their self-esteem and psychological well-being. One might as well suggest that people of color be made more like white people.

- Children with little aptitude for speech could be set up for a lifelong sense of inadequacy if they fail to learn to speak even after receiving an implant.

- The time and effort that implant recipients devote to refining their listening skills might more valuably be invested in mastering English.

- Given the fact that deaf children are still *deaf* even with a cochlear implant, there is some risk of developing an identity crisis about which "world," deaf or hearing, that they fit into as they get older. They may reject having a deaf identity based on the expectations placed on them to fit into hearing society.

Note the ironic similarity between the last points in the two lists: Implant proponents argue that deaf people who receive implants lessen their risk of isolation from hearing society. Implant opponents argue that deaf people who receive implants increase their risk of having an identity crisis about where they fit in the world. The authors have seen the latter happen more than enough times to know it can be a real problem requiring counseling.

As the authors have tried to make clear throughout this book, the critical concern is that we give our deaf children the means to function in *both* worlds. For parents to concern themselves with the risk that a deaf child will be isolated from the hearing society without being *at least equally concerned* that the child may be isolated from the Deaf society would be to fail as their children's ambassadors to the world. It is this profoundly important matter that injects the cochlear implant controversy with its great heat and significance.

Is there a way through this difficult conflict for parents attempting to do the right thing for their children?

We can only repeat: Go out, network, make contact with deaf adults and deaf children who have firsthand experience with cochlear implants. Finding them may take effort, but schools and agencies working with deaf children and adults should help. The point is to meet people with every point of view. Welcome those who contradict your own initial orientation. *Learn—learn and empathize* as much as you can. Try to imagine how a cochlear implant might affect your child, whether positive or negative.

With this advice in mind, turn now to the following real-life stories, which were imparted to the authors by recipients of cochlear implants.

Personal Experiences: The Real-Life Debate

The authors have seen wonderful benefits from cochlear implants and have talked with teenagers and young adults who were very grateful to their parents for deciding in favor of the implants. Among these individuals, there is a mixture of those who were implanted at the age of twelve to twenty-four months and those implanted by the age of five. Furthermore, all had gone through excellent cochlear implant programs, where they had been deemed ideal candidates following extensive analysis. Jara's success story is representative of this group.

Jara's Story

Jara lost her hearing at age three after a bout of spinal meningitis. Just as she was about to enter preschool, her parents had her evaluated for an implant, feeling that it would do more for her than the hearing aids she wore. The program accepted Jara, even though her grandparents on both sides were adamantly opposed to a cochlear implant. The professionals decided that because the core family was committed and had excellent community support, successful follow-through was likely.

Jara happened to have strong spoken language skills. She had begun to talk before she lost her hearing and expressed herself extremely well. A year after the surgery, she was doing very well—mostly owing to her personality, which was well suited to the training and follow-up. She seemed to enjoy it and participated fully.

Were there problems? Jara reported that the sounds from the implant were metallic and static, but with time, she adjusted to that. She was sensitive about the visible wires and apparatus, but her teachers helped her educate the other children in her class and overcome the feeling of being different. Jara hated it when children said she had a "funny voice," and she asked her parents whether it really was funny. Just different, they explained over and over. Jara seemed to grow comfortable with that.

Over time, the keys to Jara's success were the mutual respect and productive working relationships among Jara, her family, and the professional team. She had consistency in the follow-up programming and training, and no surprises occurred that couldn't be handled. The result was that Jara expressed great satisfaction with the decision.

On the other side of the coin, the authors have seen abuses of cochlear implants and have heard a good number of horror stories. One at the top of the pile involves the Reynso family, whose doctor was a zealous supporter of cochlear implants.

Brian's Story

When the Reynosas' three-year-old son, Brian, was found to be deaf, the doctor convinced the family that a cochlear implant was their only alternative, and soon after, Brian was implanted with the device. No one informed the family that not all children are good candidates for an implant, or that Brian would need extensive training to make use of it, with no guarantee of success.

Long after the operation, when it seemed that the expected "cure" had failed to materialize, the family finally wound up in a skilled audiologist's office. This professional found, to his horror, that they were expecting a miracle: complete restoration of Brian's hearing. After a few weeks of evaluations and meetings, he was even more distressed to find that Brian was not a good cochlear implant candidate at all. Hearing aids and training to develop residual hearing would have been the best choice in this case. The traumatic and expensive surgery on a three-year-old child had been in vain and even worse, a lot of time that could have been spent on developing his world knowledge and literacy skills during a critical development period had been lost.

Jasmine's Story

Jasmine, at the age of four, went through a cochlear implant program despite truly terrible communication at home. Her parents and siblings only occasionally took the time to communicate with her. Instead, they expected her implant to do the task of feeding information into her head. Even when they did talk to her, they made no effort to speak clearly or to face her, so that she could see their lips. The family had worked hard to get what they considered to be the solution to all of Jasmine's problems; Jasmine's teachers had been impressed by their diligence and enthusiasm before the operation. But once they achieved the "solution," the family felt their work was over. Needless to say, without proper audiological follow-up and family support, the cochlear implant proved to be a great disappointment.

Zeke's Story

Zeke's parents were so eager to see their twenty-four-month son in a cochlear implant program and be implanted. Four years after the surgery, however, Zeke's speech and listening skills were not what they should be. Zeke had difficulty understanding why his parents did not make the effort to communicate with him on a regular basis. Nor was the extended family taught or encouraged to communicate with Zeke. He was frequently not included in many family events but was left alone to do his own thing. Alexis, one teacher (thank goodness) in his spoken language program noticed that Zeke was not doing well, so she started teaching him to sign and persuaded the family to enroll him in a signing program. There, he thrived and started catching up to his peers, but his parents were still disappointed that Zeke was not going to be a "hearing person." We need more professionals like Zeke's teacher, Alexis, who are often aware which child is benefiting and which one is not and are willing to make and suggest changes as needed.

The Proper Assessment Procedure

If, after extensive study and networking, you decide to have your child assessed as a cochlear implant candidate, you'll need to find a responsible program that performs detailed evaluations and offers full disclosure of the results. For your information, here's a checklist of steps necessary for a responsible assessment.[§] If a program you are considering doesn't include these steps in its standard working procedures, go elsewhere.

1. The family fills out a comprehensive questionnaire.
2. An initial meeting is scheduled.
3. The child goes through medical, audiological, and radiological tests (the last, to make sure an implant can be inserted) and a hearing aid evaluation (to make sure the implant would offer significantly greater benefits than conventional hearing aids).
4. If the child is deemed a potential candidate at this stage, more tests are scheduled to assess the following:
   - the child's oral skills (to determine whether existing skills can enhance the implant's effectiveness),
   - the child's commitment to, and emotional readiness for, the necessary follow-up effort,
   - the child's motor skills,
   - the child's academic achievement and educational placement,
   - the child's communication skills, and
   - the child's social and adaptive skills.
5. Next, the program's team members conduct an assessment of the psychological and other support services available in the applicant's local community (or the family's willingness to commute if necessary).
6. Psychological factors in the family are evaluated in depth, specifically the following:
   - the expectations of the parents,
   - the expectations of the child,
   - the willingness of all family members to go through the training and follow-up,

---

§ We are indebted to Dr. Stephen D. Roberts for the recommendations from which this checklist was drawn.

- the personality characteristics of parents and child, and
- the communication habits of the family and peer group.

7. The family meets with the program's permanent team of professionals (ENT physician, teachers, psychologist, speech therapist, and audiologist) to participate in a group decision-making process. Some programs require that the child's professional support network—teachers and the school psychologist and audiologist—participate at this stage to lay the groundwork for follow-up work.

8. If a problem arises at any stage of this process, the candidate is discharged from the program.

Our Personal Opinions

In this book, the authors have tried to present all points of view impartially. However, because with regard to cochlear implants, subjective opinion, tempered by information and empathy, is the deciding factor, it seems fair to contribute our own two cents. You may find it useful to consider this personal perspective along with the many others you'll collect.

As profoundly deaf men, the authors have considered the issue of cochlear implants. Although neither author has a deaf child, suppose we had one? Would we give him or her a cochlear implant? Although we agree on many things, we respectfully disagree on this topic and will show you our reasons, in turn, below.

DAVE'S OPINION

Although I acknowledge there are indeed great success stories for cochlear implants in children, for me, the answer is *no*—and it is not complicated. For one, this entails major surgery on an infant or young child along with all of the risks entailed with anesthesia, possible infections or botched procedures, possible side effects, and just the general anxiety of having my child undergo a medical procedure. My wife and I do have hearing children, and they have undergone relatively minor medical procedures, like ear tubes for chronic infections. They were still pretty stressful events for us, like it would be for a lot of parents. There is also the expense of implants; insurance can only cover so much before there are out-of-pocket expenses for batteries, upkeep, repairs, and the eventual replacement of the processors, which may or may not be covered.

Benefits of the implant are still uncertain, and far from guaranteed. Changing a child from profoundly deaf to "hard of hearing" (*only* with the cochlear implant on) may not be a measurable advantage at all. I also question whether the potential benefits justify committing a child to hours and hours at doctor's offices and in clinics for therapy. That time could be better spent playing with siblings and learning about the world.

Some might ask, "Why would you deny your child the potential benefits?" To that, I can say it is the child's decision, not ours. If a child of mine decided to get a cochlear implant at a time when he or she is capable of making that decision, my wife and I would respect it. We would do our homework together with due diligence and find a surgeon and audiologist that respects our wishes for an ASL/English bilingual child. We have actually seen that happen with other deaf families, and the results usually worked out quite nicely, mostly because the child already had a good language foundation to build upon. The key to success for deaf children is not only about being able to hear and talk or sign but also being a literate individual with supportive parents.

PAUL'S OPINION

When we assembled the second edition of this book about twenty years ago, my original answer about cochlear implants was an emphatic *no* based on the technology and then relatively recent knowledge of professionals. There were too many variables for me to be comfortable with the idea, so I decided against it. However, I recently changed my stance after a trip to Washington DC, where I was on a tour and observed a child with an implant interacting positively with his family. It was obvious that good communication was taking place. That plus the knowledge and technological gains over the years have influenced my thinking on this. So now my answer is *yes*, I would consider implanting my deaf child, if it was the right decision. Let me explain why.

First, I want to say that the most important variable in this situation would be the parents. I had wonderful parents, who did a great job raising me with the best possible knowledge they could find for the times back during the post–World War II era. For this situation, parents would need to have positive expectations and do everything we recommend in this book, but be tempered by the reality that a cochlear implant just *might* not work out in the end. Also keep in mind that your child, even though he or she may seem to function like a hard of hearing person, is *still deaf*. If you decide to do this, then being forewarned with information is to be forearmed about what to watch out for.

Second, I need to make sure that you are aware of and knowledgeable about the existence of the "optimal window for learning language." Along the continuum of normal language development, there exists a prime period of time for language learning. We referred to it earlier in this book, and that time is the first five years of life. During this time, the brain is the most "elastic," or pliable, in its ability to learn language (referred to as the *elasticity of the brain*). The most opportune time for children to develop and learn language is during this period of brain development. That is not to say that learning language later (after five years of age) is impossible; it is just more difficult. If you want to get the most out of an implant, the prime time for implantation is within the first five years of your child's life.

I'd like to share some tidbits we learned when my wife, Anne, decided to get an implant several years ago. The first thing we did was research the surgeons, and when we found one we thought might work well with us, we interviewed him with a laundry list of questions. (You can get some ideas from this book and other sources.) Unfortunately, we were not satisfied, so we started over again until we found the one that we thought was a good match. After the surgery, we also needed a good audiologist for mapping the sound processor, so that was another process we went through. It is *extremely important* that anyone with an implant consistently and frequently go see their audiologist for mapping and equipment checks in order to get the best out of it. You wouldn't spend tens of thousands of dollars on a sports car and not keep it in top running shape, would you? You've made the decision to get a cochlear implant, so now you need to be sure that you follow through with that decision and support your child completely.

Remember, I asked you to keep your expectations tempered and watch to see how it is working out. Let your child lead the way. If all goes well, and they have the appropriate support and services, he or she should adapt to it and progress well. If your child seems not to be responding or is reacting negatively for any reason, go back and have the implant checked and evaluated until things improve. Don't try to force it to work. The last thing you need is a deaf child who grows into a deaf adult with bitter memories and resentment. Trust us, the authors know many such deaf adults. Yes, please sign with your child, and if it all works out, you could end up with a child who is fully bilingual in ASL and English. Who knows . . . your child can even end up being trilingual if they learn another spoken language. That would be wonderful!

Conclusion

We are not trying to confuse you, we just want to make sure you are *fully* informed before you make a critical decision. Deaf people, as we have shown, do have varying points of view on the issue of cochlear implants, just as they do with hearing aids or other topics. Some detest the idea of anything near their ears, and others actually cannot live without their implants or hearing aids. But remember, we all still have far more things in common than not.

Alternative paths to *everything* in life are available to your child. Your job is to find those paths, even if they take you far from the path you have followed to maturity. The parenting of any children—deaf or hearing—never means producing little clones of ourselves. Rather, the job is to foster the best in our children, different—yes, different and wonderful—as they may be.

Notes

1. Elizabeth M. Fitzpatrick, Elizabeth Johnson, and Andree Durieux-Smith, "Exploring Factors That Affect the Age of Cochlear Implantation in Children," *International Journal of Pediatric Otorhinolaryngology* 75, no. 9 (2011): 1082–087.

2. Amy Lederberg, Brenda Schick, and Patricia Spencer, "Language and Literacy Development of Deaf and Hard-of-Hearing Children: Successes and Challenges," *Developmental Psychology* 49, no. 1 (2013):15–30.

3. Peter Flipsen, "Intelligibility of Spontaneous Conversational Speech Produced by Children with Cochlear Implants: A Review," *International Journal of Pediatric Otorhinolaryngology* 72, no. 5 (2008): 559–64.

4. Patricia Spencer, Marc Marschark, and Linda Spencer, "Cochlear Implants: Advances, Issues and Implications," in *The Oxford Handbook of*

Deaf Studies, Language, and Education, vol. 1 (2nd ed.), ed. Marc Marschark and Patricia Spencer (New York: Oxford University Press, 2011): 452–70.

5. Sophie Ambrose, Mark Fey, and Laurie Eisenberg, "Phonological Awareness and Print Knowledge of Preschool Children with Cochlear Implants," *Journal of Speech, Language, and Hearing Research* 55, no. 3 (2012): 811–23.

6. Peter Blamey and Julia Sarant, "Development of Spoken Language by Deaf Children," in *The Oxford Handbook of Deaf Studies, Language, and Education*, vol. 1 (2nd ed.), ed. Marc Marschark and Patricia Spencer (New York: Oxford University Press, 2011): 241–57.

7. Tom Humphries, Poorna Kushalnagar, Gaurav Mathur, Donna Jo Napoli, Carol Padden, Christian Rathmann, and Scott Smith, "Language Acquisition for Deaf Children: Reducing the Harms of Zero Tolerance to the Use of Alternative Approaches," *Harm Reduction Journal* 9, no. 1 (2012): 1–9.

8. Ann Geers and Heather Hayes. "Reading, Writing, and Phonological Processing Skills of Adolescents with 10 or More Years of Cochlear Implant Experience," *Ear and Hearing* 32, no. 1 (2011): 49S–59S.

9. Adeline McClatchie and MaryKay Therres, *AuSpLan: A Manual for Professionals Working with Children Who Have Cochlear Implants or Amplification* (Oakland, CA: Children's Hospital & Research Center at Oakland, 2003).

10. Linda Spencer, J. Bruce Tomblin, and Bruce Gantz, "Growing Up with a Cochlear Implant: Education, Vocation, and Affiliation," *Journal of Deaf Studies and Deaf Education* 17, no. 4 (2012): 185–98.

11. John Christiansen and Irene Leigh. "Cochlear Implants and Deaf Community Perspectives," in *Cochlear Implants: Evolving Perspectives*, ed. John Christiansen and Irene Leigh (Washington DC: Gallaudet University Press, 2011): 39–55.

12. Laura-Ann Petitto, "What the Eyes Reveal about the Brain: Advances in Human Language Acquisition," webcast (Washington, DC: Laurent Clerc National Deaf Education Center, 2014). Available online at www.gallaudet.edu/clerc-center/learning-opportunities/webcasts/what-the-eyes-reveal-about-the-brain-webcast.html.

13. Julie Mitchiner, Debra Berlin Nussbaum, and Susanne Scott, Research Brief no. 6: *The Implications of Bimodal Bilingual Approaches for Children with Cochlear Implants* (Washington, DC: Visual Language and Visual Learning Science of Learning Center, 2012).

14. Gifford, René. "Who Is a Cochlear Implant Candidate?" *Hearing Journal* 64, no. 6 (2011): 16–18.

15 Boot Camp for Parents of Deaf Children with Special Needs

DEAF CHILDREN, as a population, are more likely than hearing children to have one or more disabilities other than deafness—the chances are 10 to 40 percent, as compared with 2 to 10 percent in the general population.[1] The reason for this is that some causes of deafness also are associated with other conditions, including intellectual disabilities, emotional and behavioral disorders, learning disabilities, and deaf-blindness or low vision. This chapter addresses the particular circumstances you will face as a parent if your deaf or hard of hearing child is diagnosed with one or more of these other conditions.

Many deaf children are misdiagnosed as *deaf plus*—that is, as having one or more additional disabilities—and subsequently treated as children with limited functioning. Often, the diagnosing professional simply mistakes deafness and limited communication skills for one or more of the other conditions listed above. For example, autism and deafness have many similar symptoms in very young children. These additional conditions do occur more often in deaf than hearing children (e.g., the higher rate of prematurity among deaf babies and the periodic epidemics, such as rubella, that cause not only deafness but an array of other disabilities). However, as a parent, it is important for you to remember: *Professionals make mistakes!* Before accepting an additional disability diagnosis for your child, *get another opinion!*

If you conclude that the diagnosis is correct, don't stop there. You will have much to learn, and your quest for knowledge won't end with a single spate of research. Things change as a child matures, and other problems can crop up, changing the overall diagnosis a great deal. You'll need to turn your attention to many aspects of your child's well-being that you may not have thought about much before: social-emotional development, motor development, language development, physical development, cognitive development, and the development of communication skills. With children who are deaf plus, especially those who have moderate to severe disabilities besides deafness, it is hard to get the whole picture at once and nearly impossible at the beginning. So you'll need to look for information all the time, going national (if not global) in your search. Fasten your seat belt! You're going to be an expert on your child's condition.

Much as we all wish we could depend on medical professionals and others who wear the label *expert*, we're constantly thrown back on our own resources to confirm the accuracy of diagnoses. Few people who understand intellectual disabilities or blindness or learning disabilities also understand deafness and its impact on communication. Conversely, few people who understand deafness are specialists in the ways its effects are compounded by other disabling conditions, although you are probably more likely to find one in this latter group. The interrelationships among deafness, other disabilities, and communication are so subtle and complex that few doctors, educators, or counselors have mastered them. You'll need to put a tremendous amount of effort into finding just the right professionals—the ones who *really* know what's going on with your child, how the different variables are interacting, and what the appropriate educational, medical, and social responses may be. The authors suggest starting with professionals whose primary area of expertise is deafness and then seeing if they also have expertise in the additional area(s) of disability. Much of your initial work will be that of a personnel analyst, interviewing candidates for the job of working with your child. One of the first places to look is at state schools for deaf children, as they often have programs for deaf plus or what some call *special needs students.*

You will be called upon to verify, test, challenge, and doubt every pronouncement that anyone makes about your child. Does this sound overwhelming, or even impossible? Don't despair. Remember the tried and true way: Find people who have walked the path ahead of you—deaf adults with the conditions diagnosed in your child (e.g., deaf-blind organizations) and parents whose children have been similarly diagnosed. Deaf adults with special needs can describe for you their frustrations and successes along the way from a very personal yet informative point of view, one you won't get from a professional. One deaf man the authors know, Ian, was autistic as a child; his family was extremely supportive and helped him deal with his autism and overcome it. Ian remembers vividly what it was like to grow up autistic and now is able to describe his behavior and experiences from the inside.

The Dangers of Misdiagnosis

As soon as you receive a diagnosis of deaf plus, you need to find a strong counseling program or support group, where you can hash out these matters for as long as necessary with other parents who have gone the same route. If you can't find such a support group, get on the phone or Internet and start one! Again, see if your state school for deaf students can connect you with other parents. Break through any natural resistance you may feel to discussing your problems with strangers, and *network, network, network.* Knowing you're not alone is quite beneficial for your mental and emotional health. Your child's future depends on it.

Why are we making such a fuss about consulting other parents? An important reason is that you need to be fully aware of the services available to you and your child. It is all too common for professionals to appear to know what they're talking about and appear to be familiar with the range of available services. The reality is that *very few people are properly trained and qualified to work with deaf plus children.*

The first people you will come into contact with are likely to be doctors. Although they are, of course, indispensable in pinpointing most *medical* problems, unfortunately doctors are notoriously naive about the needs of deaf and deaf plus children. The authors feel confident in asserting that 99 percent of the physicians in the United States are unaware of the information on deafness in young children available to you in this book. Understandably, parents tend to rely heavily on their pediatricians, particularly around the time of diagnosis. However, they tend to have an annoying habit of pooh-poohing parent's concerns, telling them to wait things out. For information about the combination of deafness with more subtle disabilities, especially learning disabilities, the people to track down are experienced teachers and other educational professionals, not doctors.

The danger to be avoided at all costs is misdiagnosis. Very often, deaf children are incorrectly classified as intellectually disabled, learning disabled, autistic, et cetera, only because their communication skills are undeveloped and their academic achievement low. Other deaf children who actually *have* such disabilities are classified and treated as deaf alone and consequently left without the special resources they need. (For some guidelines in your search for professionals with appropriate expertise, see "What to Expect from Professionals" on page 310.) Now let's turn to the story of Austin to see the profound, real-life consequences of one misdiagnosis.

Austin's Story

Austin's parents were terribly upset when he was diagnosed as deaf, and they brushed aside all the recommendations from professionals who urged them to begin bonding and communicating with him immediately. When Austin entered school (part of a small, rural system), he was classified as *slow* by a testing psychologist, who knew very little about deafness—a fact Austin's parents were unaware of. After eight years in the school system, always under the label *slow learner*, Austin was transferred to a vocational program at a state school for deaf students. There, the diagnosing professionals found him to be nearly without communication skills. None of the tests or other measuring tools pointed to a learning disability; however, by behavior and habit, Austin had fulfilled the first psychologist's diagnosis and become a *multidisabled* individual.

What to Expect from Professionals

From doctors and other medical personnel:

Diagnosis and treatment of physical conditions. Don't expect them to know or tell you what you should do about a deaf plus child.

From audiologists and ENT specialists:

Diagnosis regarding hearing loss. Sometimes they have information about programs and educational resources, but always double-check the information with others who know their way around.

From psychologists, counselors, and assessors:

Diagnosis of emotional, mental, and behavioral problems. They're usually not experts in the impact of deafness and its interaction with other conditions.

From teachers and other education professionals for learning disabled students:

Assessment of the learning disability. Don't expect them to understand the effects of deafness on your child's learning skills and social relationships unless specifically trained.

From teachers and other education professionals for deaf and hard of hearing students:

Don't expect them to be qualified to work with special needs students. Some of these teachers may be specifically trained or licensed in working with deaf plus children; but be sure to verify this if you are considering making them part of your team. ❏

His employment opportunities were limited to manual labor; eventually he got a job as a school janitor. This is a reflection of the power of self-fulfilling prophecies and low expectations. No one knows what would have happened if Austin's parents had taken an active interest in his education and communication skills with high expectations right from the beginning.

THE OTHER SIDE OF THE COIN

Misdiagnosis runs the other way as well: Many deaf children are deemed *normal* when they actually have additional disabilities; and many are misdiagnosed in one category (e.g., as intellectually disabled) when their condition actually falls into another (learning disabled).

As a parent, you should be aware that our system of screening children is characterized by a general lack of identification procedures for mild disabilities. The first thing you should have checked is your child's vision: Many deaf children suffer from minor, easily correctable vision defects—so many, in fact, that the authors are always running into them and recognizing their situation immediately, although we are not ophthalmologists. These vision problems often remain undiagnosed and untreated, as do mild learning disabilities in many deaf children. Poor or nonexistent diagnostic procedures place heavy burdens on deaf children. To us—and certainly to the children and those who love them—this is an avoidable tragedy.

An example will help to show how complicated it can be to deal with the subtle interactions of special needs, even when the medical diagnosis is accurate. The condition known as *attention deficit hyperactivity disorder (ADHD)* is a serious problem for deaf children, because it impedes their ability to focus their attention on intellectual tasks. It affects speech or signing skills, reading, auditory skills, speechreading—all the capabilities necessary for the child to learn. ADHD is a syndrome—a collection of symptoms—with various neurological causes. The symptoms and their severity vary greatly from child to child, and the effectiveness of interventions, such as medication, also varies. Even when medication does work, it cannot address the emotional, social, and cognitive problems that have taken hold as a result of the disorder. This means parents and teachers must deal not only with a medical situation, and not only with a communication problem, but also with a complex set of social, emotional, and educational circumstances, all of which will change as the child matures. However, ADHD can and has been successfully overcome by many deaf children.

Where another disability is present in addition to deafness, it does more than merely add to the child's problems—it creates a unique and complex interaction of variables that require subtle analysis and a customized response. Imagine how complex might be the interactions of even two or three of the following variables on a deaf child's ability to learn, communicate, and mature toward independence:

- blindness,
- intellectual disability,
- learning disability,
- communication skill level,
- IQ level,
- learning style,
- family background,
- psychological factors,
- family support,
- willingness of family members to learn alternative communication modes, and
- personality and motivation.

There is no such thing as a "typical" deaf plus child or actually any deaf child for that matter. Each one presents a unique constellation of needs. Yet only a very few education programs in the United States prepare teachers to work with deaf plus children. Most education professionals in mainstreamed settings are well prepared to help deaf or hard of hearing children, but generally they have little experience with deaf plus children. The challenge you face in planning for the education of your deaf plus child is finding those very few professionals who are competent to assess and address your child's needs or willing to become educated to better meet your child's needs. It is not easy, as the following story shows.

Rudy's Story

At birth, Rudy Howard was normal in every respect, but his parents soon began to suspect he had hearing loss. When their suspicions were confirmed, they acknowledged another intuition—of a certain slowness, although they were unable to pinpoint the problem.

The Howards sought far and wide for reliable assessments of Rudy's learning and cognitive abilities and were appalled to find how little most professionals could tell them, even while constantly subjecting Rudy to a battery of tests. The testers and diagnosticians who turned out to be the least trustworthy came up with all kinds of explanations for Rudy's slowness in learning. After many years in the system, Mrs. Howard came to understand that the universal diagnosis among reputable diagnosticians was this: "We just aren't sure *what's* going on. Like you, we have more questions than answers."

But the Howards persisted. And over the years, they learned a great deal about the learning assessment business. They discovered, for example, the following:

- Not all tests are appropriate for deaf children or are administered correctly.
- Not all testers know or respect the communication mode of the child they are testing; instead, they often administer the test in *their* preferred mode (this is actually against the Individuals with Disabilities Education Act).
- Some testers inappropriately measure a deaf child's performance against hearing norms, skewing the assessment.
- Some testers are uncomfortable with deafness, and their discomfort has a negative effect on a deaf child's test performance.
- Testers often put too much stock in tests, mistakenly believing that the scores contribute to a diagnosis.
- Testers will not take into consideration how the results of various tests interact and influence each other to give one a complete picture of the total child.
- Many testers are intimidating and insulting to parents, insisting on their own expertise, even when parents have a very clear picture of their children's capacities.
- Testers often see themselves as authorities rather than as teammates working with parents and children.

Rudy's learning problem was never accurately diagnosed, despite an accumulation of test results and evaluations that filled three carefully organized loose-leaf binders. The shared opinion seemed to be that he was of average intelligence; he never became much of a reader. Still, his story ended well. The Howards finally accepted the assessment of average intelligence and helped Rudy to concentrate on working with his hands, for which he had always showed a strong aptitude. After graduating from high school, he immediately began working in his cousin's automobile shop. He loved his new life, started saving for a new car, and became a passionate fisherman. Much of Rudy's happiness—his sense of the "rightness" of his life today—stems from his parents' eventual willingness to accept the lack of a definitive diagnosis and to focus instead on helping him develop his potential. This is an example of having high expectations for your child regardless of the diagnosis: always expecting them to do better than others will. Many parents have trouble admitting that their child has "average" or "below average" intelligence, as measured by standardized tests. They find themselves seeking more and more opinions and diagnoses over the years rather than accepting the child for who he or she may be and working with them to make the best of it.

Accentuating the positive can become a great challenge for parents of deaf plus children. You may feel that your responsibilities pull you in two directions at once. On the one hand, we're urging you to seek out the best professionals in the country and carefully monitor their feedback; on the other hand, we're urging you not to get too hung up on scores, levels, and measurements. The best approach is to guard against extremes in either direction. Ask yourself as you explore the world of professional assessments and diagnoses: "Am I losing sight of who my child really is? In trying to plan for the future, am I forgetting his or her current need for love, communication, acceptance, and reassurance?"

The story of Thomas Powell illustrates this problem in an extreme way.

Thomas's Story
Deaf from birth, Thomas gave early signs of severe learning problems that were confirmed by countless tests administered

in his special school. His parents were humiliated and frustrated for years by an education system that insisted on seeing their son solely in terms of "outcomes"—that is, test scores and measurement profiles. All the wrong decisions were made for presumably "right" reasons: Academic tests suggested certain routes, and Thomas's parents made their choices accordingly. However, Thomas never learned to read, write, speechread, or speak. His expressive signing skills never advanced beyond the first-grade level, although his receptive skills were somewhat higher. He understood American Sign Language (ASL), but he never really absorbed the structure of English.

After years, Thomas's parents saw the light. The educators were still coming up with plans based on outcomes, but the Powells decided to withdraw Thomas from the special program and enroll him in a vocational training program in a public high school. Now he works at a grocery store, where he has wonderful benefits. He owns a pickup truck, has a driver's license, and has moved into an apartment on his own. A social worker visits six hours a week to oversee his meal planning and banking.

The lesson here is that the test scores and progress reports that fill a student's file never tell the whole story. Be sure to keep track of all the scores of all the tests your child has taken. But also be sure to keep in touch with the professionals overseeing your deaf plus child's progress and ask them to supplement scores and assessments with portfolios of your child's less-quantifiable work—drawings and writings, for example—and teachers' "impressions," anecdotes about classroom interactions, and so forth.

Next we turn to Deirdre's story, a tale of success thanks to her single mother's patience and great luck in meeting the right professional early.

Deirdre's Story

Deirdre is deaf and mildly intellectually disabled. Her mother, Marie, was a determined networker and eventually met Nan Beckwith, a highly qualified specialist in working with special needs children. The two met not at a school or clinic, as you might expect, but at a fast-food restaurant waiting in line. (You never know where you might meet those influential people in your life.)

Nan became intrigued with Deirdre when she learned that the girl was not only intellectually disabled, but deaf. She didn't know much about deafness but worked with Deirdre and Marie to learn all she could—and discovered in the process how much her educational approaches and standard assessment measures left to be desired when deafness and intellectual disability were in the picture together. Working in tandem, Nan and Marie located the right professionals, and these people, in turn, helped them to find the right school. The teachers there emphasized the importance of using sign language with Deirdre.

Throughout their long association, Nan encouraged Marie to train Deirdre slowly in household chores and responsibilities. The goal was independence, Nan explained, but the pace had to match Deirdre's ability to absorb the new skills. Pacing was everything. This is an example of appropriate high expectations: keeping them just above the current level of progress and constantly moving and adjusting that bar of expectation as it is reached every time.

Today, Deirdre works in a restaurant, washing dishes, a skill she learned in an on-the-job training program at a local hospital. She rides the bus to work on her own every day and still lives with Marie. Although not considered *high-level functioning*, Deirdre takes care of her own laundry, cooks some meals, and participates in the household. These are no small returns for her mother's determined efforts, especially when you consider the alternative: complete dependence, and all the loneliness and unhappiness that implies.

Our Personal Views

The authors have visited or worked with a number of excellent programs for deaf special needs children staffed by highly dedicated teachers. Many of these people are at state schools for deaf students. You can feel the rapport among principal, teachers, parents, and students the minute you walk in the door. We strongly recommend that you never make a decision about a school or other facility without visiting it in person. Note, too, that the best facilities for deaf plus children tend to be in or near major urban cities; it may be impossible to find a good school close to home if you live in a rural area. Even if you are unable to move closer, these specialized programs may be able to provide outreach resources and *appropriate* evaluation services by qualified professionals.

The greatest investment you can make in your deaf plus child's future is to focus on two prerequisites for success in school and adult life: communication skills and independent living skills.

First, learn sign language yourself and make it available to your child. Doing this will be like buying an insurance policy—insuring that, no matter what happens in school and in life, your child will have a means to communicate. Even many hearing children with intellectual disabilities, autism, or limited verbal skills benefit from sign language. (For children who are deaf-blind, there is an approach called *tactile signing*, which relies on the placement of their hands on top of those of the other person who is signing.) Second, help your child, from the very beginning, to attain the skills required to become independent and productive.

The authors have known many parents of deaf plus children who enjoy their children tremendously at an early age but become uncomfortable around them when they grow up. The best way to provide for your child's future and for your future relationship with the child is to communicate constantly and do things together all along the line.

Many parents help their deaf plus children get work but then allow them to live isolated lives after hours. Our wish list for your child includes the kind of time-management skills and communication skills that allow deaf plus people to live active personal lives in a network of meaningful social relationships.

All of your efforts should be guided by your child's need to learn communication and independent living skills. These skill areas are the foundation for everything else your child learns. Be careful as you proceed not to become distracted from these fundamental skills, and always monitor your child's progress in them. If you notice that he or she is having difficulty communicating through sign language or is slow to gain a sense of his or her role in the household, you may need to pull in your focus and concentrate more on the basics until they are more secure.

One more point: We feel it is our responsibility to warn you about certain attitudes you may encounter. You may discover that

The Bill of Rights for Parents of Deaf Children with Special Needs

1. Remind yourself that you have done and are doing the very best you can.
2. Love, care for, and enjoy your child.
3. Allow yourself to be depressed or hostile once in a while without feeling guilty (as long as you work out of it).
4. Enjoy your own life as intensely as you can.
5. Allow your child to have his or her privacy.
6. Take time to be alone.
7. Every year, take a vacation away from the children.
8. Pay attention to your marriage, and maintain and fine-tune it with plenty of "dates" and celebrations.
9. Keep your sense of humor alive and ticking.
10. Remind yourself that your deaf plus child requires more time than your other children, and that spending that time doesn't mean you love the others any less (and tell your other children just that).
11. Try not to devote your whole life to the child—think carefully about how to parcel out your energy.
12. Feel free to tell well-meaning people that you don't want to talk about your problems. There's more to life than one situation. Celebrate life's diversity.
13. Feel free to tell educators and other professionals exactly what you think about their work, and demand that they respect your opinions.
14. Despite the deafness and the other conditions, feel free to tell your child that you don't like certain things he or she does.
15. Never give up your special interests—hobbies, passions, special projects. Protect them with your life, and use them as your re-creation. ❏

some deaf people in schools or programs for deaf students want to dissociate themselves from your child if he or she has special needs. These people are frightened by the prospect of having deafness being associated with other "disabled" people and feel the need to distance themselves.

You may wonder: How can this be? Remember, people in the Deaf world have worked hard to make it clear to the hearing world that they are in no way disabled. Many have fought so hard to break free of these labels in their own lives that they fear being thrown back into the Dark Ages by associating with people who do have disabilities that impair their functioning.

Both authors can remember how shocking and appalling it can be to run into Deaf people who cruelly rebuff deaf-blind or deaf plus people. When we were younger, we were probably expecting too much to think that Deaf folks were above this sort of attitude. Just as the hearing world is populated by saints and sinners and everything in between, so is the Deaf world. Be aware, as you venture out into the world to follow up on your leads that you may find yourself in places where you and your child are avoided or ignored. You must remember, though, that you've simply made a wrong turn—back up and try another path. There are plenty of other folks who are welcoming.

On a more optimistic note, most of the states have one or more residential schools for deaf students that can be good sources of support for a deaf plus child. Other sources are your state chapter of the Council of Exceptional Children and your state department of special education (each state has such a department, possibly under another name). Finally, a must: Subscribe to *Exceptional Parent,* an invaluable website and digital magazine (www.eparent .com).

You *will* find brilliant and qualified professionals (rare birds that they are) ready to help and even, in some cases, ready to learn. View your job as one of assembling a team to work with your child and with you. Look for the *exceptional* professional whose experience matches your child's needs. Although the commitment of time and energy will be considerable, you may find that you have entered a world where people of depth and humor enrich your life in ways you never dreamed of. This journey for the sake of your child will yield many warm moments and perhaps true friendships you would not have found on the well-traveled path.

Notes

1. Gallaudet Research Institute, *Regional and National Summary Report of Data from the 2004–2005 Annual Survey of Deaf and Hard of Hearing Children and Youth* (Washington, DC: Gallaudet Research Institute, Gallaudet University, December 2005).

Epilogue:
Final Thoughts

CONGRATULATIONS! We've now come full circle. We've told you about the major issues you will face in raising your deaf or hard of hearing child, and have told you many stories. Yet we can't quite consider our job completed without returning once more to the single, fundamental issue in raising a deaf child: *communication.*

Communication is the very heart of the difficulties—and the successes—associated with deafness. You may recall the saying quoted earlier in the book: *Being deaf is not about hearing, but about communication.* If you were puzzled by this notion then, we hope its meaning is clearer now. Therefore, we want to take this last opportunity to explore why this is the case. One need not go far to find an answer—only as far as a group of deaf adults.

Ask deaf adults with hearing parents and siblings what is the single greatest problem they remember from growing up in their families, and their answers almost always will revolve around communication. Here are some examples from interviews with them:

"My family never included me in dinner discussions, planning of family events, or anything. They just talked around me, and I guess I got used to it, but I never stopped feeling left out."

"There were so many things they thought I understood that I never got at all. And nobody thought to explain them to me.

I didn't even understand who all my aunts and uncles were until I was in my twenties."

"Nobody *ever* introduced me to another deaf person. You know, once I realized I was different from my family, I thought I was the only person in the world like me. I believed that nobody would ever understand me and I would never understand anybody in all my life. It wasn't until I went to school and learned to sign that I could have a conversation without feeling anxious and depressed—and completely, totally different."

"My parents were sticklers, perfectionists. I grew up using listening and spoken language, and I don't think I ever had one single conversation where my parents weren't correcting my speech and making sure I spoke clearly and checking my hearing aids. All the *content* got lost, the *fun* got lost, and the *meaning* got lost. Our conversations weren't about communication; they were about speaking skills, getting it *right*. All my parents seemed to care about was having me speak and lipread perfectly. It was exhausting, and it made me a nervous wreck. I got so I hated to have any kind of conversation at all."

The authors firmly believe that hearing people take the ability to communicate easily for granted. We don't blame them for that—it's easy to take for granted what you don't have to think about much. In taking communication for granted, parents of deaf and hard of hearing children may forget that the real function of communication is using language to share and exchange information, feelings, and experiences of the world.

Keep this in mind as you research educational options. Don't get mired in the politics of deaf education: The point is not to find "The One Right Way" and dismiss all others as useless or worse, but rather to find the best possible match of communication mode and education program for your child and family, so that communication can start flowing as early as possible. There will always be new ideas about deafness and deaf education. In the 1970s after decades of oral-only deaf education, total communication seemed to be the answer; more recently, digital hearing aid technology and cochlear implants are sweeping the field with new promises, only partially fulfilled. However, trends like these are transitory—and secondary. Primary is what works for your family to get you communicating with each other. Your role as parent is to see that you and your child, other siblings, extended family, and a wide range of friends and associates, both deaf and hearing, are linked together in a buzzing web of learning, guessing, and reflecting; in other words, interacting in meaningful ways.

Look for books and other published resources, whether in print or online, that embrace the whole picture—the relationship of deafness to communication, education, family, social and emotional life—in short, the issues that will have an immediate and enduring impact on your child and your family.

Parents often tell the authors that because of the fierce controversies surrounding certain issues, they wonder whether the information they gather is accurate. Our answer is always the same: Keep reading, talking, interviewing, and collecting; and especially bring your good judgment and common sense to bear on everything you learn. We also tell them to ask the *real experts*—deaf adults who have grown up with deafness and have dealt with it all their lives. No one understands the subtle and sometimes secret ins and outs of being deaf better than those who have lived it.

The authors have known many of our deaf friends most of our lives. They come from all walks of life and all over the country. Many of them grew up on wonderful terms with their families, actively communicating in just the ways described in this book. However, there are those in our group who have always felt like outsiders in their own families. Others feel cut off from particular family members who have never learned to communicate with them.

Take Patrick, for instance. Although his father knows he is bright, he sees Patrick as a mysterious individual, unlike anybody else in the family—practically an alien. The authors see Patrick as remarkably similar to his father. We see the same personality and communication habits, eccentricities of thinking, quick temper, and soft heart. The familial resemblances practically jump out and touch you. The trouble is, Patrick's father doesn't know his son, and probably never will, because he has never found a way to communicate with him. He sees an impenetrable wall around his son, a wall called "Deafness." No such wall blocks our knowledge of Patrick. For us, and for his other friends and associates who communicate with him through sign language, he is easy to know and enjoy. He is simply . . . Patrick.

Being deaf is not about hearing, but about communication.

Above all, in the end, communication is not limited to the exchange of ideas and information, or even emotion and experience. Communication is about knowing and understanding each other.

And to know first is to begin to understand.

Appendix:
Resources for Parents

Alexander Graham Bell Association for the Deaf
3417 Volta Place, NW
Washington, DC 20007-2778
202-337-5220
www.agbell.org

American Society for Deaf Children
800 Florida Avenue, NE, #2047
Washington, DC 20002-3695
1-800-942-2732 (ASDC)
http://deafchildren.org/

American Speech, Language, and Hearing Association
2200 Research Boulevard
Rockville, MD 20850-3289
800-638-8255
www.asha.org/

Association of Late Deafened Adults (ALDA)
8038 Macintosh Lane, Suite 2,
Rockford Illinois, 61107
815-332-1515
www.alda.org/

Center for Education Research Partnerships National Technical
Institute for the Deaf (NTID) Rochester Institute of Technology
52 Lomb Memorial Drive
Rochester, NY 14623-5604
585-475-6400
www.rit.edu/ntid/educatingdeafchildren/

Council for Exceptional Children
2900 Crystal Drive, Suite 1000
Arlington, VA 22202
888-232-7733
www.cec.sped.org/Tools-and-Resources/For-Families

Dawn Sign Press
6130 Nancy Ridge Drive
San Diego, CA 92121
858-625-0600
800-549-5350
www.dawnsign.com/

Federation for Children with Special Needs
529 Main Street, Suite 1M3
Boston, MA 02129
617-236-7210
http:://fcsn.org/

Gallaudet University Press
800 Florida Avenue, NE
Washington, DC 20002-3695
202-651-5488
http://gupress.gallaudet.edu

Hands and Voices
P.O. Box 3093
Boulder CO 80307
303-492-6283
866-422-0422
www.handsandvoices.org/

Harris Communications
15159 Technology Drive
Eden Prairie, MN 55344
800-825-6758
www.harriscomm.com/

Laurent Clerc National Deaf Education Center
Gallaudet University
800 Florida Avenue, NE
Washington, DC 20002
202-651-5855
www.gallaudet.edu/clerc-center.html

National Association of the Deaf
8630 Fenton Street, Suite 820
Silver Spring, MD 20910
https://nad.org/

National Cued Speech Association
1300 Pennsylvania Avenue, NW, Suite 190-713
Washington, DC 20004
800-459-3529
www.cuedspeech.org/

The S.E.E. Center
P.O. Box 1181
Los Alamitos, CA 90720
562-430-1467
www.seecenter.org/

John Tracy Clinic
806 West Adams Boulevard
Los Angeles, CA 90007
213-748-5481
www.jtc.org/

Visual Language and Visual Learning Science of Learning Center
Gallaudet University
800 Florida Avenue, NE
Washington, DC 20002-3695
202-651-5000
http://vl2parentspackage.org/

Bibliography

Andersen, Peter A., *Nonverbal Communication: Forms and Functions*, 2nd ed., Long Grove IL: Waveland Press, 2008.

Atkins, Dale V., "Siblings of the Hearing Impaired: Perspectives for Parents," *The Volta Review* 89, no. 5 (1987): 32–45.

Baker, Colin, *Foundations of Bilingual Education and Bilingualism*, 5th edition, Bristol, UK: Multilingual Matters, 2011.

Bank, Stephen, and Micheal D. Kahn, *The Sibling Bond*, New York: Basic Books, 2003.

Barra, Allen, *Yogi Berra: Eternal Yankee*, New York, NY: W.W. Norton & Company, 2009.

Berent, Gerald. "Sign Language—Spoken Language Bilingualism: Code Mixing and Mode Mixing by ASL-English Bilinguals," in *The Handbook of Bilingualism*, ed. Tej K. Bahtia and William C. Ritchie, Oxford, UK: Blackwell, 2008: 312–35.

Bornstein, Harry "Signed English," in *Manual Communication: Implications for Education*, ed. Harry Bornstein, Washington, DC: Gallaudet University Press, 1990:128–38.

Bornstein, Harry, Karen Saulnier, and Lillian Hamilton. *Comprehensive Signed English Dictionary*, Washington, DC: Gallaudet University Press, 1983.

Brueggemann, Brenda Jo, *Lend Me Your Ear: Rhetorical Constructions of Deafness*, Washington DC: Gallaudet University Press, 1999.

Cawthon, Stephanie W., and Jacqueline M. Caemmerer, "Parents' Perspectives on Transition and Postsecondary Outcomes for Their Children Who Are d/Deaf or Hard of Hearing," *American Annals of the Deaf* 159, no. 1 (2014): 7–21.

Clark, M. Diane, Marc Marschark, and Michael A. Karchmer, eds, *Context, Cognition, and Deafness*, Washington DC: Gallaudet University Press, 2001.

DesGeorges, Janet, "Family Support and Cultural Competence," in *The NCHAM e-book: A Resource Guide for Early Hearing Detection & Intervention*, ed. Les Schmeltz, Logan, UT: Utah State University, 2015: 5–6. Available online at http://infanthearing.org/ehdi-ebook /2015_ebook/17-Chapter17FamilySupport2015.pdf.

Emerson, Ralph Waldo, *Emerson: Essays and Lectures*, ed. Joel Porte, New York: Library of America, 1983.

Evans, Mariah, Jonathan Kelley, and Joanna Sikora, "Scholarly Culture and Academic Performance in 42 Nations," *Social Forces* 92, no. 4 (2014): 1573–605.

Fitzpatrick, Elizabeth, Ian D. Graham, Andrée Durieux-Smith, Doug Angus, and Doug Coyle, "Parents' Perspectives on the Impact of the Early Diagnosis of Childhood Hearing Loss," *International Journal of Audiology* 46, no. 2 (2007): 97–106.

Gallaudet Research Institute, *Regional and National Summary Report of Data from the 2004–2005 Annual Survey of Deaf and Hard of Hearing Children and Youth*, Washington, DC: Gallaudet Research Institute, Gallaudet University, December 2005.

Goldberg, David, Dennis Looney, and Natalia Lusin. "Enrollments in Languages Other than English in United States Institutions of Higher Education, Fall 2013," New York: Modern Language Association, 2015. Available online at www.mla.org/pdf/2013 _enrollment_survey.pdf.

Goldin-Meadow, Susan, *The Resilience of Language: What Gesture Creation in Deaf Children Can Tell Us about How All Children Learn Language*, New York: Psychology Press, 2005.

Gustason, Gerilee, "Signing Exact English," in *Manual Communication: Implications for Education*, ed. Harry Bornstein, Washington, DC: Gallaudet University Press, 1990.

Hart, Betty, and Todd R. Risley, "The Early Catastrophe: The 30 Million Word Gap by Age 3," *American Educator* 27, no. 1 (2003): 4–9.

Hattie, John, *Visible Learning: A Synthesis of Over 800 Meta-Analyses Relating to Achievement*, New York: Routledge, 2013.

Hoffmeister, Robert, "ASL and Its Implications for Education," in *Manual Communication: Implications for Education*, ed. Harry Bornstein, Washington, DC: Gallaudet University Press, 1990: 81–107.

Holcomb, Thomas K., *Introduction to American Deaf Culture*, New York: Oxford University Press, 2012.

Hymes, Del. "On Communicative Competence." *In Sociolinguistics: Selected Readings*, ed. J. B. Pride and Janet Holmes, Baltimore: Penguin Books, 1972.

Johnston, Jane, and John Halocha, *Early Childhood And Primary Education: Readings And Reflections*, Berkshire, England: McGraw-Hill Education, 2010.

Karlan, George. "Manual Communication with Those Who Can Hear," in *Manual Communication: Implications for Education*, ed. Harry Bornstein, Washington, DC: Gallaudet University Press, 1990: 151–85.

Kingsley, Emily Perl, *Welcome to Holland*, 1987. Available online at www.our-kids.org/Archives/Holland.html.

Koester, Lynne, and Kathryn P. Meadow-Orlans, "Parenting a Deaf Child: Stress, Strength, and Support," in *Educational and Developmental Aspects of Deafness*, ed. Donald. F. Moores and Kathryn P. Meadow-Orlans, Washington, DC: Gallaudet University Press, 1990.

Kurtzer-White, Ellen, and David Luterman, "Families and Children with Hearing Loss: Grief and Coping," *Mental Retardation and Developmental Disabilities Research Reviews* 9, no. 4 (2003): 232–35.

Lederberg, Amy, Brenda Schick, and Patricia E. Spencer, "Language and Literacy Development of Deaf and Hard-of-Hearing Children: Successes and Challenges," *Developmental Psychology* 49, no. 1 (2013): 15–30.

Leybaert, Jacqueline, and Jésus Alegria. "The Role of Cued Speech in Language Development," in *The Oxford Handbook of Deaf Studies, Language, and Education*, 2nd ed., ed. Marc Marschark and Patricia Spencer, New York: Oxford University Press, 2011: 276–89.

McAnally, Patricia L., Susan Rose, and Stephen Patrick Quigley, *Reading Practices with Deaf Learners*, Austin TX: PRO-ED, 2007.

McNeill, David, *Hand and Mind: What Gestures Reveal about Thought*, Chicago: University of Chicago Press, 1992.

Machado, Jeanne, *Early Childhood Experiences in Language Arts: Early Literacy*, Boston: Cengage Learning, 2015.

Maller, Susan. "Intellectual Assessment of Deaf People," in *Oxford Handbook of Deaf Studies, Language, and Education*, ed. Marc Marschark and Patricia Spencer, New York: Oxford University Press, 2003.

Marschark, Marc, "Do DHH Students Succeed Better in Academic and Other Assessments by Using ASL or SEE?" *Educating Deaf Children* website (2015). Available online at www.rit.edu/ntid /educatingdeafchildren/?cat=11#.

Marschark, Marc. *Raising and Educating a Deaf Child*, New York: Oxford University Press, 1997.

Mayberry, Rachel. "Early Language Acquisition and Adult Language Ability: What Sign Language Reveals about the Critical Period for Language," in *The Oxford Handbook of Deaf Studies, Language, and Education*, 2nd ed., ed. Marc Marschark and Patricia Spencer, New York: Oxford University Press, 2011: 281–91.

Mayer, Connie, and Beverly J. Trezek, *Early Literacy Development in Deaf Children*, New York: Oxford University Press, 2015.

Meadow-Orlans, Kathryn P., Marilyn Sass-Lehrer, and Donna M. Mertens, *Parents and Their Deaf Children: The Early Years*, Washington DC: Gallaudet University Press, 2003.

Miller, Paul, Tevhide Kargin, and Birkan Guldenoglu, "Deaf Native Signers Are Better Readers than Nonnative Signers: Myth or Truth?" *Journal of Deaf Studies and Deaf Education* 20, no. 2 (2015): 147–62.

Mohay, Heather, "The Interaction of Gesture and Speech in the Language Development of Two Profoundly Deaf Children," in *From Gesture to Language in Hearing and Deaf Children*, ed. Virginia Volterra and Carol. J. Erting, Washington, DC: Gallaudet University Press, 1998.

Moses, Kenneth, L., *The Dynamics of Transition and Transformation: On Loss, Grieving, Coping and Growthful Change*, Evanston, IL: Resource Networks, 1990.

Nielsen, Diane, Barbara Luetke, and Deborah S. Stryker, "The Importance of Morphemic Awareness to Reading Achievement and the Potential of Signing Morphemes to Supporting Reading Development," *Journal of Deaf Studies and Deaf Education* 16, no. 3, (2011): 275–88.

Nussbaum, Debra, Susanne Scott, and Laurene E. Simms, "The 'Why' and 'How' of an ASL/English Bimodal Bilingual Program," *Odyssey: New Directions in Deaf Education* 13 (2012): 14–19.

Nussbaum, Debra B., and Susanne M. Scott, "The Cochlear Implant Education Center: Perspectives on Effective Educational Practices," in *Cochlear Implants: Evolving Perspectives*, ed. Raylene Paludneviciene and Irene Leigh, Washington, DC: Gallaudet University Press, 2011.

Padden, C., and Tom Humphries, *Deaf in America: Voices from a Culture*, Cambridge MA: Harvard University Press, 1988.

Paludneviciene, Raylene, and Irene W. Leigh, eds, Cochlear Implants: Evolving Perspectives, Washington, DC: Gallaudet University Press, 2011.

Paul, Peter, *Language and Deafness*, 4th ed., Sudbury MA: Jones & Bartlett Publishers, 2009.

Raghuraman, Renuka Sundaram, "The Emotional Well-Being of Older Siblings of Children Who Are Deaf or Hard of Hearing and Older Siblings of Children with Typical Hearing," *The Volta Review* 108, no. 1 (2008): 5–35.

Rose, Susan, Patricia L. McAnally, and Stephen P. Quigley, *Language Learning Practices with Deaf Children*, Austin, TX: PRO-ED, 2004.

Scott, Jessica, *Beyond the Fourth Grade Glass Ceiling: Understanding Reading Comprehension among Bilingual/Bimodal Deaf and Hard of Hearing Students*, Ph.D. dissertation, Harvard University, (2015): 97–99.

Scheetz, Nanci, *Orientation to Deafness*, Boston: Allyn and Bacon, 1992.

Smith, David H. "Deaf Adults: Retrospective Narratives of School Experiences and Teacher Expectations," *Disability & Society* 28, no. 5 (2013): 674–86.

Smith, David H., and Claire L. Ramsey, "Classroom Discourse Practices of a Deaf Teacher Using American Sign Language," *Sign Language Studies* 5, no. 1 (2004): 39–62.

Spencer, Patricia Elizabeth, *A Good Start: Suggestions for Visual Conversations with Deaf and Hard of Hearing Babies and Toddlers*, Washington DC: Gallaudet University, 2001.

Weinstein, Rhona S., *Reaching Higher: The Power of Expectations in Schooling*, Cambridge MA: Harvard University Press, 2002.

Wood, Barbara, *Children and Communication: Verbal and Nonverbal Language Development*, Englewood Cliffs, NJ: Prentice-Hall 1976.

Index

Figures and tables are indicated by "f" and "t," respectively. Illustrations are indicated by italicized page numbers.